PENGUIN BOOKS

OPAL

Kathrine Beck is the author of sixteen novels, mostly mysteries. She is the mother of three grown children and is married to the English crime writer Michael Dibdin. They live in Seattle, Washington.

Kathrine Beck

PENGUIN BOOKS

Opal

A Life of Enchantment, Mystery, and Madness

PENGUIN BOOKS

Published by the Penguin Group
Penguin Group (USA) Inc., 375 Hudson Street,
New York, New York 10014, U.S.A.
Penguin Group (Canada), 10 Alcorn Avenue, Toronto,
Ontario, Canada M4V 3B2 (a division of Pearson Penguin Canada Inc.)
Penguin Books Ltd, 80 Strand, London WC2R 0RL, England
Penguin Ireland, 25 St Stephen's Green, Dublin 2, Ireland
(a division of Penguin Books Ltd)
Penguin Group (Australia), 250 Camberwell Road, Camberwell,
Victoria 3124, Australia (a division of Pearson Australia Group Pty Ltd)
Penguin Books India Pvt Ltd, 11 Community Centre,
Panchsheel Park, New Delhi - 110 017, India
Penguin Group (NZ), cnr Airborne and Rosedale Roads, Albany, Auckland,
New Zealand (a division of Pearson New Zealand Ltd)
Penguin Books (South Africa) (Pty) Ltd, 24 Sturdee Avenue, Rosebank,
Johannesburg 2196, South Africa

Penguin Books Ltd, Registered Offices: 80 Strand, London WC2R 0RL, England

First published in the United States of America by Viking Penguin,
a member of Penguin Group (USA) Inc. 2003
Published in Penguin Books 2004

1 3 5 7 9 10 8 6 4 2

THE LIBRARY OF CONGRESS HAS CATALOGED THE HARDCOVER EDITION AS FOLLOWS:
Beck, K. K.
Opal : a life of enchantment, mystery, and madness / Kathrine Beck.
p.   cm.
ISBN 0-670-03145-3 (hc.)
ISBN 0 14 30.3429 4 (pbk.)
1. Whiteley, Opal Stanley.   2. Authors, American—20th century—Biography.
3. Women naturalists—United States—Biography.   4. Princesses—France—
Miscellanea.   5. Orleans, House of—Miscellanea.   6. Diaries—Authorship.
7.Oregon—Biography.   I.Title.
PS3545.H625Z58 2003
813'.52—dc21
[B] 2003041085

Printed in the United States of America
Set in Fournier
Designed by Francesca Belanger

*S*ome minerals, when held in particular directions, reflect from single spots in their interior a coloured shining lustre, and this is what is understood by opalescence.

—Robert Jameson, *Characteristics of Minerals*

Acknowledgments

Many librarians, archivists and staff members of libraries and archives around the world helped me collect information for this book. I am grateful to all of them, including Kim Walters, of the Braun Research Library, Southwest Museum, Los Angeles; Penny Brook of the British Library Oriental and India Office Collections, who provided permission to quote from Mewar Residency Udaipur File No. 18; Nahur Singh Jasol and staff of the City Palace Museum, Udaipur; Kyle Carey of the Harvard University Archives; Ralph Drew of the *Los Angeles Times* Archives; Nicholas Graham and the staff of the Massachusetts Historical Society; William R. Ellis, Jr. of the National Archives; Todd Welch of the Oregon Historical Society; Merrialyce Blanchard, Jim Scheppke, and Craig Smith of the Oregon State Library; Margaret Kimball of the Stanford University Archives; James Fox, Hannah Dillon, Lesli Larson, Linda Long, and staff of the University of Oregon Library Special Collections; as well as the staff members of the British Library Newspaper Library; Lane County Historical Museum, Eugene, Oregon; Widener Library of the Harvard College Library; and the Library of Congress; and the Suzallo Library and University Archives at the University of Washington. Special thanks go to Judith Etherton and Ali Burdon of the University of London Library, where the bulk of Opal's papers are cataloged and preserved, and which has kindly given me permission to quote from Opal's diary and her letters and papers.

Academics who have written about Opal and shared their views with me or provided welcome expertise on aspects of her life were equally forthcoming and generous. They include Dr. Blake Allmendinger, Dr. Lynne Anderson-Inman, Dr. Cathryn Halverson, Dr. Julia Herschensohn, Dr. Juliet McMaster, and Dr. James Santucci.

My most sincere thanks also to the many people who have been drawn to the story of Opal and who have written about her or who have created works based on her story, and who freely shared their knowledge, insights, opinions, and feelings about her work and her life. In many cases they also shared papers, letters, documents, introductions, and leads. They include Richard Acton, Victoria Beatty, Jane Boulton, David Caruso, Larrance Fingerhut, Jeff Goode, Roberta Gregory, Nan Gurley, Benjamin Hoff, Elizabeth Bradburne Lawrence, Steve McQuiddy, Robert Lindsey Nassif, Ian Taylor, and Steve Williamson.

I am also grateful to the relatives and associates of people who were a part of Opal's story, and who told me what they knew and went out of their way to help me uncover facts and understand the cast of characters better. They include John Cabot, Robert C. Cabot, Michael Madden, Julia Hemenway, Ann Jackson, Julie and Terry Trujillo, Beth Bede Simkin, Elise Bede Swan, Steve Moore, Dorothy Randle, Cabot Sedgwick, Julie Clark, Tanya Van Alstine, Jimi Mathers, and Dorothy Stewart.

Special thanks also to Shriji Arvind Singhji Mewar and Sabina Bailey of the Maharana Mewar Charitable Foundation; Bill McBryde and Catherine Brady at the Office of the Official Solicitor to the Supreme Court, London; Carol Smith of Oregon Christian Endeavor; Alan Klein, Mark Thompson, and Vanessa Morán. Gregg Olsen helped launch this book, generously provided me with many important and helpful leads, and gave me some very good professional advice as well.

This book would not have been possible if it had not been for my agent, the wonderful Clare Alexander, and my editors, Wendy Wolf, who took the idea on board and gave me excellent editorial advice, and Lucia Watson, who brought her own enthusiasm for the subject and her considerable editorial expertise to the task of helping me shape a large and shifting mass of material into an actual book, as well as attending energetically and cheerfully to many other details required to get the book into production.

And to Jean Beck, Emma Marris, Andrew Marris, and Alexander Marris, thank you for all your help, encouragement, patience, and invaluable research assistance. I am especially grateful to my husband, Michael Dibdin, who helped me understand Opal and her world, provided me with many helpful insights as to how to tell her story, and tolerated the presence of Opal, always a demanding houseguest, in our midst for many months.

Opal

CHAPTER
One

*I*n February 1918, Opal Whiteley, aged twenty, and a regional celebrity known as the Little Nature Study Girl and the Sunshine Fairy, got on a Southern Pacific train in Cottage Grove, Oregon, a small town in a lush valley surrounded by green hills. Opal was headed south. Officially, she was planning to study the flora and fauna of California for the summer. Privately, she had also decided to break into the movies.

She left behind a to-do list reminding herself to get in touch with Cecil B. DeMille and took with her a portfolio of publicity photos taken at the Tolman Studios in Eugene, Oregon, for which she had served as her own art director. She was pretty, striking, and small—under five feet—with high cheekbones, a wide smile, and strong-looking, slightly prominent teeth. Her thick black hair hung down past her waist, and her eyes were described as black.

Opal had been photographed in several costumes and poses—as a barefoot, violin-playing Gypsy with autumn leaves strewn around the studio floor; as a waif in a little Dutch girl hat; in profile, barefoot again, as a dancer in a gauzy Isadora Duncan–style tunic with flowers in her hair; and as a crazed-looking ballerina in toe shoes.

The most startling image preserved from this series is Opal with dreamy eyes, her mouth in a Mona Lisa smile, her thick hair brushed back from her oval face and cascading down over a white dress and out of the frame. Her hands are extended and half open. Three huge butterflies appear to have landed there, and there is another on her shoulder and one more on her hair. But Opal isn't looking at the butterflies or at anything at all. Her eyes are unfocused. She appears to be in a trance or in communion with something unattainable by the viewer. (This may be because the butterflies were added to the photograph later.)

A lot of young Americans Opal's age were on the move in 1918. Woodrow Wilson had declared war on Germany the previous April. Doughboys and Red Cross nurses were leaving cities, farms, and small towns like Cottage Grove to take part in the bloody conflict overseas that was to determine the trajectory for the rest of the eventful twentieth century.

The trenches of France, however, never loomed large in Opal's consciousness. Her journey would be one in search of fame and glamour via a child's shimmering fairyland and half-remembered princes and princesses. No one knows for sure to what extent the magical place she found for herself was real and how much of it sprang from her own mysterious inner world. Opal never came back to Oregon after her train left town in 1918. She never saw any other Whiteleys again. Nor did she become a movie star. But she did become, very briefly, very famous.

Today those who know about Opal Whiteley are few in number, but many of them are intensely attached to her work and her memory. They do not necessarily agree among themselves about the details of her life or indeed about who she really was.

Here are some biographical "facts" about Opal Whiteley that have become accepted into the official canon. Some of them are true.

She was born sometime in 1897 and grew up in and around Cottage Grove, a logging town in Oregon, where she had arrived in 1902, when she was about four years old. She was raised by Ed and Lizzie Whiteley. The other four Whiteley children—Pearl, Faye, Cloe, and baby Elwin— were all younger.

As a child of nine or ten Opal began collecting nature specimens, chiefly butterflies and minerals, and taught younger children about them. At seventeen she was named state superintendent of an ecumenical Christian youth group and traveled throughout Oregon successfully recruiting many new members.

She also gained regional recognition as a lecturer on the natural world. She combined nature studies with the uplifting religious message that children could be brought to God through the beauty of His handiwork.

She was accepted into the University of Oregon at Eugene because of her extensive knowledge of geology, botany, and zoology, although she hadn't completed all the entrance requirements.

Opal left college during her sophomore year and went to southern California, where she taught nature classes to the children of rich families.

She took the material from her classes and put them into a self-published nature book for children, *The Fairyland Around Us*, a venture financed in part by collecting deposits from people who wanted to buy the book before it was published. Opal always had charm.

Opal had a dispute with the printer, who wanted extra money to pay for changes in the book and who finally destroyed the plates, leaving her with a partially produced book. She gathered up what had been printed, had copies bound, hand-pasted hundreds of color plates of birds and plants into them, and added handwritten captions.

In July 1919, when she was twenty-one, she went east to seek a literary career and ended up in Boston in the office of Ellery Sedgwick, editor of *The Atlantic Monthly*. She showed him a copy of *The Fairyland Around Us*, and he asked her if she had kept a childhood diary. She told him that she had but that it had been torn up by the middle Whiteley child, Faye. The pieces, Opal said, were in a hatbox in California. The pieces were sent for. Early portions of the diary were written in crayon on old paper bags and scrap paper.

Opal spent months as a houseguest of Sedgwick's mother-in-law, pasting the diary back together, and it was published in installments in *The Atlantic Monthly*. Fan mail poured in. When it was published as a book in 1920, under the title *The Story of Opal: The Journal of an Understanding Heart*, it sold briskly, and more editions were planned. By one account its sales were second only to the number one bestseller of the year, Sinclair Lewis's *Main Street*.

In the diary, which she said she had written when she was seven, readers met Opal's pets. The pig Peter Paul Rubens; Brave Horatius, the sheep herding dog; bats Pliny and Plato; Geoffroi Chaucer, the squirrel;

Lars Porsenum of Clusium, a crow; Mathilde Plantagenet, a calf; Lucian Horace Ovid Virgil, a toad; Nannerl Mozart, "a very shy mouse"; and Thomas Chatterton Jupiter Zeus, "a most dear wood rat," are but a small sample.

Many of these animals were carried around in special pockets Opal said she had secretly sewn onto her petticoats. Others, including the pig, trotted after her along the road. The crow rode on the dog's back. When they were ill, she nursed them back to health, applying large doses of Mentholatum to their injuries.

Opal's friends were not confined to the animal kingdom. Readers also met a lot of fir trees, including Queen Elinor of Castile; Good King Edward the First; Godefroi of Bouillon; Lionel, Duke of Clarence; Étienne of Blois; and Michael Angelo Sanzio Raphael, "a grand fir tree with an understanding soul." Keats was an oak.

Opal and her animal friends went on "explores," and she conducted religious services for them, based on the Roman Catholic mass in a forest "cathedral." The diary records the birth and death dates of the famous, information that she shared with plants and animals. "I so have been going to tell the plant-folks and the flower-folks about this day being the going-away day of one William Shakespeare in 1616," for example, or, "I did have thinks as how this was the going-away day of Saint François of Assisi and the borning day of Jean François Millet."

A cruel caretaker known as the mamma often foiled her plans, switching her with a hickory stick for well-intentioned deeds that went awry and assigning her daunting domestic chores, including taking care of "the mamma's baby," presumably Faye Whiteley. At one point the cruel mamma tied her up and left her out in the hot sun until she passed out and got a nosebleed. There were some kind humans, such as Sadie McKibben, a motherly woman with freckles, a blue gingham apron, and a full cookie jar, and "the man who wears gray neckties and is kind to mice." He found the notes Opal had left for the fairies in a mossy log asking for crayons and supplied her with them and with replies from the fairies. The reader knows this man was her secret benefactor but Opal herself believed in fairies. There are similar examples of the innocent

Opal's inadvertently revealing the truth to the more sophisticated reader.

The diary is written in very idiosyncratic English, which some find enchanting and others cloying: "Then I did have joy feels all over"; "I have thinks these potatoes growing here did have knowings of star-songs." Like her nature lectures to children, the book displays a strong vein of religiosity and mystical union with God through nature.

Opal also wrote of her Angel Mother and Angel Father. These ghostly figures were completely unlike the coldhearted "mamma" and the barely mentioned "papa." She tells us they taught her to love nature, gave her the knowledge she had of the greats of art, literature, and history, and watched her from afar. She wrote notes to them on gray leaves, and when she recollected what they told her before she was parted from them, she says they addressed her as "petite Françoise."

The introduction to the diary says that it was not known where Opal was born or who her parents were, but that they died when she was four, leaving behind two notebooks with their photographs. It goes on to explain that clues in the diary pointed to her father's being a naturalist "by profession or native taste" and that one of her parents was presumably French "by birth or education," because French appears in the diary. Readers were also informed that while piecing the diary, Opal had to be told the French phrases were indeed French, and she was quoted as replying, "But they can't be French! I never studied French!" Opal said she didn't know how the references got there or what they meant. Putting all the French clues together, including some in code, would lead the reader to conclude that Opal was a member of the d'Orléans family, pretenders to the throne of France, and a princess.

Some irate readers asked for their money back, saying that this was ridiculous and that the diary must have been written when she was an adult and larded with clues to allow her to call herself a princess and then passed off as the work of a precocious child. Others believed Opal's story, and still others didn't know what to believe but were fascinated. Some found the book a moving and enchanting picture of childhood and a child's relationship to God and nature. Some wept at the suffering of little Opal at the hands of the cruel "mamma." Others found it pretentious and arch.

Amid a huge storm of publicity, the Whiteley family, portrayed badly in the book, changed their names and disappeared. Plans for further installments of the diary from unpublished portions of the manuscript were abandoned under mysterious circumstances.

More than eighty years since the diary appeared, questions about Opal and her diary remain. If Opal's diary was a fraud, cooked up when she was a young adult, no one, even the most skeptical, has ever been able to prove it or explain exactly how she pulled it off.

Opal vanished from the scene, and the world lost track of her until the 1930s when she was spotted by an American woman in Udaipur, India, traveling in a royal procession. The woman asked about Opal and was told she was a princess, the granddaughter of a maharaja. Opal had many friends in high places, and she was said to have traveled to India on a special diplomatic passport, provided for her by former British Foreign Minister Lord Grey of Fallodon and American Secretary of State Charles Evans Hughes, and that she had been accepted by the duchess of Orléans as her granddaughter, and had been sent by the duchess to India.

Despite the accusations of fraud in her own time, today her diary is taken more seriously than ever. It is in print in several versions. It is taught in schools, and a teacher's guide to go with it says she was probably indeed a French princess. It has been anthologized in an ecofeminist collection and is available online. It has also attracted some attention from academia; the shredded and pasted-together diary is literally a deconstructed and reconstructed text.

Opal has inspired an Off Broadway musical, one-woman shows, and other musical compositions and plays, including one for children called *Les Opales*, in which a whole bevy of Opals appear. One fan designed an Opal Whiteley dress with silk origami butterflies attached to it, in homage to Opal's famous photograph. Benjamin Hoff, bestselling author of *The Tao of Pooh* has written about her in *The Singing Creek Where the Willows Grow*.

There are those who believe that Opal was a genius and that if her diary were read more widely, the world could become a better place.

They remember the moment they first came across Opal's diary as if it were an epiphany. For them, Opal seems to provide a mystical, even religious experience. Of course, like all religions, the cult of Opal is riddled with schisms.

Robert Nassif, who wrote *Opal*, the musical based on her diary that was produced Off Broadway, told me, "I have been under the spell of this diary for twenty-one years. It never ceases. It's a happy spell. She enchants our lives. Opalites are people who have been touched by her."

CHAPTER

Two

As an adult Opal consistently said she had been born in Rome and that her birthday was February 6, 1897. The Whiteley family said she had been born at home with a nurse in attendance at Colton, Washington, on December 11, 1897, and that she was the first of the five children of Ed and Lizzie Whiteley.

Charles Edward Whiteley and Mary Elizabeth Scott had been married by a Protestant minister on June 27, 1896, in Walla Walla, Washington. He was twenty-four, and she was twenty-one. The groom had been born in North Yamhill, Oregon; the bride in Lakeport, California. They were the children of pioneers. Although Ed's family is said to have had Native American roots—Sioux, according to one family member; a tribe from Quebec, according to another—both Ed and Lizzie are listed on the license as "White." Ed's maternal grandparents came from Canada, and on his father's side he was said to be related to Daniel Boone. Scott family photographs include handsome Mediterranean-looking people who could have been Sicilians or Arabs. Opal was very dark; an Indian colonial officer said she looked as if she were half European and half East Indian. Questions about her origins were to become central to her life.

The marriage certificate describes Ed's occupation as farmer. Lizzie had attended teacher's college but hadn't graduated and was working as a housekeeper. Soon after their marriage Ed and Lizzie moved from Walla Walla to Colton, a small German Catholic town in eastern Washington State, where Ed Whiteley had family, and he went to work for a local farmer, Doug Mustard.

There is no birth certificate for Opal Irene Whiteley or for a Margaret Whiteley, which she was apparently called for the first months of her life, until Lizzie had a quarrel with the Whiteley aunt who had suggested the name. After that, Margaret became Opal, the first of numerous name changes.

In the first year of Opal's life, Lizzie Whiteley went home to her parents in Oregon, taking the baby with her for about six weeks, apparently because of strains in the marriage. Ed Whiteley sent gifts, a pearl-handled pen for his wife and a gold pin for the baby at Christmas in 1898. Lizzie returned to her husband in due course. Another child, Pearl Whiteley, whose birth was officially registered, was born on September 4, 1899. In 1902 the family moved from Colton to Oregon, near the town of Cottage Grove. Cottage Grove, at the less fertile end of the lush Willamette Valley, was more dependent on mining and logging than on agriculture. This gave it a rougher edge. A population of transient single men lived there alongside families.

If it had been left to nature, the area would have been covered with a dense forest of Douglas firs, but when the pioneers arrived, the Indians had already burned large chunks of the forest in order to create grassy meadows to attract deer and other game. It gave the place somewhat the look of the English countryside—green lawns and spreading oak trees—alongside stands of dark conifers: fir and cedar.

Opal stayed first with Lizzie Whiteley's parents, Leonidas and Acseh (pronounced Axie) Scott in a pretty square white farmhouse that still stands, although the current owners have remodeled it with a huge Palladian window and some new wings, much to the horror of local traditionalists. It is near a picturesque covered bridge crossing a rushing creek with overhanging greenery.

Today the area around Cottage Grove is beautifully verdant, with open fields and woods of deciduous and evergreen trees, interlaced with rushing creeks, backed by gentle hills. The white farmhouse is across the road from a bike path that in Opal's childhood was a railway line. Buster Keaton's classic silent film *The General*, the plot of which revolves around railroad action, was filmed there in 1926. For an idea of what it looked like nearer to Opal's era, the scenery on view in *The General* reveals the same lush beauty in the surrounding countryside, but the town, dotted with charming wood bungalows, is also full of crude stumps and fir trees with branches hacked off at alarming angles, testimony to the ongoing logging in the area and to a frontier ruggedness that has since vanished from the landscape.

Logging was phased out in the area during the 1980s. Now the town's biggest industry is yurt building. The wooden yurts, portable round dwellings based on the homes of the natives of the Mongolian steppes, are sold to individuals as well as to the U.S. military and the Oregon Parks and Recreation Department, which rents them to campers. The manufacturer's promotional materials say that the yurt is "more than a product, it is a concept connecting ancient wisdom and practicality with modern technology." In Opal's day, no one used "ancient wisdom" to promote local commodities. The idea was to get minerals out of the ground and chop down the trees and sell them.

Lizzie Whiteley and the two little girls, Opal and Pearl, left Colton by train. Ed Whiteley and his sister Mary Simpson stayed behind and packed. In the move, some lace doilies were torn, and an album that contained family pictures and stood on a stand in the parlor was damaged. Lizzie Whiteley never forgave Ed and Mary for their carelessness. That family album and those lace doilies reveal a lot about Lizzie. She tried very hard to provide a civilized, refined domestic life for her family, and it just wasn't always possible.

Pioneer accounts reveal that women often went west reluctantly and resentfully, forced to pull up stakes and shed most of their possessions by their husbands, who were excited by the prospect of free land. Many pioneer diaries noted that the women were making the journey under protest and that the Oregon Trail was pathetically littered with cast-off family heirlooms that had had to be jettisoned so the beleaguered oxen could pull the heavy wagons.

Although Lizzie herself was born in the West, she seems to have felt some of this pioneer woman resentment. The grown Opal remembered her mother's bitterness that her family, southerners who had come west after the Civil War, had lost social status. Lizzie may well have been a sort of pioneer version of Scarlett O'Hara or Blanche DuBois, an archetypal déclassé southern woman. In later life Opal went fiercely after what she perceived to be her own stolen aristocratic credentials.

After spending some time in the white farmhouse with Lizzie's parents, the Whiteley family moved often around the Cottage Grove area. Opal lived in small logging communities with pretty names like Wendling, Walden, Dorena, and Star, where Lizzie Whiteley was the postmistress. Opal later said that she had lived in lots of lumber camps, but this was an exaggeration. Generally, she lived in small communities around Cottage Grove, where schools and other amenities were available, while her father was away at the actual camps with the loggers and camp cooks.

Turn-of-the-century logging camps were temporary bases of operation. Teams of mostly single men worked ten-to fourteen-hour days in the dark, often wet and muddy forests. The work was hard and dangerous. At the end of the day they came back to camp for the high-calorie meals they needed to keep going, then slept in crowded, smoky, damp bunkhouses. Conditions were often harsh and unhygienic. The Industrial Workers of the World, or Wobblies, found the logging camps fertile organizing grounds.

Ed Whiteley was a logger who had little education but who had worked his way up to supervisor in logging camps. He was regarded by the locals as respectable and somewhat aloof, hardworking, and not rowdy and hard-drinking as some lumberjacks were. He had a reputation for being a good storyteller and was remembered as kind, helpful, and calm. He was also said to have had at times a somewhat difficult and "changeable" personality, and was also reported to have alcoholic tendencies, but he didn't drink or smoke.

Though Ed was hardworking and steadily employed, the family had periods of poverty. Around Opal's sixth birthday, the Whiteleys lived in what was referred to as a house tent, and the Oregon rains sometimes got into the tent. Ed, a proud man, was ashamed that they'd lived in the tent and later denied it. Sometimes the Whiteleys had trouble putting food on the table. Had the Whiteleys been around today, they would no doubt have had a big Visa balance, but in the days before consumer credit and unemployment benefits, these financial ups and downs meant that sometimes the Whiteley children had no shoes.

The Whiteleys worked hard to maintain standards and respectability, and they seem to have been admired by the community for their efforts. The children were recalled by neighbors as always being spotlessly clean, and the little girls' long, neat ringlets were much admired. This adherence to high standards of cleanliness, while considered admirable by the neighbors, is portrayed more sinisterly in the published childhood diary *The Story of Opal*. The "mamma" is an obsessive housekeeper, always after Opal to do her chores—washing, scrubbing, churning butter, minding "the mamma's baby," sewing up the carpet, weeding—and beating her when they are done wrong. What is more appalling is that Opal is also beaten when she tries to help and inadvertently makes a bigger mess.

Besides the diary, the case for Opal's having been an abused child rests with a 1921 newspaper interview with Lizzie's mother, Acseh Scott, in which she claimed that Opal was such a stubborn, difficult child that Lizzie got tired while switching her and Mrs. Scott had to step in and continue. Another reporter covering the story at the time later claimed that she was "cruelly misquoted" and that the neighbors said Lizzie never laid a hand on her children. Whiteley relatives today fiercely resent the allegation that she was beaten.

In 1920, University of Oregon psychology professor Edmund Conklin interviewed neighbors while researching a paper on foster-parent fantasies. Lizzie was described by Conklin as "cultured and refined." Neighbors later remembered her as quiet, pretty, fond of books, a good cook and housekeeper who read fairy tales and poetry to her children. The local grocer remembered her as being very well spoken.

Conklin also noted that Lizzie Whiteley was capable of odd behavior, such as bolting from the house if people she didn't like came calling. Someone else said she even hid in trees, and one neighbor said she had behaved "like an Indian," which in a local context would mean that she was reserved, unsmiling, and, by the norms of the white population, unsociable and avoiding eye contact.

The Story of Opal says, "There are no rows and rows of books in this house, like Angel Mother and Angel Father had. There is only three books here. One is a cookbook and one is a doctor-book and one is a almanac." There were, however, reports that Lizzie owned a copy of Macaulay's *Lays of Ancient Rome*, a favorite of the time, and indeed, in the diary, several of Opal's animal friends bear names from this book.

We know Opal had childhood books because two of them have survived, left behind in a box of her books and papers now at the University of Oregon Library. *Our Babies' Bible ABC: First Steps for Little Feet* is written, interestingly, under the pseudonym "An Angel Mother," the name in her diaries of Opal's ghostly birth mother.

The other one, titled *The Little Housemaid*, is inscribed to Opal from an aunt in 1903 when she was five. It is full of killjoy admonitions for little girls to stay close to home, pitch in, and help Mother.

That message didn't take with Opal. In the diary she wants to turn her back on domesticity, "go on explores," and find spiritual calm in the fields and woods, and Opal had a lifelong aversion to housework. Julie Trujillo, a cousin who lives in Cottage Grove on Scott Lane, named for her great-grandparents, told me that her grandmother Ethel Scott, a schoolteacher and Lizzie's sister-in-law, said Opal was "the laziest child ever born." When pursuing what interested her, however, Opal was later to display manic energy, working for many hours at a time until she collapsed, exhausted.

Opal's first school was in Wendling, where she proved to be a good student, getting through the material for first and second grade in one year. Her teacher, Miss Daugherty, who read stories from Greek mythology to the children, said later she was bright and dreamy and an early reader. By the age of seven, if Opal is to be believed, she was also an early writer, composing her diary in crayoned block letters on scraps of butcher paper and successfully hiding it from her family.

When Opal was nine or ten, she began collecting insects and butterflies, deputizing other children to help her. She became obsessed by her collecting. Soon Opal was to decide on her life's work, becoming, in the process, a local personality referred to by her neighbors as the Little Nature Study Girl.

During Opal's childhood, Americans were taking another look at nature. Four years before she was born, historian Frederick Jackson

Turner famously announced that the West was closed and had been won. When she was four, Oregon's Crater Lake became a national park. Two years later, when the citizens of Oregon noticed they had killed off all the native elk, they opened an elk preserve and stocked it with elk from Montana. Americans were touring the West in Model T Fords and sending their children to summer camps where they sometimes dressed as Indians and learned nature lore, something the real pioneers would have found bizarre.

A true child of her era, Opal read bestselling novels of the day extolling the beauties of nature and ran her own summer day camp for the children of the community with the approval of their mothers, while their fathers toiled in lumber camps, exploiting the forest as fast as they could.

In 1913, when Opal was fifteen, Lily Black, Opal's high school teacher in Dorena, a town long since vanished under an artificial lake, wrote the Oregon state librarian, Cornelia Marvin, about the traveling library service operated by the state for the benefit of country schools. Miss Marvin pioneered the idea of books by mail, establishing the first free mail-order library service in the nation and sending out books to snowbound shepherds and inmates in the state penitentiary as well as to schoolchildren.

Miss Black was looking for reference books that she said the district couldn't afford to buy, especially works on English and ancient history, physical geography, and English literature. She said she also had one student who wanted books for her independent study of geology.

Soon after that, a postcard, or, as they were called at the time, a postal, from Opal arrived at the library in Salem, addressed to "Dear Sirs." It asked for federal bulletins on geology and explained that the sender was fifteen years old, in her second year of high school, and planned to "make a home study of Geology and to study the Geology of this Valley." The term "Geology" seemed to refer not exclusively to the study of minerals but to natural history in general.

A lengthy correspondence ensued, in which "Dear Sirs" became "Dear Miss Marvin" and later "Dear Friend." Soon, besides ordering and renewing an astonishing number of books with titles such as *Strolls by Starlight and Sunshine*, *The Friendly Stars*, *Boy Mineral Collectors*, and *Half Hours with the Lower Animals*, and sending in the fifteen cents' postage required, Opal was confiding in her new librarian friend Cornelia Marvin about her activities and her ambitions.

Opal had spent the preceding summer teaching nature classes to younger children. She wrote to Miss Marvin that local mothers had encouraged her to write nature articles for children on butterflies, trees, mosses, flowers, lichens, fish, and birds. Someone at the library circled all the subjects she wanted to write about in her letter, and it is pleasant to imagine Miss Marvin or a colleague, in Gibson girl blouse and long skirt, Opal's letter in hand, flipping through the card catalog in long wooden boxes and going to the shelves to fetch the volumes to mail to Miss Opal Whiteley, Star, Oregon.

At sixteen, Opal wrote Miss Marvin, "I desire to take up as my life work the training and teaching of children. I want also to teach them about the beauties of God's Outdoors, of the birds, trees, flowers, of insects, shells and rocks. I want to help them to be a blessing to the world to make the hearts of their parents glad and to grow into noble pure manhood and womanhood."

She asked for a list of good illustrated books about flowers and birds and then described her plans further: "I desire to write for other people the lessons I have learned from little children and of the great things I have gained from God's Outdoors, and to write for little children. Could you tell me two or three good books on this subject which would be well for a beginner to study? I have a great many child-friends. And I keep their sayings and little stories of their daily life in notebooks for future refarance [*sic*]. I have found this very helpful."

Opal appears to have been very successful as a teacher of natural history to children. Existing letters from parents indicate that Opal did a terrific job. Even a lifetime later the children she taught remembered her affectionately, and more impressively, they also remembered the love of nature she had given them. She took the children out into the woods to gather specimens and grub in the dirt. Photographs of her classes evoke a period charm as little boys in knickerbockers and girls with big hair bows and in white dresses clamber around fields beside old farmhouses in a sort of happy chaos. Opal took her teaching seriously. Besides getting materials from the state library, she also sent away to Washington, D.C., for teaching materials from the federal government.

She wrote to Miss Marvin in the spring of 1914, "Mother and Father have given me a small room . . . for my nature study. I have finished a work table for the room and am now putting up shelves, making a book case, and building a window seat by one of the windows. When I have finished these I will begin work on the large screen cage to keep the butterflies and larvae this summer.

"That butterfly book was certainly helpful to me," the letter went on. "There were many butterflies which I observed last summer but did not know the names of that the book enabled me to learn much more of their habits and their families to which they belonged. The Library Commission is doing a grand work."

Opal's teacher, Lily Black, who had arranged for Opal to get library services, later wrote in a long letter that she felt especially close to her pupil. Opal would visit her after school in the bungalow where she lived and sometimes spend the night. Black reported that although Opal was studious, she didn't always apply herself. She did not like Latin (her only B among straight As, according to her report card). Neither did she care for history, finding wars and bloodshed unpleasant. And while she took great pains with her compositions, she didn't always stay on the assigned topic. When it came to natural history, however, her photographic memory and her enthusiasm kicked in, and she overwhelmed everyone, including the teacher. Sometimes her teacher simply turned the class over to her, and "then the rest of us just listened." Opal knew the names of an astonishing number of plant and animal species.

Opal's collection had grown to thousands of specimens, and more were always forthcoming from little children in the community. She took the children off on exploring expeditions, and "there was not a mother in the valley but would not trust her with her children." The children themselves also seemed to be crazy about her.

When it came to her peers, however, Opal was rather isolated. She did not have many friends her own age and Miss Black wrote that she played with younger children "in order to study them, she would say." The younger children of the community also provided an audience. In her teens Opal's dramatic flair became evident. She was known for eye-catching floppy hats and is said to have put on plays by herself, rigging up a makeshift curtain. Her one-woman shows involved several costume changes. She played characters from history or novels. These performances were given to younger neighbor children, who, it is said, didn't always get the gist of the performances. The older girls in town would taunt her, according to Miss Black, "even to her face." Apparently, Opal, even when she did know she was being insulted by these mean teenage girls, was pleasant to them, and her teacher wondered how she could be so forgiving. Miss Black noted that Opal wasn't interested in boys, except in a "brotherly" way. Opal's classmates later reported the same thing. The boys liked Opal, though, and would do anything for her, according to her teacher.

In 1914, when Opal was sixteen, Lizzie gave birth to a boy, Elwin, who joined the family of four girls. Lizzie was suffering from breast cancer and perhaps tuberculosis as well. She went into Cottage Grove to have the baby but was in such bad health she wasn't expected to return alive. Until her death three years later, Lizzie was always ill. Opal herself, later in life, said Lizzie had an open wound on her breast that required dressing. There is nothing to suggest she received any medical care or painkillers.

Lizzie relied a lot on Opal, the eldest, to take care of such things as going into town to pay bills. Miss Black says Ed Whiteley was not much in evidence, and he may have been working in the woods. Sometimes Opal was kept out of school to stay home and look after the younger children.

Throughout this period, Lily Black said, Faye Whiteley was "a trial." It is a cruel fact known to social workers that adolescents sometimes become angry, aggressive, and impossible while their parents are dying, turning what is already a horrible situation into a complete hell. Faye seems to have taken out her rage against Opal, who was acting as surrogate mother. Lily Black witnessed Faye's persecution of Opal and mentioned her breaking into Opal's locked workroom full of specimens and tearing up many of the choicest examples. Opal sometimes squirreled away her cocoons in her desk at school to keep them out of Faye's clutches.

The out-of-control Faye, Lizzie dying a painful death, a new baby in the house, Ed Whiteley's frequent absences, the expectation that as the eldest she would help hold everything together, and contempt from her peers: all seem a lot for a sixteen-year-old to bear. Opal's letters of the period, however, paint a much rosier picture. They are full of enthusiastic descriptions of the natural surroundings and speak happily of her work with nature, younger children, and her "darling" baby brother. Sometimes they include a Bible verse.

"I live in a little valley nestled among the hills. I love to live among the hills and their peace and their strength have entered into my life," she wrote to a friend in Portland. "I wish you could see our hills in the sunset's golden glow or again beneath the pale moon beams light." Opal often sounds almost like a sugary character in a children's book of the period, expressing such sentiments as "Truly the children are jewels in God's kingdom teaching us great lessons by their childlike faith and willingness to help."

Opal kept lists of her reading, and they include many bestsellers of the period, including the works of Gene Stratton-Porter, whom she was later accused of plagiarizing, and who she said was her favorite. Stratton-Porter, whose real first name was Geneva, wrote sentimental, moralistic tales emphasizing a love of nature and traditional values. The books were routinely dismissed as lowbrow and panned by the critics, but they sold like mad, with sales peaking in 1912, during Opal's girlhood. Devoted readers praised them as uplifting and heartwarming, and their author was rich and famous.

Stratton-Porter, a generation older than Opal, grew up on a farm in Indiana, taming wild birds, exploring the natural world, and resisting domesticity, much like Opal. A corpulent woman with alarming, shaggy eyebrows, she believed that it was her mission to lead female readers to an appreciation of nature, writing, "I came into the world at a time when womanhood was in fierce recoil against the hardships of pioneer life as it edged its way westward."

In *Freckles*, an orphan lad creates his own forest "cathedral," just as Opal of the diary does, and later turns out to have been from an aristocratic European family. (Besides sharing a reverence for nature and a hatred of housework, Opal and her idol Gene-Stratton Porter both insisted on their aristocratic origins to a doubting world. Stratton-Porter maintained against all evidence that she was descended from a duke, tarted up her official bio with fake genealogy, and even designed her own phony coat of arms.)

Dr. Cathryn Halverson, author of the scholarly *Maverick Autobiographies and the American West, 1902–1936: Mary MacLane, Opal Whiteley, and Juanita Harrison*, has noted that the young Opal's life reads uncannily like that of the heroine of a Stratton-Porter novel, Elnora Comstock of *Girl of the Limberlost*.

Plucky Elnora lives with her impoverished and mean-spirited mother (a mean mom is always a surefire winner in a book for teenage girls) out in the sticks but finds solace in nature. She goes into an abandoned swamp, revels in its beauty, and hides a key to a box of nature specimens in a mossy log in the forest, not unlike the log described in the diary in which crayons appear "from the fairies."

Elnora learns to grow moths and butterflies from cocoons to sell to wealthy collectors, allowing her to go into the town, attend high school, and eventually triumph over the snobbish town girls.

Opal later had herself photographed playing a borrowed violin (holding the bow in a manner that indicated complete ignorance of the instrument), surrounded by autumn leaves, and told people she played out in the forest, just as in the book Elnora plays a "Song of the Limberlost" on her violin out in the forest.

Whether she was out in the forest serenading nature or not, Lily Black reported that Opal didn't go to teen parties or dances. Her social activities were centered on church. By the following year her church activities had given Opal her very first brush with fame, and those unpleasant high school girls—and who can be more unpleasant?—were left in the dust.

 O pal's idol Gene Stratton-Porter leveraged her natural midwestern surroundings into bestsellerdom, made lucrative movie deals, and eventually moved to Hollywood, leaving Mr. Porter, her dull banker husband, behind. While Stratton-Porter was crazy about the Limberlost swamp near her home, she is also in the tradition of regional writers who wrote about the West and its nature in glowing terms, romanticizing the environment in order to be able to leave it.

Opal's childhood passion for nature was no doubt also genuine, but it is also true that by her teens Opal displayed a strong ambition to be somebody and, like Stratton-Porter, she resourcefully used whatever was around toward that end. In Cottage Grove there wasn't much, but there was plenty of nature, and with her characteristic thoroughness and manic energy, Opal had thrown herself into what she always called her nature work, which consisted of gathering specimens, teaching children about nature, especially the names of plants and insects and birds, and becoming a personality in the process.

Another exit strategy from Cottage Grove for an ambitious teenage girl was religion. Opal was very religious from girlhood on. As tiny children Opal and Pearl went to a church of the denomination known as the Christian Church or the Disciples of Christ, an offshoot of Methodism with roots in Ohio, Kentucky, and Pennsylvania and characterized by a lack of central authority and an evangelistic bent.

Interestingly, Scottish-born John Muir, the American naturalist a generation older than Opal, was raised in the same denomination.

John Muir has been credited by a historian of the West, Ferenc Morton Szasz, with starting "a religion of Nature," which persists as a part of contemporary American thought with which many Opalites identify. Szasz, in his book *Religion in the Modern American West*, says that John Muir's theology was characterized by "a reverence for the majesty of creation" and "his vision of the interconnectedness of all life" and was related directly to the Disciples of Christ, with their emphasis on free will when it came to personal salvation, emotionalism, and the discarding of many "manmade" aspects of religion. Muir's prose is full of biblical and evangelical references and infused with the idea of salvation through nature, as were both Opal's diary and her work teaching children.

Although Opal's and Pearl's feet dangled from the pew far above the floor, sometimes without shoes, Opal astounded church members by her ability to march up to the front of the church and recite long Bible passages. One neighbor actually believed that her incredible memory for Scripture was some sort of miracle and that the Bible had been transmitted into her memory all at once, presumably by the Holy Ghost. (Her nature-loving coreligionist John Muir had memorized all of the New Testament and most of the Old Testament by age eleven.)

In the winter of 1911, when she was thirteen, Opal became a local officer in Junior Christian Endeavor, which has been described suspiciously by Opal fans with a New Age bent as "fundamentalist," but in fact was a broad-based, mainstream Protestant movement with some progressive tendencies.

Junior Christian Endeavor was an ecumenical prepackaged church youth program, particularly suited to small towns. Cottage Grove had Presbyterian, Methodist, Christian, and Baptist churches. Through Junior Christian Endeavor, the kids from all these denominations could participate in one youth program.

Founded in Portland, Maine, in 1881 by a Congregationalist minister, Junior Christian Endeavor launched two new ideas: church programs just for youth and the idea of letting kids run things themselves or at least think they are doing so. They were ideas whose time had come. Better transportation and communication made a national movement possible. The popularity of Junior Christian Endeavor also reflected an increasing emphasis on young people as a separate segment of society, to be marketed to separately.

Its broad success in Opal's day was no doubt due to the fact that it provided an opportunity for adolescent coed socializing. (Conservative, primarily southern Christians objected to it for this reason and were also unhappy with the fact that girls had prominent leadership roles.) From the very beginning, chapters had social committees as well as prayer committees. There were also state, national, and international conventions.

The setup seemed perfect for teenagers and their parents. The teenagers got to run their own operation, expand their social circle, travel away from their hometowns, and elude a certain amount of parental supervision in service of a cause their parents couldn't fault. For the parents, there was the consolation that in an increasingly mobile society, where keeping an eye on teenagers was becoming more difficult, their children were hanging out with wholesome, respectable, church-going kids, not the dreaded "wrong crowd." After all, a quick jaunt in a Model T could carry them far away from the parental eye. Better that they were involved in church work than smoking, drinking, and doing the bunny hug, the grizzly bear, the turkey trot, or other animalistic rag-time dances. The positive tone was reflected in the Junior Christian Endeavor motto, "Onward and Upward."

Opal's route to fame in the organization began unglamorously. At thirteen she was secretary of the local chapter of Junior Christian Endeavor. Her hastily scrawled minutes of a 1911 meeting read, "Junior was opened by singing songs No. 165 and 142 after which [illegible] stood and lead [*sic*] us in prayer. Last Sundays lesson was then reviewed by the Supt. The bible lesson was read and explained followed by the lesson story read by Clifford. We then sang song 168. Bible story reviewed by Sup. Mission story read by Virgil Powell . . . Penny March collection 3¢. Roll was called. Leader for next Sunday Ruth. Sang Song No. 203. Said Benediction."

But within a few years her Junior Christian Endeavor work, in combination with her little nature girl persona, allowed Opal to turn herself from a small-town, working-class girl from a struggling family, unpopular with the other girls, into a teen celebrity. For Opal Whiteley, who later said that at seventeen she had never been to Eugene, the college town about twenty-five miles away, the Christian Endeavor movement was her ticket out of town and the beginning of her career as a regional personality.

Opal attended her first Christian Endeavor convention that year. She achieved state office on the Resolutions Committee, work that she performed by one account with "striking self-assurance," unintimidated by the city kids despite her own "backwoods" environment, but still coming across as "girlishly natural and unsophisticated." She had a good grasp of parliamentary procedure, and she could wow a crowd.

Opal's speeches have been described as mesmerizing. She is said to have spoken quickly, "like a waterfall," and seemed to sizzle with quick energy. Audiences were enchanted by the combination of her tiny size and abundant enthusiasm. Her rapid movement, small size, and dark good looks with flashing dark eyes make her sound like Rima the bird-girl, the heroine of a popular novel of the day, W. H. Hudson's *Green Mansions*, who darted fetchingly around the forest primeval.

Opal's ability to enchant was enormous. Asked to describe why she was so charming, people said she had an engaging combination of innocence and intelligence, and she was often described as a child-woman. They also remarked on her enthusiasm and eagerness. "I just don't know how to describe it. She is so interested and enthusiastic that it looks as if her soul were too large for her body and kind of overflows through her eyes," said someone who knew her at this period.

While in Eugene for that Christian Endeavor convention, Opal also visited the university. There too her charm knocked out a crowd of professors. She was so captivating she made the *Eugene Register-Guard*, which wrote:

Tutored by nature, a tiny 17-year old mountain girl, her hair down her back, has opened the eyes of the Eugene teaching profession and left it gasping for breath. Educated by herself in the forests of the Cascade Mountains [this seems a little unfair to Lily Black, who taught her Latin and ancient and European history at Dorena], she has made a college education appear artificial and insignificant, university professors admit. Entrance rules have been cast aside; scholarships are proposed.

"This experience happens to a university but once in a generation," declared Warren D. Smith, head of the university geology department. "She knows more about geology than do many students that have graduated from my department. She may become one of the greatest minds Oregon has ever produced. She will be an investment for the university."

The Oregonian, a Portland paper with a statewide circulation, picked up the story. SELF TAUGHT NATURE EXPERT OF 17 ASTONISHES UNIVERSITY FACULTY; HAS FINE COLLECTIONS OF SPECIMENS AND IDEAS FOR INSTRUCTION OF YOUTH ARE DECLARED TO BE ULTRA MODERN, read the headline.

Dr. Smith of the geology department was quoted as saying he had let her look through a microscope, presumably for the first time, and "she became highly excited." Opal hadn't passed geometry, a college requirement, but Dr. Smith announced that there were "no entrance rules that can keep her out of the university."

Readers throughout the state learned that Opal had a fantastic memory, which she trained by memorizing three poems a week. Her favorite poets were Wordsworth and Longfellow. She attributed much of her interest in nature to her late uncle Henry Pearson, a miner, and said her constant companions as she roamed the forests were her little sister Cloe and her white dog, Dandy.

A few months later, after a stunningly well-received speech about God and nature, Opal was elected the Oregon chairman of Junior Christian Endeavor. She immediately announced a statewide tour to promote the organization and take her message of God's handiwork revealed in nature to the children of Oregon.

Her next press coverage came from Elbert Bede, the editor and publisher of the *Cottage Grove Sentinel*. The eyes of Opalites tend to narrow at the mention of his name. They are not happy with the way Bede portrayed Opal in his almost half century of covering her. In his 1987 book on Opal, Benjamin Hoff called him "a character assassin." Playwright and composer Robert Nassif, who wrote the musical *Opal*, said to me,

"What a strange, jealous, pathetic, uneducated man. . . . I know these people who are jealous of any success . . . resentful that they have been left behind."

Some Opalites say Bede later questioned Opal's claims and her integrity not because of envy but because she spurned his advances. If the dark forces of envy, lust, and revenge were part of Bede's makeup, he managed to hide it pretty well. He appears to have been an extroverted, cheerful, sociable man, a kind of Norman Rockwell–style 1920s boosterish small-town gee-whiz optimist. Opal was the biggest story that had ever hit his beat, even surpassing Buster Keaton's coming to town to film *The General*. Bede went after it with his characteristic enthusiasm and made the most of it in the purplish newspaper prose of the day.

When Bede died in 1967 at the age of eighty-six, his obituary in the *Sentinel* quoted someone who knew him: "He was a comic, a character, a great ladies' man, full of hell but smart and shrewd." He was also eulogized as "a man that believed in bettering things all the time. He was honest. He liked to help people and went around visiting the sick and persons with other troubles. He worked very hard in putting over municipal projects." Another obituary noted his "sparkling wit."

Bede apparently relished small-town life. Always civic-minded and a joiner, he served on the city council and at the Chamber of Commerce and was the reading clerk in the state legislature. A lifelong Episcopalian, he went to church every Sunday, and he was a fanatical golfer. In the heyday of men's lodges in small-town America, he was also an avid Mason and a Shriner. After a stint as a customs official on Lake Superior, Bede decided to become a small-town newspaper editor. He went west in 1911 to scout around for a suitable place to settle. He put a down payment on the *Bellingham Herald* in Washington and caught the train back to Minnesota to fetch his young family, but a stop along the way in Cottage Grove convinced him to forfeit his down payment on the *Herald* and to buy the *Sentinel*.

Bede first met Opal in 1915. In his 1954 book *Fabulous Opal Whiteley: From Logging Camp to Princess of India* he describes this meeting:

Opal gave me a rapid, unhesitant description of her plans for Junior Endeavor for the state, already well advanced although she had been in office but a few hours. She was going out among the children of Oregon to tell them of God. She was going to interest them in Christian Endeavor through stories of His creatures that roam the fields, flutter in the air, burrow in the earth, inhabit the waters. She was going to give them messages whispered by the flowers and trees, the flowing streams, the rocks of the hillsides, the fairies of the air, the shells of the sea.

"How did you get your plans laid so quickly?" I asked.

Her reply indicated that the honor of the office scarcely had taken her by surprise and that its duties were faced without misgivings.

"I have been planning this for years," she said.

He wrote that his first impression of her was that of a "vibrant, fluttery, whimsical maid, informed strangely beyond her years, deeply earnest and seriously religious," but when he looked back later, her long-term planning struck him as perhaps indicative of a certain steely ambition.

He sold a version of his 1915 interview to California's *Sunset Magazine* for its "Interesting Westerners" column. In the accompanying picture, the seventeen-year-old Opal looks plump and sweet with a wide smile. She is wearing her hair parted in the middle and drawn back in a rather dowdy bun. Bede, sounding as enchanted as the Junior Endeavor set and the faculty at the University of Oregon, called her "a little slip of a girl" and told his readers about her isolated life in the woods, where she had "been preparing herself for the teaching of young people by studying Nature . . . the flowers, the birds, the butterflies, the rocks, the skies. . . . She found that by explaining the mysteries of Nature she interested the little boys and girls in the maker of Nature. . . . Many a lesson was taught while the children watched the unfolding of a butterfly from its chrysalis." He summed up by saying: "Miss Whiteley has a remarkable face, not for its unusual beauty, but for its innocence, its intelligence and its eagerness."

He sold a third version of the story to *The Oregonian*. In this version he downplayed the religious angle but emphasized that Opal was "a prodigy" who had managed to teach herself all about science in the out-of-doors. The article implied she had never been to school but had simply flitted around the forest, absorbing knowledge, and it said she had done this "with no one to assist her" and "without even a parent's guidance. . . . Miss Whiteley's school has been the great outdoors." This is at odds with the known facts: Opal did indeed go to school, had lots of books sent her from the state library, and lived with the Whiteleys, whom she called Mother and Papa.

With this excellent advance publicity, Opal hit the road for the Junior Endeavor society, traveling all over Oregon, giving pep talks as well as motivating local groups to start new Junior Endeavor societies. She had an expense account and did her own scheduling, writing ahead to local Endeavor members to meet her at the train station. Reportedly, she made four or five of these trips a month. Opal was a phenomenal promoter. During the two years of her tenure, the number of Junior Christian Endeavor societies in Oregon rose from fifteen to one hundred.

Having made a big success of her Christian Endeavor work, Opal now aspired to go to college. She needed some more high school credits, and she had to pass geometry to enter the University of Oregon in Eugene. Despite the gushing professors' insistence that admittance requirements should be waived for the charming young woman who had waltzed through their laboratories, Opal was told by less dazzled officials in admissions that she had to get her remaining high school credits. She went to Cottage Grove High School in town to get the extra credits she needed.

In Cottage Grove, Opal's worldly ambitions were given a further boost when a Mrs. Jean Morris Ellis came to town. Mrs. Ellis was a lecturer and pop psychologist and proof that there is nothing new about the self-help movement.

In her eccentrically punctuated brochure, Mrs. Ellis claimed to have a message for "The Young Man or Woman too large for their present place" and "ANYBODY AND EVERYBODY Heartsick or Discouraged."

For Opal, Mrs. Ellis was both a source of advice on making something of herself and, as a successful female lecturer, a role model. Mrs. Ellis billed herself as a "vocational advisor and character analyst," and her flyer offered a dozen lectures on subjects such as body language, telepathy, and sex.

Mrs. Ellis's photograph reveals a serious-looking woman with big dark, sad eyes under low, level brows. Her hair is arranged in a topknot, and she wears a stiff black dress trimmed with a lot of white lace and a long bead necklace. She rather resembles the battle-ax-grand dame chaperone in a silent movie comedy, but she was described as "a decoration to her noble and unique vocation."

After her lectures, members of the audience could get, for an additional two dollars, private counseling appointments in which they could receive "a special and intimate personal message." "It has meant success to thousands, why not you?" asked the brochure.

Opal took Mrs. Ellis up on the offer and received a "Descriptive Chart." This document included several pages of boilerplate advice that would not be unfamiliar to anyone who has been forced to listen to a corporate trainer or motivational speaker: "Have faith in your own genius," "Make every obstacle a stepping stone."

Opal had her brain measured (21⅝ by 14 inches), which I assume means that Mrs. Ellis ran a tape measure around the circumference of her skull, and was rated on a one to seven scale on forty-three character traits. Mrs. Ellis rated her highly on most of them, but she was encouraged to work to cultivate a sense of humor and to improve her bone and muscular system and circulatory system.

Mrs. Ellis also provided a chart describing the kind of husband Opal should be looking for. He should be tall, fair, and of medium build, and his skull should measure twenty-three inches around. It isn't clear whether this was an optimum or a minimum circumference.

She was also given a list of suitable occupations to follow, including Ellis's own glamorous and lucrative profession—lecturer, which Opal was already doing on the Christian Endeavor expense account. Opal thought enough of this document to store it with a friend, so that Faye wouldn't tear it up. Opal was ambitious and concerned about the future. The year she was seventeen had been a busy, successful time, and Opal seemed to have burst into the world and begun to dazzle it. Opal herself, however, later remembered it as a grim time full of hardship and disappointment. In notes for an autobiography, written in her thirties, Opal, referring to herself as F. for Françoise, the name she then used, described 1915, the year she was seventeen and elected Junior Christian Endeavor superintendent.

Self Study. Wanted to enter University of Oregon at Eugene where F. went to Christian Endeavor Convention. Admission impossible—not having qualified. . . . Left Whiteleys to do housework at Eugene as Mr. W. was out of work—only salted salmon for children. University of Oregon refused admission so Dr. Smith of Geol. Department requested that Françoise be admitted as a special student. <u>Refused</u>.

Returned to Whiteleys summer of 1915 owing to overwork at Eugene at the house of a Mrs. David Auld, a society woman. F. only servant, washing, cleaning, scrubbing steps $3.50 a week. Whiteley at Donahue lumber camp. . . . Star Oregon. Mrs. Whiteley ill. Looked after 4 children.

Autumn 1915 all moved to Cottage Grove . . . Stayed at CG High School 2½ months.

[Here Opal apparently got her high school diploma and passed all the rest of her required courses except geometry.]

In 1916 Opal had a nervous breakdown. She later said that she spoke to a group of Junior Endeavorers even though she was hoarse, and the next day her voice left her. She became completely mute for three or four months. There had been an earlier time when Opal had severe bronchitis and spoke only in a whisper. Although Opal had previously campaigned for an Oregon state initiative to ban alcohol, putting up "Oregon Dry" posters around town, neighbors gave her some wine, saying it was grape juice and would be good for her throat. Opal drank it, and her voice was immediately restored.

The 1916 episode of mutism, however, was much more than laryngitis. After her voice had come back, Opal wrote G. Evert Baker, a lawyer involved in Junior Christian Endeavor work, that her hearing had also gone. She appears to have become anorexic as well. "I solemnly promise you Mamma and Daddy Baker, that I will not get so busy in my work that I do not have time to eat." Revealing her public position on her origins at that time, she added, "I had to solemnly promise my own Daddy that last week." Unable to speak or hear and eating very little for three or four months sounds as though she were in a catatonic state. According to Ed Whiteley, her voice came back all at once, three months later, and she was back on the hustings.

In her adult notebook covering this period Opal described the episode this way: "Cruelty of Mrs. W. and her mother Mrs. Scott, beaten hair brush, lost hearing and speech four months, shock. Taken to doctor at Crewel—operated on nose."

During the summer of 1916, Opal taught nature classes in Heppner, Oregon. Opal lived with Maude MacDonald, a poorly educated, good-hearted minister's wife who shared Opal's love of nature and religion. The mother of two boys, Mrs. MacDonald treated Opal like a daughter and loved her for the rest of her life. Mrs. MacDonald's letters reveal her to be a kind, energetic soul, making pies for lonely bachelor neighbors on Christmas Eve. She enjoyed pressing plants, flowers, and fungi and sending them to her correspondents, painting slightly garish nature scenes on her writing paper, and composing inspiring little poems. Mrs. MacDonald wrote Opal for many years, addressing her as "girlie," and giving her motherly advice.

The letters are full of reminiscences of that halcyon summer of 1916. Mrs. MacDonald never forgot about the happy times they had had and tried to get Opal to return to her farm. Among her memories was Opal's naming a tree at the entrance to the farm Geoffrey Chaucer, in the manner of the little girl of the diary. The only jarring note about the visit, reported later by Mrs. MacDonald, was that Opal would have terrible nightmares and awaken screaming in the middle of the night. At one point she insisted that a mysterious man was stalking her and trying to get inside the MacDonalds' house and do her harm.

At the end of her summer with the MacDonalds, Opal was going off to college. After two tries she had finally arranged to be admitted even though she hadn't strictly fulfilled all the entrance requirements. She seems to have charmed her way in and was admitted on the understanding she would have to pass high school geometry at some point.

By her own account, freshman year was a disaster, marked by grinding poverty and the demands of her family. She got a twenty-five-dollar loan to pay for a year's fees but said she lived in a one-room hovel with no sheets. Editor Ellery Sedgwick, later her publisher, who had had a much different undergraduate experience at Harvard, reported with horror that the room contained nothing but a cot, and her curtains were newspapers. She lived on milk, peanut butter, and bread. She owned no clothes but those she wore.

A month after school started, according to Opal's later account, "Mrs. Whiteley and 3 children turned up . . . & lived in this room with Françoise who had to earn her money working consequently had to miss classes." Opal said Lizzie Whiteley was acting unbalanced and destroyed her study notes "as she felt learning would eventually take F. away from them." In November she set Opal off on a wild-goose chase, getting her to rent a cart and horse for six dollars and move the entire family and all their possessions to a new home in nearby Springfield and then, changing her mind the morning of the next day, got Opal to rent the horse and cart again for another six dollars and move everybody to another house entirely. "Mrs. W. had cancer (open). F. worked again odd jobs—sold ferns [to florists]—missed school."

Opal's public image at school was less troubled. She was considered a campus personality and was remembered years later for her old-fashioned girlish look and her unspoiled manner, although some found it phony. Years later a University of Oregon alumna described her as a proto-hippie. It was at this time that she began to be photographed in various striking poses and costumes. She was also remembered by one professor as walking the halls with photographers following her and snapping her picture. Another professor wrote, "[T]he university faculty recalled Opal as a girl withdrawn from normal campus activities, but intensely preoccupied with her own private affairs. We remembered her appearance—her dark gypsy coloring, her small vigorous physique, her eager smile." He said the faculty had already heard of her nature classes for children and her lectures.

Benjamin Hoff reported that the wife of the university president came upon Opal on her knees singing, entranced by an earthworm, and that she leaped out of the classroom in pursuit of butterflies and perched in trees, reading books.

Opal had changed from the demure seventeen-year-old described by Bede to somebody considerably slicker. A 1917 article by her in the *Christian Endeavor Bulletin* reveals that first of all, her publicity shot had changed from the plump, wholesome image that accompanied Bede's 1915 stories about her. After two years on the road, the nineteen-year-old Opal looked a lot more sophisticated, with a much more fetching coiffure swept back from her forehead and arranged over one shoulder.

Artful corkscrew curls dangled at the ears. She had also learned not to smile so broadly for the camera, which tended to make her teeth look too prominent.

The article over her byline, "What About Your Juniors?," was a pitch to Endeavorers who, despite Opal's efforts, still hadn't established a Junior Endeavor society in their town. She was full of the certainty and confidence of a seasoned salesman, with some of the boosterish Jean Morris Ellis tone of positive thinking. She wrote "To build firmly the foundation for the success of your Senior Endeavor Society, why not get the children of your community together for a Junior Endeavor Society[?] Oh! You need not worry about them not being interested in Christian Endeavor. You just give them a glimpse of what Christian Endeavor means and you will have a band of loyal willing workers. . . .

"What! You have no Junior committee. Well—get one into existence just as quickly as possible. . . . It's mighty fine the way the Oregon Endeavorers sing that inspiring song 'I'm here on business for my King.' I put the Junior Endeavor work before you as a business proposition. Are you going to make this worthwhile investment for your king?"

Through her religious work she had made friends all over the state, and at conventions she met Endeavorers from around the country. A young man from Massachusetts named Fred Lynch became a pen pal, who proudly reported that he too had become a state superintendent and asked solicitously about her health after her breakdown.

She even had a brief romance. Steve Pearson, a relative of her aunt's husband from Winchester, Oregon, was a fisherman who liked working on cars. He said he would send pictures of an outing they had taken to Crater Lake, although interestingly, he wrote he had to mail them from out of town so someone named Rhoda wouldn't find out and tear them up. (Years later, when Opal was in her thirties, she asked Mrs. MacDonald to check up on Steve and Rhoda and tell her what had become of them. Mrs. MacDonald told her that "S.P." hadn't been "the right man" for her.)

Opal got fan mail from people her age who declared it a privilege to have met her. Other correspondents were like real friends, filling her in on how their school football teams were doing and asking about mutual acquaintances. After a bumpy start, as the weird kid in a small town, saddled with heavy responsibilities at home, Opal seemed to have come into her own socially.

Opal used her visibility to promote her nature lectures. An announcement in the June 1917 *Christian Endeavor Bulletin* mentioned that Miss Whiteley "is making as her life work a study of the various things of nature that should interest us," adding that she had decided that "during the months of October, November, and December she will travel in different parts of Oregon, California, Idaho and Washington, giving lectures on her Nature Study Work." As she was also in her sophomore year at the university, this was an ambitious schedule indeed.

Opal turned out to be a natural self-promoter. To ensure advance publicity, she distributed her photo to local papers around the state, instructing editors to pass it on to the next town, and she charged an admission fee, which she presumably did not do on Christian Endeavor trips.

In the same issue of the *Christian Endeavor Bulletin* promoting her tour, there was an announcement under the headline MRS. WHITELEY PASSES AWAY: "Perhaps there is no State Worker more loved by the Endeavor Members of Oregon than our little Junior Superintendent, Opal Whiteley." The article also took note of the fact that "her Grandfather . . . on the Mother's side" died the following day. The article asked for prayers and gestures of sympathy for Opal, which duly arrived. There was no indication, however, that her nature lecture tour would be called off, although she did cancel her plans to attend a Junior Christian Endeavor convention in New York City soon afterward. In Opal's own, much darker account of this time, she stated that she paid for the funeral herself, borrowing ninety dollars from Steve Pearson.

After Opal had begun traveling on the Junior Christian Endeavor circuit again, a woman she stayed with reported that she woke up hysterical in the middle of the night, calling for her mother, and had to be soothed. Old acquaintances later said that Opal often put flowers on Lizzie's grave at this period.

Despite these signs of grief, the family had been upset because Lizzie's mother, Grandma Scott, had told Opal that Lizzie would not last out the day and that she should stay home so as to be at her mother's side when she died. Opal had refused to stay home, saying her schoolwork was too important, and Lizzie did indeed die that day while Opal was away.

*J*ust before the beginning of her sophomore year, Opal wrote that school was scheduled to begin in a few days, she was very lonesome, and she was living by herself in a house with a bedroom, combined kitchen and dining room, workroom, and study. Opal, never keen on housework, told her correspondent that since it was more economical to keep house than to board, she was working "all the time," piling up wood for the winter, and canning peaches, plums, and tomatoes. The house, across the street from campus at 1703 Franklin, was loaned to her rent-free by admirers, a couple called the Hunts, who also brought her gifts of food. The house was full of her nature specimens—according to Elbert Bede, more than sixteen thousand of them.

In Eugene, Opal was in contact with the rest of the Whiteleys, and some of their letters survive. They indicate that despite what Opal said about them in the years to come, the family clearly felt affection for her.

After her breakdown, Ed Whiteley's father in Washington State wrote a concerned letter and suggested she could get a job as a schoolteacher near his home. Ed Whiteley's mother, Mrs. Patrick (who was divorced from Ed's father), wrote an encouraging letter from Santa Rosa, where she lived with her second husband.

She urged her, "Do be careful and not overdo yourself again and have another nervous breakdown."

The Whiteley sisters wrote too. Faye, despite her record as a holy terror, apparently cared about Opal, although her feelings may not have been reciprocated, as she often began her letters with "Why don't you write?"

Opal was often encouraged to visit home. More than once the Whiteley girls wrote that Ed Whiteley would pay her fare home and promised her a nice home-cooked meal.

The girls also wrote her often that they were sending a box of home-made treats or said that if she visited they would send her home with one. They were after Opal to act as a shopping scout and personal shopper for them in Eugene, asking what hats cost, and what kind of coats were in style. The girls wanted her to get some wallpaper samples. They had an oatmeal color and texture in mind. The family had just moved, and the girls were decorating. They also wanted prices on flowerpots, jardinieres, and leather to be made into sofa pillows.

Faye wanted a picture taken of "all of us girls together" and asked Opal once more to come visit and bring her camera, and let them know about the wallpaper.

Early in the school year Opal had an accident with a coal fire and got a cinder in her eye. When Pearl heard about it, she wrote to ask how much the operation cost and enclosed five dollars.

Opal later said that she was poor and hungry and that her family treated her badly during this period. According to author Benjamin Hoff, her family lost interest in her around this time. But these letters seem to indicate the family was trying its best, despite the fact that Ed Whiteley was unemployed for a while after a mill where he worked burned down in Cottage Grove. The Whiteley girls' repeated pleas for Opal to write, to visit, and to send those wallpaper samples makes it pretty clear that it was she who was drifting apart from them.

Opal was developing new interests. Shortly after moving into the house on Franklin, she bought a subscription to *Motion Picture Classics* magazine. Opal and a girlfriend named Bertha were dabbling in what was called mood photography, photography with artistic content as opposed to snapshots. Opal, wearing a bathing suit, would arrange her long hair strategically to achieve a nude Lady Godiva look for these shots, although she was said to be personally very modest. She also rented a typewriter from the Remington typewriter company, whose collection department was soon dunning her for the three-dollar-a-month rental fee. In notebooks she scrawled pseudonyms based on surnames from the Whiteley and Scott genealogy and ideas for literary projects based on childhood memories and her nature studies. She made lists of photographs she intended to have taken of herself in various costumes, include one of herself sobbing.

A list of books she read includes, in addition to the titles *Everyday Butterflies*, *The Charm of the Hills*, and *How to Study Birds*, such items as *Heredity in Relation to Eugenics*, *Heredity and Eugenics*, *Parenthood and Race Culture*, and *Practical Eugenics*.

She corresponded with the Eugenics Record Office of Cold Spring Harbor, Long Island, New York, which sent her something called the "Record of Family Traits' schedules," which Opal was supposed to fill out and return. The office also promised to mail her two copies of the "Family Distribution of Personal Traits," a more elaborate form that required several months to complete. The Eugenics Record Office, founded in 1910, was a center for research into heredity, much of it now discredited. Among other projects, it kept boxes of file cards with names, birthplaces, birth dates, illnesses, and special abilities taken from forms sent in by people like Opal, a sort of human DNA mapping project on three-by-five cards.

Opal became preoccupied with tracing the family and changed her middle name from Irene to Stanley, a name from the Whiteley family tree that she reckoned could be traced back to 1277 and connected to the seventeenth earl of Derby. She also explored various family trees among French royalty.

Along with this search for her roots in 1917 came the first recorded instance of Opal's saying she was adopted. She apparently announced this to Mrs. Hunt, the woman who had loaned her the house near campus, who said she could well believe it, because Opal was of a very different temperament than the Whiteleys.

Her lifelong habit of not returning books began and reflected her changing personality. She borrowed books all over Oregon, and from her professors in Eugene, forcing their owners to beg for their return. Among other complaints, an overdue notice for *Useful Birds and Their Protection* arrived from the University of Oregon Library, to be archived years later in its special collections department, and an epic battle over long-overdue materials was under way with Cornelia Marvin, Opal's old friend at the state library in Salem.

Between 1916 and 1918, Cornelia Marvin wrote a brace of libraries and educational institutions trying to find a good address for Opal, who ignored her demand for either the return of *Nature's Garden* or the three dollars it cost. Miss Marvin hinted broadly that since her previous letters had not been returned, Opal had received them and ignored them. After about a year and a half's worth of silence, Opal finally did write back, but she insisted that *Nature's Garden* had been returned years ago, hedging a bit by adding that it had been mailed by someone else for her because she was ill at the time.

This cut no ice with Miss Marvin, who suggested that she check at the post office where it had been mailed and that in any case Opal must be confusing it with other material that she had returned. Miss Marvin, perhaps remembering the pleasant correspondence she had had with Opal when she was younger, not to mention the many volumes she had shipped to the lumber camps, as well as the many six-month renewals she had allowed, was taking this one personally. Opal had become a teenage celebrity in part with Miss Marvin's help, and instead of gratitude, the librarian was being treated cavalierly. *Nature's Garden* became to Miss Marvin what Moby Dick was to Captain Ahab.

She wrote the Eugene public library to ask if Opal borrowed from them and ended grimly, "I want to make her pay it since she does not even pay attention to the letters."

In the end Opal won. Miss Marvin learned that Opal had been found and been reminded to write to her. Opal agreed, but there is no evidence she ever did so. Her borrowing card at the state library rests there now among the Opal Whiteley papers. A well-worn strip of yellow cardboard with titles and date stamps, it also records a list of letters sent in vain and a note initialed by Miss Marvin instructing not to send a requested book. Finally, across the top, in letters whose blottiness indicates the force with which the pen was used, is scrawled "Dead Beat!!! No more books *ever*."

Miss Marvin got her revenge some years later, when she asked Ellery Sedgwick for some of the original manuscript pages of the diary, perhaps with an eye to detecting fraud. He refused but sent an order form for a published copy. Miss Marvin informed him that the Oregon State Library would not be adding *The Story of Opal: The Journal of an Understanding Heart* to its collections. (In 1928, at age fifty-four, the strong-willed Cornelia Marvin resigned her post as state librarian to become wife and political adviser to her boss, the governor of Oregon.)

Besides losing books, Opal was falling apart in other ways, skipping classes and racking up incompletes at the university, but she kept up her overachiever image and exhibited manic energy, reading and studying so much that she ate standing up with a book in her hand. Psychology Professor Conklin summed up her college career tersely in his report. He said she completed about one year of credits, borrowed "an incredible number" of books; had trouble making friends, borrowed outfits in which to be photographed, and "tried unsuccessfully to live with one or more Eugene women and do housework."

Here is Opal's later account of her sophomore year: "Very poor—no food—hard work—poor effort at University. Faye Whiteley stole petticoat in December 1917—In February 1918 only decent green dress, drawers, toothbrush. F. decided to go to California."

In February, Opal got on the train for California. She borrowed $150 for the trip from the Cottage Grove bank. A relative of her friend Nellie Hemenway cosigned for the loan. Nellie, who was part of Opal's life for many decades, packed her some snacks to eat on the train and went to see her off. Nellie was a University of Oregon graduate and an aspiring writer who worked for a while writing articles for Elbert Bede's newspaper. Even though she was seven years older and came from a more sophisticated and affluent background than Opal, Nellie found Opal fascinating and tended to hero-worship her. Nellie's nephew told me that initially Nellie found Opal "glamorous." After Nellie and Opal said good-bye, they never saw each other again, although they corresponded for more than fifty years. The two girls from Cottage Grove were to lead very different lives.

In early March, after Opal had already gone, *The Oregonian* printed an interview with her under the headline UNIVERSITY GIRL PLANS MUSEUM AS AID TO CHILDREN OF OREGON IN STUDYING NATURE. There are two pictures of Opal, one looking wholesome and perky with a wide smile, a thick braid over one shoulder, and a broad-brimmed hat on her head; the other her barefoot Isadora Duncan dance pose with flowers woven into her hair over the caption "Interpreting the Spirit of Nature in the Dance."

The article explained that Opal Whiteley, who had been affectionately known as the Sunshine Fairy since childhood, was establishing a children's nature museum in Eugene the following autumn. The museum would include specimens of minerals, fossils, flowers, butterflies, and insects from around the state, and it would be run by children under the direction of the "Phusis Philoi" (lovers of nature) club which "Miss Whiteley has just organized at the university among girls interested in science, art, and music." The article went on to describe Opal's childhood and her early pets and said she had named them after characters in history and opera, citing a lizard named Rigoletto.

Of Lizzie, Opal was quoted as saying: "My dearest girl chum was my mother. In my love of music, art, poetry, biography, the drama, history, she was in close sympathy with me and we had many wonderful twilight hours together before her homegoing last year." However, according to Opal, Lizzie had opposed her nature work "since she had planned a different career for me." Opal didn't say what it was.

The article said Miss Whiteley was off to California to do research work there "in the Sierra Nevada and San Bernardino Mountains, in the Yosemite, the Catalina Islands, and the Mohave Desert." Opal was to give nature lectures while in California and planned to return in September to begin the children's museum and go back to the university. Opal was quoted as saying, "I want to say to my many friends in Oregon, that I'm not saying good-bye to Oregon but am taking Oregon right along with me."

Opal's first stop in California was Oakland, where she stayed with Mr. and Mrs. Awbrey, old Cottage Grove friends who knew her through church work. She visited "nature collections" at the University of California at Berkeley and across the bay at Stanford. She went on to Los Angeles, arriving at night in a torrential rainstorm, and wrote to her friend Nellie that she walked to Sunday school through flooded streets the next morning.

She was staying with a Mrs. Stephens who let rooms, the sister of a woman in Cottage Grove. Opal later wrote ominously: "F. stayed there a few days until discovering she was a bad woman."

Opal then went to a house in Hollywood that took in boarders. Maud and Frank Bales and Elisa Harwood, Mrs. Bales's daughter by her first husband, lived on DeLongpre Avenue, just a block off Sunset Boulevard, a pretty, quiet street of wooden bungalows surrounded by small gardens and wood fences.

The Bales family was from Cottage Grove, and Opal knew them slightly. Maud Harwood Bales had instigated the couple's move to California. She wanted to make a gentleman farmer out of her second husband, Frank, but he knew nothing about farming and was of a more mechanical bent. Eventually the Baleses moved to the San Fernando Valley and the town of Owensmouth, now Canoga Park, then a hub of chicken ranching. But in 1918 they lived in Hollywood and took in boarders, something the genteel Mrs. Bales found a little embarrassing.

Opal told them she only had thirty dollars, was doing research work in Los Angeles in connection with her work at the University of Oregon, and was returning there in September, and they said she could stay until then. Maud, a woman with cultural interests, was initially charmed by Opal and was delighted to have her join her household.

The Baleses turned over the bedroom of twelve-year-old Elisa Harwood to Opal. It was a small but pretty room with four windows looking out over Sunset Boulevard to the Hollywood Hills. Opal later said that she was charged $4.50 a week for room and board and was also supposed to tutor Elisa. Opal had a huge collection of boxes with her, which she hadn't unpacked at Mrs. Stephens's house. They were full of papers and nature specimens. She was given half the storeroom over the garage in which to deploy these items. Elisa and Mrs. Bales's former brother-in-law, Mr. Harwood, helped Opal unpack the boxes, and he also rigged up shelves and tables on which she could arrange her specimens and papers.

Maud Bales had led a fairly adventurous life, including a stint helping build a railroad in Venezuela, but it was marked by thwarted ambition and disappointment. She was an Englishwoman, the eldest girl in a family of ten. Her father, she said, was "foreign correspondent" for

Bayliss Jones & Bayliss, a Wolverhampton manufacturer of metal gates, fences, and railings. She had received very little education, partly because the two siblings who followed her were very talented and good-looking, the implication being that scant family resources were considered better spent on them. Her services were needed at home, but she read a lot of books when household duties allowed. In many ways Mrs. Bales's complaints about her childhood were similar to those Opal later made about hers: an uncaring family, the domestic drudgery that often fell on an eldest girl, and family discouragement of her intellectual interests.

Soon after Opal arrived at the Bales home, she wrote her friend Nellie Hemenway a glowing letter about her new situation. She described Mrs. Bales as "a dear friend, a delightful English lady" and added that she had discovered wonderful flowers in the desert, was doing very interesting "research work" in the San Bernardino Mountains, was attending Sunday school, and was finding many new birds, flowers, moths, and butterflies. Twice a week she went to the coast to pursue "my study of conchology. I find many interesting things in the sea."

Nellie Hemenway had written Opal a rather worshipful letter, confiding that she too had literary ambitions and was at work on some stories. She also wanted to write a profile of Opal and asked if that would be all right. Opal replied with a patronizing "You wrote about writing article concerning my work. Should be more pleased to have you write it than anyone I know."

Opal, armed with her publicity shots from the Tolman Studios in Eugene, spent the first six weeks at the Baleses' trying to break into the movies. Mrs. Bales noted the presence of many envelopes Opal had addressed to movie stars, but Opal never made it into the movies. Later in life she claimed she'd told Cecil B. DeMille she wanted to make nature movies for children, and when he told her it wasn't practical, she shelved the idea.

Quickly abandoning her Hollywood hopes, Opal amazed Mrs. Bales by cracking the forbidding social facade of southern California women's clubs—the Friday Morning Club and the Shell Club—and giving nature lectures to members, after which she formed outdoor nature classes for their children. Mrs. Bales thought it ironic that Opal's naiveté had made this possible. Not knowing how exclusive these clubs were had emboldened her.

Opal was never intimidated by rank or social standing and always considered herself the equal of anyone. She was also never afraid to ask for anything. Her combination of forthright demands coupled with girlish charm proved to be an effective one-two punch. It's not clear if her brazenness was naive or calculated or somehow a bit of both.

Elbert Bede, whose source was almost certainly Mrs. Bales, reported that after arriving in Los Angeles, Opal compiled a list of important people from the local *Who's Who* and set out to meet them without appointments or introductions, simply walking into their offices and introducing herself. She carried autobiographical information and even talking points to use when chatting with these prospective friends and supporters. Two wealthy retired gentlemen volunteered to drive her to these meetings. They were said to have been flattered into helping. When she took the liberty of calling one of them, a correct Englishman, by his first name, he dropped her immediately. The other man quit chauffeuring her around town when he discovered she was making cold calls.

Opal described her appearance at the time as rakishly bohemian with her hair in two braids down her back, "hatless, sandles [*sic*], white stockings, old blue dress, no petticoat." She said she observed houses in the neighborhood from which children left to go to school and asked their parents to hire her to teach nature lessons to the children in groups of six.

The nature classes were a great success. Through her work Opal met well-heeled Los Angeles clubwomen, many of whom helped her and sent her money for many years. They included a Mrs. F. W. Flint, a Mrs. Daniel Murphy, and Miss Marie Mullen, who served as president of the family business, the tony Mullen & Bluett haberdashery. Opal also is said to have befriended Mrs. Jesse Lasky and to have taught the legendary producer's children. Things went well with the nature classes until the summer, when the children were out of school and the students seemed to be unavailable. Around this time, encouraged, she said, by the mothers of her pupils, Opal began to put together her nature lectures into a book.

Opal decided to publish it herself and to presell copies, beginning, in her words, to "tramp for orders." According to Mrs. Bales, she wrote letters to the rich and famous, containing newspaper clippings about herself and asking for money to support her work. After she asked John D. Rockefeller for the curiously unround figure of $999, Mrs. Bales told her to stop writing begging letters from the Bales address.

While she was preselling and writing the book, in the spring of 1918, Opal began an incredible work jag that lasted for many months. Mrs. Bales later said she spent many days researching in the Los Angeles Public Library and then wrote well into the night, twelve hours at a time.

At the end of May, Opal wrote Nellie Hemenway that "my first nature book, 'The Fairyland Around Us' has gone to press and will be ready for distribution in August." She proposed that Nellie try to get some stories about Opal into the Eugene and Portland papers. She suggested the headline WITH OREGON'S NATURE GIRL IN THE SOUTH and said she'd send seven or eight photos to accompany the articles.

Opal was becoming less popular around the Bales home. She was enjoined from doing any housework, as she was extremely clumsy, and that was probably just fine with her. Mrs. Bales was irked when she loaned Opal a book and discovered it later with a cut lemon facedown on it. Maud Bales said that "one by one" the other boarders took a dislike to Opal that "in some cases became a positive antipathy." Mrs. Bales finally told them they had to be nice to Opal, who would be there only until September 1.

Frank Bales's niece Dorothy Randle grew up in Cottage Grove. Born in 1916, she recalled watching the filming of Buster Keaton's *The General* as a ten-year-old. She also remembered her uncle Frank and aunt Maud and her stepcousin Elisa, but never met Opal. In the early 1970s Mrs. Randle came across a copy of the published diary. She wasn't particularly taken with the diary itself, telling me that Opal's "imagination was greater than her capabilities," but grew very curious about Opal's life. She tracked down Elisa specifically to ask her about Opal.

Elisa has since died, but according to Mrs. Randle, she described Opal as "kind of demanding." She said Elisa told her that "the gal had the ability to captivate everyone. Everyone was clamoring to see her and have her stay with them. A week later, they'd say, 'Come and get her.' . . . Opal wowed everybody, and they couldn't stand her in a week."

Elisa, who might well have been annoyed at having to give up her room, was less than enchanted with Opal. Mrs. Randle said, "She was supposed to be a genius, but Opal didn't know how to get around the town on streetcars." She quoted Elisa as saying, "Me, a little nine-year-old girl, [*sic*] had to go get her and take her back. She didn't know where the heck she was. She didn't have the brains to do it."

Just as Opal's earlier rapport with librarian Cornelia Marvin had gone bad, so did her relationship with Mrs. Bales, once her "delightful friend." She later wrote: "In Aug 1918 F. left Mrs. Bales as she was unkind to F. laughed at appearance etc." She never forgave Mrs. Bales for implying that she had "helped F. gratis as a charity . . . and that F. was immoral, out at night. F. was often out late at night getting orders on foot and correcting galley proof." When Opal finally left in August, she left a huge collection of boxes behind in the storage area of the Bales garage. And Mrs. Bales said she had finished her book.

CHAPTER
Five

*A*uthor Benjamin Hoff, one of the Opal's greatest champions, has pointed out that *The Fairyland Around Us* may well have been influenced by a turn-of-the-century children's bestseller *The Fairy-Land of Science* by Arabella B. Buckley. Like Opal, Buckley taught science to children, but she seems to have been more interested in physics and chemistry and the mechanics of botany than was Opal, whose concern was always with field observations and species identification.

Buckley's book, like Opal's, was meant as a collection of her nature classes in book form. It reads like a straight lecture, including lots of questions, such as "What work do the sunbeams do for us?" and "Can you imagine these water particles . . . rising up and getting entangled among the air-atoms?" It includes a chapter called "A Drop of Water and Its Travels," identical in concept to Opal's chapter "Raindrop's Journey," in which the reader follows a drop of water from its snowflake form atop a mountain through long lists of flora and fauna and finally out to sea.

Buckley also touched on the spiritual aspects of the study of science: "We are all groping dimly for the Unseen Power, but no one who loves nature and studies it can ever feel alone or unloved in the world . . . even the little child who lives with nature and gazes on her with open eye, must rise in some sense or other through nature to nature's God." But whereas Opal always described *The Fairyland Around Us* as a book about nature based on her classes, very much like Buckley's, it didn't turn out that way at all. Opal may have thought she was writing a book like Buckley's, but Opal's book is marked by the fact that she was a personality within the work. She was depicted in a frontispiece with the studio shot of herself barefoot and playing the violin in a circle of autumn leaves. Except for one brief period in her life, Opal was never able to separate herself and her image from anything she produced, and most of her efforts seem also to be attempts at marketing her own personality.

It is dedicated "To you little children over the world who are dreaming of a fairyland far distant and who are longing to know the fairies, this book of the fairyland around us in God's outdoors is dedicated and also to you grown-ups who have kept your faith in childhood and who are seeking inspiration for your work in the everyday things around you this book is dedicated by one who loves this fairyland around us and who has found therein a bigger vision of life and of life's supreme joy—service."

Much of it is in the form of a nature diary with entries dated by month and day but not year, and it features a bizarre dual point of view. It is written in the voices of Opal the child and of Opal the adult nature teacher. One minute little Opal and her child companions are clambering around an Edenic landscape observing nature and playing happy games, and the next minute Opal's teacher voice bursts in with "Do you know why they are called Coral Roots? Do you know any other saprophytes besides Coral Roots?" The effect is odd.

May 29th—We met a number of Wild Radish Fairies today. Their ancestors dwelt in the gardens here about and these, their children, have traveled beyond the gardens. Did you know that Radish is a cousin to Mustard, Spring Beauty, Rock Cress and Lace Pod?

June 15th—We children love to go to the meadow where the Buttercups grow—Don't you just like to cuddle among the Buttercups? We do. Did you know that Buttercup has other names? Cuckoo flower, Crowfoot, Kindcup, Butter Flower and Goldcup. Scientists call her Ranunculus.

July 29th—I've found several centipedes today around decayed stumps and pieces of old hollow logs. Centipedes haven't as many legs as millipedes but what they have are larger. Centipedes belong to the class Chilopoda. Centipedes are neither worms, insects nor bugs but they are Centipedes.

Can't we always call them by their right name, Centipedes? Three times I've started to raise Centipedes, but something always happens to them before they become grown-up, and they disappear. And Uncle, who has much sympathy with my nature study, thinks that I had best wait until I am older to have a Centipede Farm.

In the diary entries, Opal, sometimes alone but often part of a group she refers to as "we children," observes plants and animals, holds parties for flowers ("Have you held a reception for Buttercup fairies and invited their cousins, Meadow Rue, Marsh Marigold, Larkspur, Columbine, Virgin's Bower and Wind Flower?"), raises caterpillars, feeds birds, and tends wounded animals in an animal hospital. Her child companions memorize and recite in unison nature poems by a wide variety of authors, including Keats, Tennyson, Browning, Wordsworth, and Shakespeare, as well as contemporary bestselling writers like Gene Stratton-Porter and Ella Wheeler Wilcox, and eccentric Oregon poet Joaquin Miller. They also perform ceremonies. "To-day has been one of our pledge days—that is when we children assemble together in our pledge of friendship. How many tree fairies do you know all along the way?"

Opal's interest in classification was evident. "When I went along the road to-day I was thinking about the classification of things—and it is so interesting, the way in which the individual fairies are grouped. . . . On the way home from school we had an argument about who belonged to the Reptile class of the animal kingdom—and our argument became heated." Together the children christen masses of individual plants and animals. Discussing some recently hatched lizards, the diary says, "We named these forty from Assyrian, Egyptian, Chaldean, and Babylonian rulers—and seven were also given a second name from the Bible."

The book also contains childhood episodes in straight prose form but in an adult voice. In one of them, Opal climbs to the top of a hundred-foot fir tree and visits Heron Town, where she frolics among nesting herons, feeds them, observes their eggs and nests, and cuddles two squawking babies in her arms.

There are also slightly slapsticky mishaps that seem to be an attempt at humor. In Heron Town, Opal's pet toad, Balthazar, which she sets down on a branch for a moment, is eaten by one of the herons, so startling Opal that she falls and gets lodged on a limb farther down the tree before climbing right back up again.

Religion is there too: "How glad it makes our hearts as we travel the open road to see the fields of wheat along the way and listen to the music of the wheat—We talked of the wheat in our Cathedral service this last Lord's day." The prose takes a biblical turn now and then, as in "the Mole eateth of worms and insects," and, of a border of goldenrod plants, "We children go unto them. . . ."

Added to these various Opal voices are a long essay about her forest cathedral and some chunks of fiction about a miniature little girl named Liloriole, a Thumbelina-like creature embracing birds, visiting bats and flying squirrels and wandering through nature with her friend Twilight, naming things and explaining their Latin names.

Technically it is a disaster, and the prose is uneven and often arch with many sentences starting with " 'Tis" and " 'Twas." Mind-numbing too are the long lists of species and their classifications. It also has the appearance of having been put together hastily. At the end, for example, there is a list of "Books by the same author to be published at a later date," and four of the thirteen titles are chapters in *The Fairyland Around Us*. Despite the scattered nature of the book, there are some charming bits of imagery and it serves as a guide to what Opal's classes must have been like.

Also interesting are the glimpses it reveals of her childhood as she was presenting it in 1918. In sharp contrast with her published diary and her later statements, Opal's childhood here is portrayed as idyllic. Instead of being a solitary, misunderstood waif, the Opal of *Fairyland* has lots of friends and refers warmly to her family, including a loving grandfather who "twinkles," a kindly grandmother, a helpful uncle who teaches her about nature, her sister Pearl, Daddy, "darling Mamma," and her tiny great-grandmother, who reminisces about her southern upbringing: "The negro mammy would carry her about the plantation and tell her about the little folk of the field and the woods." Opal's great-grandmother, who lived nearby, was indeed tiny and had grown up in the South.

Physical punishment, a big part of *The Story of Opal*, is here too, but while in the published diary it is the stuff of tragedy, in *The Fairyland Around Us* these episodes are light and comic and dismissed. In one passage Opal, writing as an adult remembering her childhood, tells a story about her pet raccoon, Achilles, who steals a steak out of the refrigerator, for which Opal is beaten with a switch and sent to bed without supper. The grown-up Opal adds: "Of course I deserved the spanking for leaving the [refrigerator] door open."

It is a tribute to Opal's continuing charm that this obscure work is now available online. David Caruso, who lives in what he calls "a community of yurts in the wilderness" about fifteen miles from Cottage Grove, home of modern yurt manufacturing, is a Web designer and database manager, but he works only ten hours a week for money. "My main focus in life is dreaming," he told me. "I have millions of dream journals." Caruso is twenty-eight, with long, center-parted hair and a beard, and is a devoted Opalite.

He was at a writers' gathering and heard a man he called "a beatnik poet" reading from *The Story of Opal*. Like other Opalites, he fell in love with the prose immediately. He read the diary as slowly as he could to make it last. Later he went to the Knight Library at the University of Oregon and looked at one of the two copies of *The Fairyland Around Us* there.

It is a very rare book. Fewer than a dozen are known to exist today—a handful in libraries and two that I know of in private hands. Caruso has made the text accessible to everyone, however, by taking his laptop to the library and typing it all, then putting it on the Web with lots of photographs of the various species of flora and fauna listed in the book, as well as historic photographs of Opal.

Of *The Story of Opal*, a much darker book than *Fairyland*, he told me: "I think one of the reasons she felt this was her mission . . . is because deep down she was deeply hurt by the fact that the adults around her were killing her friends. . . . I mean all the lambs she gave names to . . . those lambs were probably raised up, sold, killed, eaten. And the trees, they chopped down the trees, you know, she had the trees that comforted her—that she had deep, deep relationships with, and no one could understand—and that she talked about a little bit in her diary but the depths of which you have to go inside of yourself to find. They cannot be conveyed."

I asked him if the diary was a painful book for him. He replied, "Yeah, I think Opal's story resonates with a lot of people, the way a lot of people feel. Opal just amplifies it."

In a happier vein, Caruso showed me a book by a female Indian guru. "This is like Opal who healed. She is very similar to Opal. The same love of nature, same altruism, everything. Her parents were also very abusive to her. Constant punishment. Constant work. But somehow she came out of it, and now she's like this internationally renowned guru." Caruso has met and presumably been hugged by Ammachi, whose nickname is the Hugging Saint. The motherly woman, who resembles a happy, plump Opal, is estimated to have hugged more than twenty million people in her career.

"I always had this fantasy," Caruso told me. "You know, Opal was probably within twenty or thirty miles of Jung. I wish they could have gotten together. Jung was Swiss. He was in Switzerland, so she must have went right through that area where he was and right at the time when he had his own private practice . . . I think he would have found Opal interesting and she would have found him helpful."

Like many Opalites, Caruso wishes he could go back in time and rescue the young Opal. In putting *The Fairyland Around Us* online, he has rescued her forgotten early work.

CHAPTER Six

Opal's Hollywood landlady, Mrs. Bales, believed that Opal had gone to stay with a patent attorney's family. She was wrong. However, Opal did operate from a patent attorney's office. Two of her new Los Angeles friends were Beulah and James Townsend. He had been a Socialist and Prohibitionist candidate for public office, was an advocate of "the Montessori Method of juvenile instruction," and claimed as an interest "the advancement of the cause of planetary long range weather forecasting." He and his considerably younger wife had three children to whom Opal gave nature classes. Townsend provided Opal with rent-free space in his law offices in downtown Los Angeles, as well as the occasional loan. Opal's long career of receiving support from wealthy and eccentric well-wishers was now firmly established.

Opal had written *Fairyland* in a matter of months. She had managed to raise nine thousand dollars to have it printed and bound. It was to be lavishly illustrated with color plates, and there were to be two versions, one in buckram and the other a deluxe green suede model. Her office was to serve as the base of operations for getting the book produced and distributed as well as a mail drop. She had a furnished three-room suite on the seventh floor of the San Fernando Building, her own phone line, and a business checking account with the address printed on the checks. Built in 1907, the eight-story white Renaissance Revival building at the corner of Fourth and Main boasted twenty-two-foot ceilings in the lobby and was an undeniably chic address. Opal spent many hours there in 1918 and 1919, but she actually lived somewhere else, and, perhaps because of its reputation, she seldom told anyone about her new home.

El Alisal was a castlelike stone house, designed to last a thousand years. Named after a clump of giant sycamore trees that shadowed the courtyard, it had been constructed entirely by its owner, Charles Fletcher Lummis, writer, editor, Hispanophile, Indian rights activist, historic preservationist, legendary party giver, and southern California booster who coined the slogan "See America First."

For information about Opal's colorful mentor and landlord, I'm indebted in large part to Mark Thompson and his biography *American Character: The Curious Life of Charles Fletcher Lummis and the Rediscovery of the Southwest*. Thompson's task was formidable. Lummis operated at a manic pace for decades, corresponded with thousands of people, and kept two sets of diaries, somewhat the way crooked businessmen keep two sets of books.

Lummis's home, El Alisal, was a monument to what was later called Arroyo Culture, a movement that developed in the 1890s along the Arroyo Seco, or dry riverbed, between Pasadena and Los Angeles when the two towns were separated by a wild and beautiful natural landscape. The area was an American enclave of the English Arts and Crafts movement of John Ruskin and William Morris, with an infusion of the Spanish and Indian past of the Southwest. These were the people behind the Mission Revival, who discovered and embellished picturesque neglected local history going back to the days when Spain ruled California.

El Alisal was built of native river rock from the arroyo with sturdy, earthquake-proof arches, a tower, stone fireplaces, handcrafted windows and doors, and the incorporation of bits and pieces from original Spanish missions, including a handsome bell. The surrounding gardens featured native and Mediterranean plants, including a species of banana. The inside was full of Navajo rugs, Indian pottery, and the Mission-Style furniture prized by the bohemian Arroyo culture set of which Lummis was a key member.

In its heyday El Alisal was the site of a busy salon featuring a live-in company of Spanish dancers and lots of red wine. Guests included Douglas Fairbanks; Madame Helena Modjeska, a famous Polish actress who had come to California to start a commune near the present-day Disneyland; John Philip Sousa; Clarence Darrow; Will Rogers; John Muir; William Lloyd Garrison; and Frederic Remington, as well as Opal's fellow Oregonian Joaquin Miller.

Sixty-four years before a young Opal fled rural Lane County, Oregon, for California, a teenage Joaquin Miller had done the same, seeking literary fame in San Francisco. Eventually they both headed east, Miller with business cards proclaiming him "The Byron of the Rockies."

Joaquin Miller was briefly lionized in the early 1870s by literary London, where he retailed tall tales of exotic western adventures and cut a wide sexual swath while resident Americans like Mark Twain and Bret Harte rolled their eyes at English credulity. A 1953 biography by M. M. Marberry, *Splendid Poseur*, says Miller dazzled London society in outfits of sombreros, buckskins, and buffalo robes, bristling with bowie knives. He once appeared at a reception Constance Rothschild threw for him wearing a red flannel shirt and blue overalls and carrying a miner's pick.

He had a hit there with his book of poems, *Songs of the Sierras*, and counted Robert Browning, Anthony Trollope, Lily Langtry, Oscar Wilde, and the Rossettis among his friends and acquaintances. Like Opal after him, he turned the disadvantage of birth in a far-flung corner of the world to his advantage by exploiting the romance of the wilderness, thus ensuring that he never need actually live there. Miller kept his Wild West act going for years, ending up with the appellation "Poet of the Sierras."

Opal, however, after leveraging her logging camp days into literary fame, shed her northwestern background as completely as she could, renaming herself and explaining that she wasn't really from there at all. Of three flamboyant authors to come out of Lane County, Oregon, only Ken Kesey went home again to die in Lane County.

Charles Lummis was a New Englander by birth. He had spent his college summers working at a resort in the White Mountains of New Hampshire, where he was employed in the printshop, turning out announcements and hotel menus. There he had his first brush with fame, printing some of his youthful poetry on thin sheets of birch bark for a rustic look, sewing the books together, and selling them in the resort gift shop. Lummis sent copies of *Birch Bark Poems* to famous poets of the day, including Whitman and Longfellow. This got him attention and some enthusiastic blurbs, and the proceeds of the book and journalism paid his way at Harvard.

His arrival in the West was characteristically flashy. Lummis proposed to Colonel Harrison Gray Otis, publisher and editor of the *Los Angeles Daily Times*, that he walk from Ohio to Los Angeles and write a series of articles about the journey. Colonel Otis liked the idea and said a job as city editor at the *Times* would be waiting for him when he arrived. In 1884 the twenty-five-year-old Lummis set out from Cincinnati for his forty-three-day, 3,507-mile walk.

In the following decades Lummis covered the campaign against Geronimo in Arizona; lived among the Pueblo Indians; penetrated the secret crucifixion cult, the Penitentes, in New Mexico; and went on scientific and archaeological expeditions to Peru and Guatemala.

He crusaded for the restoration of Spanish missions, battled for the rights of Native Americans, and edited the magazine *Land of Sunshine*, later titled *Out West*, which helped launch the careers of many young writers. He also founded the Southwest Museum, in part to house his huge collection of Indian and southwestern artifacts, including his massive photo collection and the wax cylinders on which he had recorded Spanish music of the Southwest as sung by shepherds and cowboys.

A small, well-formed man with light eyes, wavy hair, and an eagle-like profile, Lummis cut an eccentric figure in his Spanish-style green corduroy suits, accessorized with a scarlet Navajo sash, sombrero, and turquoise jewelry. For parties he occasionally wore buckskin outfits and tight, flared Spanish-style trousers in the manner of the Las Vegas Elvis, although he usually wore jeans at home.

The household Opal was joining was financially unstable. The fifty-nine-year-old Lummis's career was in shreds, and his freelance journalism wasn't selling. He was living on about three dollars a day. He had lost his last day job as city librarian of Los Angeles ten years before, after embarrassing sexual indiscretions that were made public during his messy second divorce and because of his habit of phoning in his job from home well before the era of officially sanctioned telecommuting.

Lummis's diary entries for the period Opal lived under his roof reveal him trying to negotiate loans, returning "bad rubber bands" to the store for credit, entering a jingle contest for a patent medicine, and cutting the chickens' rations.

He received a small stipend from the Southwest Museum and otherwise lived off scant royalty checks, egg money from the short-rationed chickens, the odd twenty-five dollars for an article, and rent from the occasional boarder, such as Opal. Despite the grim economic picture, Lummis continued to entertain as lavishly as he could, albeit with a slightly less distinguished guest list, almost exclusively consisting of women, many of them Los Angeles city librarians he had met on his last real job.

El Alisal was an emotional as well as a financial disaster area. The members of the household were like characters in a grim play about bad interpersonal relationships. Opal's arrival added a new plot element.

The third Mrs. Lummis, the former Gertrude Redit, was an Englishwoman who had begun working at El Alisal as a secretary in 1903 and moved into the house seven years later in 1910, soon after the departure of the second Mrs. Lummis. Gertrude and Charles had finally married in 1915, but the marriage soon hit the rocks. Gertrude had left Lummis for a while in 1917 but had come back by the time Opal arrived.

During Opal's sojourn at El Alisal, Gertrude went out to work to earn money as a secretary. Lummis expected her to come home after a day spent typing and type up his daily public diary musings, dictated by him from his private diary in code, which was written half in English and half in idiosyncratic Spanish. Lummis viewed her reluctance to pull this second shift as completely unreasonable.

The couple bickered, mostly about the typing, and Gertrude was often out or spending the night at her mother's. On at least one occasion Lummis expressed skepticism about her alleged whereabouts, but whether he suspected she was having an affair or was simply complaining that she wasn't there to do his secretarial work is unclear.

Also living at El Alisal was Lummis's son by Eve, his second wife. He was christened Jordan, but Indian friends had nicknamed him Quimu, a name that stuck. Lummis didn't get along with his son any better than he did with Gertrude.

Eighteen-year-old Quimu chafed under his father's constant demands and was engaged in a struggle for independence. A handy kid who seemed to be able to make or fix anything, Quimu held a full-time job with the Edison Company and was also expected to keep the labor-intensive El Alisal operation going by sawing wood, irrigating a vast garden, making sure lamps were filled, and repairing and renovating everything from the cement foundations of the house to damaged pepper plants. (Lummis was a pioneer in Southwest cuisine and wrote an early treatise on chilies.)

The egomaniacal Lummis was in constant competition with his nearly grown son. When Quimu attached tar paper incorrectly while performing a roofing job, Lummis was delighted. He frankly admitted he always took special pleasure in any rare example of Quimu's incompetence.

Around the time Opal arrived, Quimu, no doubt eager to get away from his overbearing father, wanted to join the marines and serve in the world war then under way. Lummis connived in an underhanded way to prevent him from enlisting, getting him to go to college instead. He studied at the nearby Throop Polytechnic Institute, forerunner of the California Institute of Technology.

Also on hand was the cook, Elena, the Mexican widow of an Andalusian troubadour named Amate, whom Lummis had taken in years before as a sort of court minstrel. Amate had died, but not before he had shot to death another member of the household, a Pueblo Indian named Procopio, in a dispute over a garden hose. Panchita, the daughter of Elena and the late Amate, also lived at El Alisal. She was seven years old when Opal arrived. Panchita was a disturbed child who set fires, stole food and money, assaulted schoolmates, teased the dog, ran away, set back the clocks, and vandalized objects around the house, once carving away at something so vigorously she permanently damaged the knife she had stolen to do the job with.

The vast number of animals on the place made life even more strenuous. There were squirrels whose cotton batten bedding had to be changed, a pond with fish that came when whistled at and needed to be fed regularly, cats, a dog named Snickerdoodle, chickens, a centenarian tortoise named Methuselam, and, living in the ivy on the walls of the house, a collection of horned toads for which live flies needed to be caught on a regular basis because the toads wouldn't eat anything that had been swatted.

Opal first visited the place in the spring of 1918, while she was still living with Mrs. Bales. Lummis liked her at once. He wrote: ". . . that curious little Opal Whiteley came out for quite a visit and liked the house." Lummis described her as sporting "sane heels and black hair down her back" and said she looked about fourteen years old. As an ice-breaker Opal brought along some moths she had raised from the cocoon stage and a portfolio of pressed seaweed. Lummis responded warmly and said she was "a nice quiet girl and really appreciates things. So I gave her an hour and showed her things because she can understand them, And instead of being 14, as she looks, she says she is 20."

Opal was back in mid-August. She had dinner and showed the Lummises her dummy for *The Fairyland Around Us*. Lummis described her this time as looking twelve and saying she was nineteen. He was impressed when he heard that "this nervy little thing" was having an edition of seven thousand books printed up, to be sold at three dollars each. She said she had collected deposits on sixty-five hundred copies. Networking, Opal told him that she'd tried to get an appointment and some career help from Lummis's friend Hector Alliot, the head of the Southwest Museum, but that he wouldn't see her. Lummis, unaware of how socially fearless Opal was, advised her to be more assertive and later made a point of bringing up Opal when he had dinner with Alliot, who called her "a fibulator," presumably slang for a liar.

Opal moved into the first-floor guest room as a paying boarder in late August. At first, she spent very little time at El Alisal, habitually leaving before anyone else awoke and returning late. She was teaching classes and working in her suite of offices downtown and spent most of her spare time reading and writing.

In September, Opal was working at El Alisal instead of her office. In those pre-air-conditioning days it was too hot in town. After returning from a Charlie Chaplin film, because the line for Theda Bara's *Salome* was too long—Lummis was always a sucker for brunettes—Lummis came home to find her "wading in papers."

Opal was also enjoying a social life. Before taking off for an overnight jaunt with friends to a party in Venice, she assured Lummis, "prayerfully," he wrote, that she wouldn't dance because she didn't know how to. On her return the next day, she asked Lummis for a lot of names of people who might be interested in her book, which she wrote down. He called her "an earnest little thing." In October she left again for a few days of "gadding," and she attended some of Lummis's parties, where cheap red wine flowed. Although earlier she had crusaded for temperance, she was now known to drink a glass of wine.

Lummis and Opal became chummier. He noted in his private diary in Spanish that "she converses with me a lot." He developed the habit of waiting up for her with dinner and hot chocolate or wine when she came home late. They were generally alone. The long-suffering Gertrude, who, unlike Lummis, had to get up early to go to work, conked out well before he did, and Quimu was out of the house around this period as members of his wartime class at the Throop Institute were away receiving military training.

Lummis biographer Mark Thompson told me that Opal was just Lummis's type: "dark and exotic . . . And he liked free-spirited, starving-artist types he could mentor." Lummis was what was characterized in his day as a sex fiend and today as a sexual predator. Throughout most of his life he effortlessly attracted a steady supply of willing and eager young women of an intellectual and adventurous bent. They included a variety of protégées, secretaries, and students at the summer sessions of the School of American Archaeology where he led expeditions into the Southwest. He had no problem luring girls into his tent and causing other campers to complain about the noise of their couplings.

In 1909, ten years before Opal's arrival, Lummis's second wife and Quimu's mother, Eve, was annoyed to discover that Lummis kept a record of his sex life with her in his diary; the Spanish word for "heaven," *cielo*, was his code word for marital sex. He also kept a record of his many extramarital adventures, using the Greek alphabet to spell out words in Spanish, a not-so-secret code. Eve was able to identify twenty to fifty lovers. At the time she was unwittingly sharing him with two secretaries, one of whom was Gertrude.

But Lummis had slowed down considerably by the time Opal arrived at El Alisal in 1918. His diary for that year includes a yearly *cielo* wrap-up in the back of his diary, and he was down to four marital encounters a year. He was straightforward about the fact of his impotence in a letter to his wife when she accused him of some infidelity. His extramarital adventures seemed to be a thing of the past, but some of Lummis's Greek sex code does appears next to Opal's name during the time he was getting cozier with her. On October 3, Opal and Lummis had one of their late-night suppers *à deux*. The diary records that Opal also asked for some career advice, which Lummis provided. And the word θαδικκαο appears next to her name.

But what did Lummis's little Greek notation, which translates into misspelled Spanish for knee, mean? I turned the problem over to Vanessa Morán, a docent at El Alisal, now a historic site. Because of her job, Vanessa knew all about Lummis. As a native Spanish speaker and a student of Spanish literature at UCLA, studying the complexities of grammar and syntax, she had already taken an interest in his peculiar brand of Spanish culled from many regional dialects of the Southwest.

Vanessa discovered how his code worked and from his earlier sex diaries identified his pattern of seduction. He liked to have women sit on his lap while he fondled them in various ways, and he used the word for knees, sometimes misspelled, to describe the activity. His descriptions of his lap dancing experiences in his earlier sex diary are reminiscent of high school petting sessions, indicating how "far" he got. The code word meant that on October 3, after everyone else had gone to bed and Opal asked Lummis for advice on her career, she ended up in his lap. Vanessa also discovered Greek letters next to Opal's name later that week, on October 9, spelling out Spanish slang for breasts, the equivalent of "tits."

Fondling Opal apparently jump-started Lummis's libido. That week he had sex with Gertrude after a five-month hiatus. He recorded no more erotic interaction between him and Opal, and the Greek letters don't reappear. From the time of these late-night gropings, however, Lummis exhibited great enthusiasm for the thirty-eight years younger Opal and began actively championing *The Fairyland Around Us*.

Lummis began his campaign to launch Opal's book by inviting over his friend David Starr Jordan, the president of Stanford University and a famous naturalist of the day. Lummis noted that Jordan "got quite thick with Opal." Lummis suggested that Opal show Starr the dummy of her book, which she duly did, giving him a sales pitch along with it. Lummis wrote that "she is a good propagandist and could make a living selling books for anyone, herself included." Lummis then asked Jordan if he would write a foreword for the book, and Jordan agreed.

Lummis was delighted to be able to help Opal, noting that "A Foreward from the greatest living naturalist for a little 19-year old girl dipping into Nature Studies is Going Some. And that did my heart a great deal of good." Jordan's six-hundred-word introduction arrived a few days later. "Very glad of it," commented Lummis. "The little girl deserves it and this is worth big money for her." To David Starr Jordan he wrote: "Our little Opal is very much delighted with the 'Foreword' and deeply grateful. She is very genuine, and is working hard to be correct; but the important thing, really, is that she has the child's point of view, and will, I think, succeed in her desire to interest children in all their Little Next-door Neighbors."

Opal now began a period of work that would have killed an ordinary mortal. Lummis soon began to worry that she was overdoing it. "Opal is chasing around in a way that will break her back," he wrote. As he himself was notoriously hyperactive and fond of chiding others as slackers, this is rather extraordinary. Opal went off to the office early and came back late, usually leaving at dawn and arriving back any time from 9:00 P.M. to 1:00 in the morning. Lummis said she was "working like a team of oxen."

Opal's behavior during this period is disturbing and seems to be a clear indication of mania. She soon developed a pattern of working twelve- and fourteen-hour days away from El Alisal, without eating, and kept it up for months. Her practice was to phone Lummis before she left the San Fernando Building and ask him to reheat her dinner. She'd arrive home late and bolt a huge meal—what Lummis called "her six pound suppers." One night she scarfed up four potatoes, five slices of bread and butter, a corncob, two tomatoes, and lots of beans, meat, and lettuce.

The deadly Spanish influenza epidemic, which eventually killed more than half a million Americans, was under way. Lummis was concerned that overwork had weakened Opal's resistance, making her more likely to catch it, and less likely to recover if she did. After one absence that lasted from 9:00 A.M. to midnight, he was worried he still hadn't heard from her. "I don't know what time she will get back," he wrote. "It will be a good job when she gets her book out and can rest a little."

But instead of collapsing, she just quickened her pace. By the end of November she was pulling overnighters at the downtown office, once working all day, all night, and the next day on one glass of milk.

What isn't clear is what she was actually doing.

According to Mrs. Bales, her book had been finished months before and was in the proof stage. She was checking proofs for weeks throughout October, both at El Alisal and at the printer, apparently making lots of changes. In November she was indexing, and at the same time her papers were recorded as being scattered all over her room and in Quimu's den, which she seemed to have taken on as a home office while he was away for military training. That the book was not entirely in print at this point is indicated by the fact that Lummis was still working on his own foreword to the book, which was to appear alongside David Starr Jordan's.

Opal was now having disputes with the printer, Mr. Smith, over money, perhaps because of all the changes, and the whole project was over budget. Because there was no money for the color plates she wanted, the book was printed with captionless blanks where the illustrations were to have gone. Opal then bought colored pictures of birds and plants from an educational supply house and, ignoring the copyright notifications on them, pasted them into the blank spots and wrote captions beneath them by hand.

Simply proofing the book should not have taken the many hours she was putting in. Pasting in the many plates by hand and scrawling captions on them would have been a monumental task for the print run of seven thousand Opal envisioned, but the mass-market buckram version never materialized, only the green suede deluxe model, four hundred of which were planned.

Elbert Bede, who investigated the matter as thoroughly as he could, said there were fewer than one hundred copies in all, but he wasn't able to find out why. By all accounts, the printer, fed up with Opal's changes and her failure to pay him, destroyed the plates, and she was able to salvage only the makings of this limited number of copies. The pasting and captioning of these hundred copies went on for many months after the period of frenetic activity recorded by Lummis.

So what was she doing at the San Fernando Building? Was she at work faking the childhood diary written in giant crayoned letters on butcher paper in her private three-room suite? Those who believe Opal faked her childhood diary generally believe this period was when she did it.

Bede later hinted, without naming names, that Lummis might have helped her, in a conscious hoax. An examination of Lummis's diaries, however, makes it clear he didn't help her fake it and that he didn't really know what took up the bulk of her time because she spent it at her office downtown. Nowhere in Lummis's diaries is there any hint that she was scrawling in crayons on butcher paper any time at El Alisal, although she was said to be operating in a sea of papers that were strewn everywhere.

In early December, arriving home after ten for yet another supper reheated by the obliging Lummis, she finally had a copy of the bound *Fairyland* with her. Lummis thought the pasted-in color plates looked "sloppy" and was alarmed by the lumpy appearance of the volume. He told her he wouldn't let her send it to his old Harvard classmate and friend Theodore Roosevelt for a blurb until it had time to flatten out.

Soon, however, he wrote TR a cover letter, explaining to the retired president that she had put together the book, "financing herself with advance orders, reading own proofs, bossing make-up, mounting insets etc. day and night. If you think she's on the right track, I know a word from you would be a Glory, and she's genuine."

A few days later, emulating the technique that had worked so well for her mentor Lummis with his own youthful *Birch Bark Poems*, Opal sent a copy of the book to Lord Rayleigh, a distinguished British scientist, with an enclosed letter. It illustrates how Opal marketed her book, and herself as a little child of the woods, eventually collecting an impressive collection of blurbs that she printed in a brochure.

Dear Lord: I am sending to you this one of the first of my books to come from the press. I am a little American girl whom you do not know—but I thought you would like my book of our out-of-doors. Nearly all my life has been spent in the woods and fields, learning of the ways of our birds, flowers, butterflies, and trees. All these have been my friends—and many of life's lessons I have learned from them. I have found in God's outdoors a fairyland around us. And great has been my joy each day so that I wanted to help other children—and grownups, who still kept their faith in childhood to find this same joy. So each day I wrote down the things that I saw—and here in this book are recorded these things of the everyday life in the woods and fields as I have watched them day after day and year after year since I was four year old and now I am twenty. It would give me great happiness to know what you thought of 'The Fairyland Around Us.'

She went on to fish for blurbs, asking what his impression of certain sections of the book were. "I would be glad to know if you liked 'The Joyous Blue'—'Twilight and then Night,' and 'In the Early Morning.' "

The brochure she compiled included blurbs from a varied group, including movie star Douglas Fairbanks; bestselling authors of the day, such as Gene Stratton-Porter, Booth Tarkington, Mary Roberts Rinehart, and Kate Douglas Wiggin; the president of France; the queens of Belgium and Spain; former presidents Taft and Theodore Roosevelt; and Lord Rayleigh, who was quoted: "A wonderful sympathy with the wild life about her."

Lummis provided the names and addresses from his special celebrity file. Unlike the letter asking for a blurb from Roosevelt, which came from Lummis, Opal wrote to the others on the list herself, using the San Fernando Building as her return address. A few of the letters from which these blurbs were drawn survive. The president of France had a secretary jot a note of thanks and appreciation on his visiting card, and someone in the queen of Belgium's office wrote an effusive thank-you letter praising the book. While the enthusiastic comments from famous people in Opal's brochure were no doubt real, the blurbs were apparently taken from thank-you letters, edited to read in the third person, and the endorsers had no idea their testimonials would appear in the brochure.

In mid-December, Opal was still putting in fourteen- to eighteen-hour days, starting at five or six in the morning, now pasting more plates into already bound volumes. She had help from a volunteer, Ruth Gentle, the daughter of another lawyer in Mr. Townsend's office. Lummis noted that he was generally the only one up when she came home to see that what he publicly called "this crazy, lovable, overdoing child" didn't starve. In his private diary, he was less charitable. Opal had begun to irritate him. He complained about how much she ate and was annoyed when she wasn't available to guard the house against the destructive Panchita so he could go out and try to negotiate a bank loan. He also noted that whenever his friends came over, she monopolized the conversation talking about her book, and he referred to her strewn-about belongings as a pigsty.

On Christmas Day 1918, Opal received a telegram, read it, and announced that a grandmother and grandfather on different sides of the family had died. This simply wasn't true. Opal's maternal grandparents lived on into the 1930s and 1940s. Her paternal grandparents were already dead, the grandmother having died in 1917, the grandfather two months before. The maternal great-grandparents whom she had visited in Oregon had been dead since 1911 and 1917.

The most likely explanation is that this telegram from the Whiteleys, arriving as it did on Christmas Day, simply wished her a Merry Christmas. After all, it was the first Christmas the Whiteley children had ever spent without her. Visibly sad, she said that she wanted to take a long walk on the beach and invited Quimu to accompany her. The story about not one but two dead grandparents was probably a ruse to get some sympathy from Quimu, recently returned to the household, and to spend some time alone with him. He was a blond, blue-eyed young man, with thoroughly modern, hunky surfer good looks, and Opal had a crush on him. Quimu, however, declined to take her for a beach walk, dead grandparents or no dead grandparents, and announced he planned to study instead. After this rejection, Lummis reported, "So she was all trembly & wd go to the Beach [alone] & miss the Turkey." He recorded that she was all cheered up by dinnertime.

Despite the arrival of the Christmas Day telegram from the Whiteleys, Opal was very vague about her origins. She gave the Lummises the impression that she didn't really know who her family was and once told Gertrude Lummis that her parents were Italian. Opal was not, however, entirely cut off from the Whiteleys, whom she had portrayed with such fondness in *Fairyland*, which she and Lummis were now enthusiastically promoting. She sent cards to little Elwin, which his sisters read to him because he was too young to read and which he saved. A letter from Faye Whiteley from around this time asked plaintively for a copy of the new book.

The day after Christmas, Opal was apparently completely over any grief she might have had about the dead grandparents and was back on her killer schedule. She rose at dawn and left for the day and night.

By New Year's Eve Opal had caught the dreaded Spanish influenza. Lummis was very solicitous and bossy, shooing away people who came to see her. He arranged for a hot bath, hot-water bottle, lunch in bed, and "pictures to look at." Opal insisted on getting up, but Lummis kept sending her back to bed.

A few days later Lummis was calling Opal "a pest for attention," but he still felt protective of her, and when Mr. Smith, her "pirate of a publisher," came around a week into her illness, trying to collect his money, Lummis took great satisfaction in telling him off and sending him away. "Now he understands there's a man on the job, he is singing in a lower key," wrote Lummis.

The next day a letter from Theodore Roosevelt about Opal's book arrived. This was made more dramatic by the fact Roosevelt had died while the letter was in the mail. Teddy Roosevelt's critique of Opal Whiteley's *The Fairyland Around Us* was one of his last acts on earth. Opal later quoted him in her brochure. "Really excellent qualities" is the phrase she lifted from the letter. Perhaps if TR had lived, she would not have been so audacious, for the sentence from which she plucked the phrase reads in totality: "I don't like to write in praise of the really excellent qualities of the book until I find just what all this means."

Roosevelt objected strongly to the fact that bird species from various regions seemed to be commingling. "It is unfortunate that the young authoress has not been particular about her localities," he wrote. "If the diaries are, as they would naturally supposed to be, written in one place, there are quite impossible combinations of birds. . . . I gather that she finds bobolinks ordinary summer visitors in Oregon." He suggested that if this was not the case, "there should be a sharp correction in the book." To this typed letter, TR added in his own hand, "and we must know that she has seen what she says she has seen, and not merely read of it in books." Roosevelt thought she had faked a childhood diary.

Remarkably, Lummis, still excited about promoting Opal, thought Roosevelt's letter could be helpful. He retyped the letter in its entirety and sent it off as a press release to, presumably among other papers, *The Kansas City Star*, Lummis added a lame explanation for Roosevelt's criticism. "The points he raises are practically covered in other parts of the book, which he did not see." In his public round-robin diary his defense of Opal was different but equally unconvincing: "He questions some of the birds that Opal put in there—and very properly—because she had fights with her own University professors until the Department sent experts and verified her discovery."

At this point Opal had stacks of copies of her books bound in green suede around the house. When going off to discuss settlement of a debt of $225, Lummis helped himself to "Opals" from the den mantel for payment in kind. There is no record if this settled the debt to the satisfaction of his creditor. He took a few more "Opals" with him the next day when he went out to see about getting a loan.

That month *The Oregonian* ran a a piece about the book, which indicates that Opal's publicity mill was still grinding and that she hadn't been forgotten in Oregon. "GIRL 20 COMPLETES BOOK ON FAIRYLAND. KNOWN THROUGHOUT THE STATE AS A NATURE STUDENT." Readers were reminded of the Sunshine Fairy, and there was a long quote from Lummis, including "I think there is nothing quite like it in the English language." The article also said that Opal was teaching a class of children at Venice Beach about shells and that her next book would be *Fairies of the Sea*.

By the end of January, a month after catching the flu, Opal was well again. She abandoned her schedule of long hours at the San Fernando Building and was now spending a lot of time with Quimu. Lummis soon suspected that they were lovers. He recorded indignantly that Opal and Quimu had slept together in Quimu's den, in an outbuilding behind the main house. A few days later he wrote in Spanish that she is "with him (Q) several hours before and after lunch and without the lights for

¾ hour!" (The exclamation point is Lummis's.) A few days later Opal again spent the morning hours in Quimu's den, and to Lummis's disgust she bolted her lunch, eating both courses—potato and pie—at the same time in order to rush back "to get up to Q's den with him." Following another long session behind closed doors, after which Opal emerged with a nosebleed, Lummis grew even more agitated.

After five months of waiting up for her, feeding her, nursing her, promoting her career, and even covering for her when Teddy Roosevelt pointed out errors in her book, Lummis turned on his protégée and addressed the fact that she was way behind on her rent. He arranged for Gertrude to give her a bill. There was no suggestion that he'd allow her to settle the debt with "Opals" from the den mantel as he had been attempting to do with his own creditors.

The sexually impotent Lummis, who earlier had groped Opal in the kitchen as the household slept, took what he believed to be her consummated relationship with his strapping young son as a personal betrayal, and he was disgusted and angry. Around then Opal noticed that the key to her bedroom door was missing. She told Quimu, who warned her that Lummis was scheming to get into her bedroom. Handyman Quimu installed a latch from the inside and told her to kick his father in the testicles if he tried anything.

In his personal diary entry for January 30, Lummis wrote in English, "D———d Opal has put screweye in my tulipwood door," and on February 1, in Spanish, "I scolded Opal about the mistreatment of the tulipwood door—very insolent—and I am going to remove the hook screwed into the doors."

The chilling level of suppressed feeling in the household is reflected by the fact that Quimu, who apparently thought his father was capable of and possibly planning to assault Opal sexually, nevertheless pitched in for the party Lummis was throwing that evening, plucking four geese for a stew and sawing some salvaged timber for the fireplace.

Lummis was irritated and insulted, however, that Quimu didn't attend the gathering, which featured a lot of singing and dancing. Opal showed up for the meal, but as soon as it was over, she claimed she was sick and excused herself, presumably to join Quimu. Lummis, furious with both of them, assumed she was faking.

A few days later the fraught drama, featuring father-son rivalry, sexual jealousy, and anger, came to a head. Here is Opal's version of what happened next.

Lummis bad man. His son told F. he feared his father might harm her. One evening F. noticed key of big salon door leading into her room was missing. She told Quimu, the son, who was certain his father had taken it. Quimu drove a large nail into big cypress salon door. There was another door giving on to the patio which could be barred and bolted. F went to sleep but CL tried salon door in night but could not force it. Next morning F. told Mrs. Lummis who told F. that her husband had promised her never to molest F. She was L's fourth wife. [Opal got this detail wrong. She was number three, but he had fathered a child with another woman before number one, which may have confused Opal.] F. said she would not stay another night in house. She said she would sleep in her own room adj. to F. (She often slept in garden—tree) F. suggested office [presumably her office space in the San Fernando Building] but Mrs. L was afraid. . . . At 9 PM F. returned, servants told her Mrs. L was asleep—so went to bed—nails in door still there, bolted outer door and went to bed.

Opal wrote she was tired and fell asleep only to wake up to find Lummis "holding her by her shoulders." Her narrative continued. "F. had been told by Quimu to kick between legs which she did & jumped out of the window. Storm—went up to Quimu's room where Quimu put her to bed. Quimu stayed in room with foot on trap door."

Lummis biographer Mark Thompson told me, "I took one look at her picture, and I was afraid her story was true." Besides Opal's being the physical type Lummis fancied, Thompson said Lummis had "a split personality" as far as women were concerned. "On the one hand he launched the literary careers of quite a few women and his wives were strong and intelligent. Yet the other side wanted to control everyone and particularly women. He subjected them to various types of abuse—psychological and otherwise." One of the Lummis wives is said to have slept with a knife under her pillow.

The next day Opal announced she'd be moving out. Lummis noted irritably that in five months, she'd paid only twenty dollars, owing him forty-five more. He referred to Opal's residence there as "a losing game of Gertrude's seeking" and wrote that Opal was going to "a woman friend to live as her guest." "She didn't even say thank-you," he wrote crabbily in Spanish in his diary. Moving on to other matters, he added casually, "Phones out of whack upstairs."

Opal's abrupt departure from El Alisal repeated the pattern she had established at the Baleses'. After a period in which she had captivated and brought out protective instincts in others, ill will set in. There were many more stormy departures to come.

El Alisal is now the headquarters of the Historical Society of Southern California. The house and gardens are preserved much as they were, on decreased acreage. It is surrounded by the Pasadena Freeway and a lively Hispanic neighborhood where kids skateboard and ride their bikes. Nearby is a Burger King in the same style as El Alisal, with a half wall of big round beach rocks, or perhaps modern versions of beach rocks made from some space age composite material.

The room where Opal lived is a small, pretty, square room with a stone fireplace fitted into the corner and topped by a triangular wooden mantel with misty bas-relief nudes in the art nouveau style, around its curved opening. The room is now an office with filing cabinets, a desk, and computer. An air conditioner is wedged into the hand-carved window frame that Opal jumped out of. It's far up enough that no one would decide to jump out of it unless highly motivated, but not so far up as to kill anyone.

Signs of Quimu's handiwork are visible. The doorframe has had a chunk of the original wood removed to accommodate some screw holes to allow it to be locked from the inside. Also in evidence in the house is the trapdoor Quimu stood on to protect her from his rampaging father. Quimu slept in a round tower that led to the main salon through the trapdoor and down a ladder.

Lummis's rivalry with his son, simmering for months, had come to a boil. The dynamic of their already charged rivalry changed, with Opal now in the mix as the apex of an emotional triangle. Whether she and

Quimu saw each other again isn't known. He went on to marry, raise a family, and become an engineer. In later years he is said to have had little good to say about his father.

What is known is that Opal fled El Alisal to the Townsends, who were already providing her with office space. Opal later said that they set her up in a cheap unfurnished rented room in the arty community of Garvanza, now known as Highland Park. She was still working at her downtown office, and she wrote Nellie Hemenway from there. "I have on hand material for the article now and if you are ready I will send it at once. Now Nellie dear—take a great big breath for I have wonderful news. (Don't tell anyone until the article is done) Now take another big breath. This is what a very, very busy English statesman wrote me Jan 20, 1919. The letter came this week. 'I wish to congratulate you on your beautiful nature book with its lovely illustrations and upon your having at so early a period learned the secrets of beauty and happiness. This lovely book is the work of one who knows how to interpret the music of the great harpstrings of the Creator.' " Her admirer was Lord Curzon of Kedleston, and Opal explained to Nellie that he was "Head of Oxford University, England; Lord President of the Kings Counsel [*sic*]; Leader of the House of Lords in parliament and for 7 years was viceroy of India." She reported to Nellie that more admiring letters had arrived from the chancellor of Cambridge University, and the president of Cornell University.

The dramas of the Lummis family behind her, Opal soon fell in with a new crowd. They were theosophists. Theosophy, the cauldron from which much of today's New Age thinking emerged, was founded in New York in 1875 by journalist and lawyer Colonel Henry Steel Olcott and his friend Madame Helena P. Blavatsky, an eccentric Russian noblewoman and former séance assistant who claimed to have learned esoteric secrets from Tibetan and Indian "masters." Heavy on the occult, theosophy combines the traditions of various religions and postulates an "Ancient Wisdom" that highly evolved hidden masters reveal sparingly to spiritually advanced people. They communicated with Madame Blavatsky through handwritten notes that appeared in her apartment.

Soon riddled by schisms and offshoots that have lasted to the present day, theosophy includes such elements as astral projection and paranormal powers. Its influence lingers with the popularity of concepts that it introduced to Europe and America, such as Atlantis, karma, and reincarnation, as well as the practice of cremation.

A Mrs. McMillan, the wife of an engineer from Winnipeg, who wintered in southern California, introduced Opal to the group. They were immediately charmed by her and quickly became convinced that she had psychic powers.

Mrs. McMillan was described by University of Oregon Professor Edmund Conklin, who interviewed her for his study of Opal in 1920, as an "amateur poet, nature lover, psychic, etc." She saw a copy of *The Fairyland Around Us* several months after Opal left the Lummis home and eventually met her at the Virginia Hotel in Long Beach, California. A friendship ensued. Mrs. McMillan, later living in a Los Angeles hotel, had then lost touch with Opal but tracked her down by phone.

Opal declined several invitations to visit her friend at her hotel, and when Mrs. McMillan pressed her, Opal confessed that she couldn't come because she didn't have a hat to wear. Mrs. McMillan urged her to come anyway. She was shocked to see Opal, who was pale, emaciated, wearing "clothing scarcely fit to be seen," and hatless. She was also very hungry. "Very poor. Nearly starved," Opal wrote later of this period.

While her letter to Nellie had been bubbly and optimistic, she told Mrs. McMillan she was broke, that her printer was after her for money, and that she was putting in long hours pasting pictures into her book. She said she was sleeping on the floor in an attic room in Pasadena. Mrs. McMillan fed her, clothed her, gave her money, and introduced her to Dr. Coulson Turnbull. Mrs. McMillan reported that Opal and Dr. Turnbull saw fairies and wood nymphs in Los Angeles parks, and that both were clairvoyant.

Coulson Turnbull was a prominent southern California theosophist of the period and author of what is arguably the most unreadable novel in the English language, *Sema-Kanda Threshold Memories: A Mystic's Story*. It somehow manages to rattle on cheerfully without any evident narrative, as it chronicles the spiritual journey of Semi-Kanda, a native of North Atlantis, throughout all time, with stops in Renaissance Rome and colonial North America, where an Indian sage named Running Water dispenses wisdom near the site of present-day Buffalo, New York.

The book also features weird temple ceremonies along the lines of *The Magic Flute*. Theosophy borrowed heavily from Freemasonry.

Professor Conklin asked Mrs. McMillan what she knew of Opal's origins. "Mrs. McMillan, as one is inclined to expect," he reported, "interprets Opal as being the reincarnation of some genius of earlier times, and that the apparently inexplicable in her knowledge is due to recollections from her former incarnation, or to her clairvoyant powers."

During this time Opal's story about her origins was still evolving. She told Mrs. McMillan that she was born in France and her parents were rich. Her parents separated and the father sent Opal to America "in the care of either an old grandmother or an old nurse." Opal was switched in a hospital with the real Opal shortly after the birth. The real Opal died and Lizzie Whiteley was unaware of the substitution. Lizzie was abusive and all of the children turned against her except Opal. Ed Whiteley knew the secret and kept it hidden. Opal said she was estranged from the family.

Opal also told her new friend that the Whiteleys were Roman Catholic, information that would have been a big surprise to the old Junior Christian Endeavor crowd back in Oregon.

Around this time Opal had another frightening encounter with a lecherous older man. Mrs. Townsend's stepfather, Willard C. James, came by Opal's office with a note from Mrs. Townsend saying that she and the children had gone "by a roundabout way" to Santa Monica, where Opal was to teach a nature class at the beach. Opal innocently accompanied Mr. James to the beach house to meet them. There the maid said Mrs. Townsend and the children had been there but had gone for a walk along the beach and would return at dusk. Opal says she was confused when the maid prepared dinner for thirteen but there didn't seem to be anybody in the house other than the housekeeper and two servants.

"Waited long for dinner," wrote Opal. "After dinner, Mr. James made many proposals to F. Mr. J. tried to embrace F. but F. rushed out into the pier and hid in the sea the rest of the night behind pier posts. F. stayed in water 3 or 4 hours + returned to Los Angeles after dawn unnoticed."

After her horrible night under the Santa Monica pier, Opal says she went to see Mrs. Townsend, her assailant's stepdaughter, just as she had immediately complained to Gertrude Lummis after Lummis's first, foiled attempt to break down her door, but this time she received little sympathy. "Frightened F. returned to LA and went to see Mrs. Townsend who had always been her good friend. Mrs. T said that as F had no money and that James her adopted father was a decent sort she thought it would be a good thing for F. He never harmed girls but only wanted to cuddle them."

A few months later, in July 1919, Nellie Hemenway received a post-card written by a Mrs. Phillips. The return address was St. Vincent Hospital on Sunset Boulevard. "My Dear Miss Hemenway," it read, "I am writing for Miss Opal Whiteley who is in this hospital because of overwork." The postcard asked Nellie not to tell the Whiteleys she was in the hospital, so as to avoid worrying them.

Opal appeared to have had another breakdown. According to both Maud Bales and Charles Lummis, she had been putting in incredibly long hours on writing and research and pasting in pictures. Her activities between February and July are less well documented, but she was still at work in the San Fernando Building and told Mrs. McMillan that she was also working in her bare Pasadena attic.

It sounds like a case of a collapse following a period of manic activity, similar to what had happened to Opal after she had thrown herself into her Christian Endeavor work in Oregon and ended up mute and deaf and anorexic. Opal said later she had been in the hospital with a back injury, caused by her leap from the window at El Alisal, and maintained that "steels" were inserted into or attached to her spine or were perhaps part of an orthopedic corset of some kind.

Soon after she was released from the hospital, Opal was interviewed by *Los Angeles Times* feature writer John Steven McGroarty, who has been described by California historian Kevin Starr as "a genial journalist and a dreamy poet of the lo! hark! school." McGroarty, who wrote a long-running pageant about California missions, *The Mission Play*, was known as the "poet of Verdugo Hills."

The quadruple-barreled headline read, NATURE'S TALE IS TOLD ANEW. GIRL WITH MESSAGE FROM THE WILDS IS VISITOR HERE. WRITES CHRONICLE OF DOINGS OF HER DUMB FRIENDS. PUBLISHED BOOK HERSELF, THEN DOES HER OWN SELLING.

McGroarty was completely enchanted. "Smaller in stature than Mary Pickford, of whom she somehow reminds one, there is a young girl in Los Angeles who has written a book that will stand among the great masterpieces of literature," he wrote. "And startling as her achievement is, it is not yet so startling as the story of her own life. It is a story that would be tragic were it not that it had been saved from being so by the gladness and the wonder of her soul."

McGroarty, who predicted that *The Fairyland Around Us* would become a standard text in schools, hadn't heard about Lily Black's teaching her Latin or getting her library books. He wrote, "One might be readily forgiven for the suspicion that a girl so young and who had scant opportunity for education and literary training could possibly have written so great a book. . . . [B]ut there is no chance for suspicion. There cannot be the slightest doubt that that she saw and experienced everything in the book and that it is the product of her own pen."

Did McGroarty read the book? If everything in the book was true, as he claimed, then the rest of his article must be false. The child Opal as portrayed in *The Fairyland Around Us* was surrounded by loving relatives who encouraged her nature studies, a family prosperous enough to own, at the turn of the century, a refrigerator in which they kept juicy steaks. The Opal of her book had led a happy childhood with lots of friends and was taught the names of the species she observed in school.

Los Angeles Times readers were told, however, that she had come from a background of poverty, deprivation, and abuse, had received no education, and was in fact an orphan with a mysterious past. "Here was a child that drifted God knows how, into a lumber camp in Oregon where the people and their ways were rough and harsh," said McGroarty. "She had no companions that could in any way be congenial and so she went out and made companions of the things in the wild that were around her. She was chastised for doing it, but she did not let that deter her."

Opal's life had become a shambles after her first breakdown three years before in 1916. After that she had been unable to focus, had grandiose projects that she never quite pulled off, woke up screaming in the night, thought people were after her, and couldn't cope with daily life. Staying in school, holding a job, returning library books—they all defeated her. But one would never know it from her publicity. Meeting people, and in her promotional efforts, as well as in *The Fairyland Around Us*, she always projected a bouncy, happy image.

Back in Eugene, a period she later claimed was miserable for her, she had billed herself as the Sunshine Fairy. The interview with McGroarty, soon after what was probably her second breakdown, marked a radical departure for Opal. Now the Sunshine Fairy was a pathetic orphan who had been abused and misunderstood and had grown up in ignorance and poverty and been surrounded by cruel louts. McGroarty described her as "very poor and very frail" and wrote that after her spinal injury (the result, he reported, of a fall, not a leap) "the doctors said she couldn't live." But he said that Opal was now in good hands, cared for by "a sweet souled woman" and entertained by "fine people" in homes in Altadena and Oak Knoll.

The article was accompanied by a very attractive studio photograph of Opal in a fetching hat, looking like a young movie star of the period with what appears to be a lipsticked cupid's-bow mouth. Gone is the eager smile. Now she's looking soulful and sexy. McGroarty added that Opal was "on the way to full recovery of her health." Armed with clippings of this newspaper story, which also announced that any publisher who got the rights to *The Fairyland Around Us* would be "fortunate," Opal was indeed soon well enough to travel.

Like the moths and butterflies she raised from cocoons, Opal had a tendency to emerge from her breakdowns—periods of dormancy and collapse—with an altered persona. There was a brand-new Opal, very different from the happy little Sunshine Fairy of *The Fairyland Around Us*. The new Opal was sad little Opal, the abused orphan. Had she been putting a sugary spin on her childhood before, and was this the real Opal, now facing her past more honestly, perhaps "recovering" memory? Or did she now see a reasonably happy past through a depression-induced veil of sadness? A third possibility is that Opal realized that the Little Nature Study Girl as plucky victim was even more interesting than the happy Little Nature Study Girl and, in a new, cynical, grieving postwar world, more fashionable as well.

The sweet, sentimental, uplifting tales of Gene Stratton-Porter were going out of fashion. The bestselling author's sales were slipping.

Newer, darker voices were being heard. Perhaps Opal was simply reflecting a new mood for a new time.

Opal's emergences from her cocoons of collapse were characterized not just by metamorphosis but by flight. Shortly after the interview with McGroarty, she left California forever.

Within a few weeks, Opal had arrived in Boston. Mrs. McMillan, her theosophist friend from Winnipeg, said the crowd around Dr. Turnbull had financed her trip. Several Los Angeles clubwomen said they also took up a collection for this purpose. Opal's fund-raising was usually broad-based, and perhaps she had help from several quarters. In later years she said very firmly on many occasions that King Camp Gillette, inventor of the safety razor with the disposable blade, had financed the trip east.

Besides being a millionaire inventor, Gillette was a wacky utopianist and one of a long line of rich eccentrics who were attracted to Opal over the years. He was the author of *The Human Drift*, dedicated to "all mankind," in which he laid out his capitalistic, socialist, globalizationist thesis that the world should be organized into one huge corporation, with everyone on the planet a stockholder. This, he believed, would lead to greater efficiency as well as allow everyone to work a shorter workweek.

His motto was "United Intelligence and Material Equality." His vision included the population of North America all living in one giant city with forty thousand beehivelike apartment buildings, each containing thousands of homes and gardens. The city, Metropolis, would be conveniently situated next to Niagara Falls, which would provide hydroelectric power. For a time Gillette served as the president of the corporation that was to take over the world and fuse all human economic activity into one big company.

Opal said that she had once refused an invitation from Gillette and his wife on the ground that the lecherous old Willard C. James who had frightened her that horrible evening in Santa Monica and driven her to take refuge under the pier would be present. James was an old friend of Gillette and Opal told him exactly how badly James had behaved. She said that when Gillette questioned James, James denied everything, and Gillette believed him, but Opal said he had already promised her the money for the trip east and didn't back out.

Gillette's involvement may explain the fact that Opal went to Boston to seek her fortune, rather than the more obvious New York. Boston was where Gillette had made his own fortune and where he still had business interests and contacts, some of whom helped Opal get launched. Indeed Gillette may have bundled Opal out of town to avoid involving his friend Willard C. James in a scandal. If so, it wouldn't be the only time Opal would be urged to leave town under such circumstances.

Opal stayed at first in Winchester with some people named Forbes, associated with the Forbes Lithography Manufacturing Company of Boston. A month before, in June, the Forbeses had received a letter from Maurice Van Ploten of Los Angeles, writing at his wife's behest and asking the Forbeses to keep an eye out for Opal, emphasizing his concern about her personal safety in a strange city. Van Ploten was part of the theosophist set and served with Coulson Turnbull on the board of a gun-toting Vancouver Island cult, the Aquarian Foundation. Mr. Forbes's sister, Cora Marsh, also wrote, asking the Forbeses to meet the train. She told her brother that Opal was "a young genius," "a sweet, pure, good little girl," and said she might be on crutches as her back had nearly been broken when she leaped out of a window to save herself from the unwanted attentions of "a beast of a man" to whom she was trying to sell a copy of *The Fairyland Around Us*.

The reason Opal was going to Boston, according to Mrs. Marsh, was that a publisher had paid for her transportation to go see him. However, this mysterious man had forbidden her to tell anyone his name as he would then be besieged by aspiring authors. This ridiculous story no doubt originated with Opal, whose fanciful explanations often revolved around secrets that must not be revealed.

Opal stayed with the Forbeses for three and a half weeks. During that time she received a dunning notice from the University of Oregon dated August 11. Could she please pay off her note for a student loan from an alumni group for fifty dollars? This represented tuition for both her freshman and sophomore years. Returning veterans from the war needed the money, and the university wanted repayment by October 1.

Opal arranged to pay off the debt in two installments. She explained that she was about to sign a contract in either September or October 1920 "for one of my books" and said that by July or September 1920 she'd be getting royalties. This is all rather odd as she hadn't even written her future publisher, Ellery Sedgwick, for an appointment by that time and didn't have a contract with him until months later. Perhaps she had received some encouragement from another publisher. What is more puzzling is the phrase "one of my books," for at that time only *The Fairyland Around Us* existed in complete form. Her next work, the "real" diary, was presumably still in scraps in a hatbox back in Los Angeles.

In a card postmarked August 13, Opal wrote a Cottage Grove woman, Mrs. Virgil White, that "I have been working on a book." This again does not fit in with the official history because *The Fairyland Around Us* was already finished, and she still had not met Sedgwick, who presumably asked about a diary. What was she working on?

Within a month she left the Forbeses, who remained her friends, and rented a room in Cambridge from two maiden ladies, the Misses Salter, whom she had met through an associate of King Camp Gillette's. There she received a letter from D. T. Awbery in Oakland, California. Opal had stayed at the Awbreys' on her way to Los Angeles. Mr. Awbrey wrote that he had received her card and had, at her request, mailed "the books you left in the office." These books were eleven copies of *The Fairyland Around Us*. In addition, he enclosed two books "on the French language" that she had also left and that he presumed she would like to have.

Opal began making the rounds of editorial offices looking for literary work, using *The Fairyland Around Us* as a sort of portfolio. The editor of *Youth's Companion* suggested she see Ellery Sedgwick at *The Atlantic Monthly*. She wrote him on September 16, asking for an appointment, and he wrote back that he could see her on the twenty-fourth.

Sedgwick's family had lived in Stockbridge, Massachusetts, for seven generations. A graduate of Groton and Harvard, Sedgwick had taught classics at Groton before going into publishing. He had a long and successful career as editor of *The Atlantic*, which he owned. He once told an interviewer that when he took it on in 1909, it was read only by "old fogies." He had increased circulation from fifteen thousand to one hundred thousand by 1921 and attributed his success to his getting younger writers. In thoroughly modern fashion, he tracked his progress with demographic research to determine the age of his readership. He was Ernest Hemingway's first American publisher and is credited with discovering many other new writers. Sedgwick was extremely well connected. Among his papers are letters from Rudyard Kipling, John Galsworthy, Winston Churchill, Virginia Woolf, Felix Frankfurter, and Franklin and Eleanor Roosevelt.

When Opal arrived in Sedgwick's office, she found a man in his late forties, balding, dapper, mustachioed, and a cigar smoker, with a lot of energy and a heavyweight literary reputation. He described this fateful meeting in his 1946 memoir, *The Happy Profession*. He didn't agree with McGroarty, the poet of Verdugo Hills, that publishing *Fairyland* would be a good business move. After dismissing the book's charms, he took note of Opal's.

He wrote, "About Opal Whiteley herself, there was something to attract even the attention of a man of business—something very young and eager and fluttering, like a bird in a thicket." Here is how he reported the subsequent conversation:

"I'm afraid we can't do anything with the book. But you must have had an interesting life. You have lived much in the woods?"

"Yes, in lots of lumber camps."

"How many?"

"Nineteen. At least we moved nineteen times."

It was hard not to be interested now. One close question followed another regarding the surroundings of her girlhood. The answers were so detailed, so sharply remembered, that the next question was natural.

"If you remember like that, you must have kept a diary."

Her eyes opened wide. "Yes, always. I do still."

"Then it is not this book I want, but the diary."

She caught her breath. "It's destroyed. It's all torn up." Tears were in her eye.

"You loved it?"

"Yes; I told it everything."

"Then you kept the pieces."

The guess was easy (what child whose doll is rent asunder throws away the sawdust?), but she looked amazed.

"Yes, I have kept everything. The pieces are all stored in Los Angeles."

This dramatic report of the encounter forms the basis of the myth of Opal. But actually it didn't happen that way at all. It couldn't have.

Opal's letter asking for the appointment is preserved in *The Atlantic Monthly* files, now at the Massachusetts Historical Society. Sedgwick knew she kept a childhood diary before he even met her because she had told him so in her letter. In the September 16 letter asking for an appointment in the coming week Opal explained, "Nearly all my life I have lived in companionship with the trees and birds and other folk about in the fields and woods around the lumber camps in the Cascades of Oregon. And each day as I watched and listened I wrote down what I saw and heard."

That certainly sounds like a childhood diary and is very similar to what she wrote Lord Rayleigh when she sent him his promotional copy of *Fairyland*: "So each day I wrote down the things that I saw—and here in this book are recorded these things of the everyday life in the woods and fields as I have watched them day after day and year after year since I was four years old and now I am twenty."

In her letter to Sedgwick she didn't seem to be pitching *The Fairyland Around Us* although she said she would bring it with her, adding, "And from it you can know how I write and of the days in the lumber camps." In a PS she added, "You may be interested in knowing that President Poincaré of France, G. Clemenceau, Earl Curzon of Kedleston and some others have been interested in reading my journal of days in the lumber camps."

It is likely she used the same wording to them as she had to Lord Rayleigh and told them she had kept a childhood diary, and in their replies they had expressed an interest in this document. Opal's letter to Sedgwick reads as if she might actually have gone to pitch him an actual juvenile diary on which *Fairyland* had been based.

Sedgwick's enthusiasm was piqued by the attractive young woman's eager, fluttering qualities, but he was certainly also aware that a current publishing phenomenon was the bestselling novella *Young Visiters* [*sic*] by adorable nine-year-old Daisy Ashford, discovered in a long-lost childhood copybook, and published first in England with an introduction by James Barrie.

Sedgwick got Opal to wire Los Angeles right away. She later wrote that it was Marie Mullen, the president of the Mullen & Bluett department store in Los Angeles, who was sent the telegram.

About a week later Sedgwick, still thinking about the diary, wrote to tell Opal to be sure to get "all of your material which could by any possibility be published. I am much interested in the matter, and shall cheerfully pay carrying charges." He also told her that he wanted to take a look at it as soon as it arrived and that he wanted first crack at it, for it should be published as a whole.

Opal answered that she had sent for additional material, "for *all* of my material which could by any possibility be published as you suggested my doing in your letter." She continued, "It brings me much happiness to know that you are interested in my work." She seemed to have had time to think about their interview and skew her pitch a little differently, away from the spiritual connection of nature and childhood to a grittier account of life in the wilds of Oregon. "You may have wondered the other day why I did not remember more of the incidents of the everyday life of the camp—but you see I was concentrating upon the nature study and having thousands of things to remember in that, I only recorded the daily life of the camp as a matter of course in the journal day by day with the observation notes of the fields and woods."

She assured him that she was "holding back *all material that you may consider it as a whole*—and I am making no arrangements for publication of portions of it as I had first planned to do." In a postscript she said, "As soon as the box of manuscripts and journals arrive I will telephone."

On October 14, Opal said that a package of material from California arrived at the Misses Salters' house, and presumably Opal telephoned to announce its arrival. The next day Opal wrote her new editor that she had learned of yet another cache of material from "one of the girls to whom I had written concerning the forwarding of my manuscript." This person had apparently discovered a small package of "fragments of the journal" when unpacking boxes of nature specimens. At this point the diary was said to have been packed in one box, later referred to by Sedgwick as a hatbox.

In the same letter Opal made it very clear that she did not consider herself a Whiteley, blaming the destruction of the diary on "one of the girls of the family with whom I lived all those years." She went on to say that she had begun piecing the diary together on the floor and in one day had ended up with about eight thousand words worth of material to send him, pretty amazing inasmuch as the few remaining sample pages show there are about ten words to a page, so she must have pieced together eight hundred pages in twenty-four hours.

From her apologetic explanation for having forgotten so much about the lumber camp because she was emphasizing nature studies, it would appear that Opal had gone in there pitching a book about nature, and Sedgwick was more interested in the lumber camp angle.

Sedgwick had an admirable history of encouraging outsider writers. In fact, he had reinvigorated *The Atlantic Monthly* by looking for fresh material, often from eloquent autodidacts far from the eastern seaboard. He had bought articles from a self-educated African American domestic worker, Juanita Harrison, who saved up her money to travel around the world, learning French and Italian at the YWCA; a Wyoming homesteader named Elinore Rupert; and Cloudesly Johns, a literate hobo. Throughout his association with Opal, it is clear that he envisioned Cottage Grove, Oregon, as a place of picturesque primitive squalor, and in this first letter, reporting on the first day's results of piecing and typing, Opal seems to be giving him what she thought he wanted.

She mentioned "Shorty, the very tall man who helped us in the nursery and with funerals—when he was not too drunk," and "Joe Cole, who cut off the tail of a fox terrier dog and also the tail of my pet mouse Oliver Cromwell." In actual fact, all of Oliver Cromwell, as well as

Shorty and Joe Cole, never made it into the published diary, although the "borning day" of the real Cromwell was noted. Neither did a hooker-with-a-heart-of-gold character make the final cut. Opal described her as "the woman of ill-fame who was so kind to me and helped me with the nursery and hospital and allowed me to hide my pets in her woodshed when they were hurt and I did not dare take them home."

Two weeks later, after having met with him, Opal wrote Sedgwick that she had a new method of piecing together the diary so that instead of sentence fragments, he could have complete scenes. The scenes she provided as examples are written in fairly standard prose and describe logging operations in Oregon. Some of the material is clearly not written in diary form at all, or from the point of view of a child, indicated by use of the past tense, such as "Our house was very close to the millpond," or of a phrase that reveals an adult sensibility, such as "All buildings in the camp are of rough lumber and have no paint on them. After the first winter they begin to get gray." Whatever document she may have been piecing together when she came up with this material, it wasn't a diary, and it wasn't written by a child.

Opal suggested scenes describing her carrying warm dinners to the logging men, watching them "bucking trees and snaking logs," and watching "the send-up man and the sky-hooker." She said Sedgwick "spoke of wanting, for the reader, who knows nothing of what I have told you, a picture of the camp as a whole." She reported that she had five or six of these scenes at six hundred to eleven hundred words each and was piecing them together "for the young lady to type and bring in to you next Tuesday."

Sedgwick wrote back approvingly. "I think your plan very promising." He suggested grouping incidents together "described by you at a certain age. There would be novelty in the idea of your enlarging appreciation and understanding of the life about you." He also advised her to "adopt chronological order" but not "slavishly" and concluded that he was "confident of the success of our scheme." He must have liked what he saw, because ten days later he told her he planned to publish a book of her childhood writings, not just a magazine series. He also expressed concern about her overworking herself.

Opal was overjoyed to hear about the book deal. She told him she could not "write in words how happy it makes me." By this point *Atlantic Monthly* secretary Gertrude Tompson was coming over regularly to type up pieced-together materials onto little cards, which Opal then filed in boxes.

A few days later Sedgwick seems to have zeroed in on the period of the diary he felt most promising, "the seven-year-old period." Opal assured him she would begin concentrating on the scraps from this period at once.

By November 19, a week later, Opal had a book contract for "a diary kept during the childhood of the author." It offered her a 10 percent royalty on the first five thousand copies sold, with increasing percentages above that number, but no advance, although Sedgwick later said he gave her some money for meat because he was under the impression food at the Salter sisters consisted mostly of milk and porridge. The contract also divided the British rights and film rights fifty-fifty between the author and *The Atlantic Monthly*.

Sedgwick was excited about the book, which he called "the most illuminating chronicle of childhood that I have seen in twenty years of reading manuscripts." He was also worried about his author's health. Besides Opal's general weakness ascribed to her Dickensian diet, she was suffering from her spinal complaint and was run-down and overworked.

Sedgwick arranged to have her spend Thanksgiving weekend with his family, at his mother-in-law Mrs. Cabot's home for a good rest. His wife, Mabel, took Opal to a doctor, who announced that her general health was "critical" and that she needed rest and better food. The mysterious spinal complaint, Sedgwick learned later, was the result of "an attempted assault upon her under peculiar and distressing circumstances at Los Angeles," but he didn't know everything about her late-night jump out the window at El Alisal. Later, when he made a thorough investigation of her life, he never discovered she had lived there. Sedgwick's doctor removed the mysterious orthopedic "steels" that she had acquired during her Los Angeles hospitalization and prescribed exercise.

After the Thanksgiving weekend proved so salubrious, Sedgwick came up with the idea of moving Opal from the Salters' to his mother-in-law's home for the foreseeable future to continue piecing together the diary at a place where she could be properly fed.

Opal said that her friends the Forbeses didn't approve of the new arrangement, on the ground that as a guest of Sedgwick's family she wouldn't really be a freelance. They thought that Sedgwick instead should have offered her some money to live on. According to Opal, they wanted to review the contract she had signed, but Sedgwick wouldn't allow it.

At Mrs. Cabot's the piecing together of the diary continued. Sedgwick estimated that there might have been half a million pieces. When she finished, the pages were typed up, according to Sedgwick, "with no change whatever other than omissions, the adoption of reasonable rules of capitalization (the manuscript for many years had nothing but capitals), and the addition of punctuation, of which the manuscript is entirely innocent." Because all but a few pages of the diary have been lost, we must rely on him to a great extent for a description. He says he thought it was about a quarter of a million words long. The paper was a collection of wrapping paper, old envelopes, and "butcher's bags pressed and sliced in two."

Besides Mrs. Cabot, the household consisted of three servants and three trained nurses, and the house was on a large estate four miles from Boston. Sedgwick later referred to his mother-in-law as "an invalid living for many years unconscious of the world about her." Opal, writing later, simply scrawled "insane" next to Mrs. Cabot's name. Apparently she was practically comatose. There were other Cabots' houses on the estate, but it hardly sounds like a festive venue for a young girl eager to make a splash in the world and meet interesting people.

Opal later wrote that the move cramped her style and put her under Sedgwick's control. She claimed that Sedgwick told her she couldn't go to the symphony with friends or accept an invitation to the theater from Mrs. Forbes, but must decline and work. He was such a slave driver, Opal claimed, that he would call her from Boston and insist she work nights on the diary, even though the doctor treating her spinal problems had prescribed rest.

Mrs. Henry Cabot, who also lived in the compound, took her for walks, but Opal felt left out because the Henry Cabots didn't have her over when all the young members of the family were there for Christmas dinner. Instead she was invited to the Sedgwicks' in Boston, and when they left at 3:00 P.M. to make family calls, Opal had to return alone to the insane Mrs. Cabot's, undoubtedly knowing that young people were having a good time at the Henry Cabots' nearby. Opal remained bitter about this feeling of exclusion for many years.

Ellery Sedgwick did arrange for her to meet one interesting person, however, the statesman Viscount Grey of Fallodon. Grey, a former British foreign minister, was a bit of a sad sack at this point in his life. On the eve of World War I he had written his famous "The lights have gone out all over Europe. They will not be lit again in our time." He had come to America in September 1919, emerging from political retirement to serve as a special ambassador to the United States. He tried to promote British policy on Ireland and foster American participation in the League of Nations, doomed after a rancorous struggle between Republicans and Democrats, exacerbated by President Wilson's stroke. Grey was to leave in failure in January 1920, but in December 1919 he was in Boston and met Opal.

Disenchanted by the horrors of a war in which millions of young people had died to little apparent purpose, and thwarted in his attempts to make the postwar world a better place, he was primed to find someone of Opal's youth, full of promise for a better future, enchanting. He was a widower between wives. His eccentric first wife, Dorothy, who was said not only to hate children but to dislike even the sight of them, had died after fracturing her skull in a carriage accident in 1906. The couple had been childless, and, to this end, celibate, at her wish.

Grey loved nature. He grew potatoes and took a keen interest in trees and birds. In one famous photograph he looks very pleased to be wearing a live duck on his head, its webby feet firmly planted on his tweed hat. When he referred to his failed diplomatic mission in America, one of his complaints was that he had hardly seen any trees. He adored Wordsworth and shared his vision of childhood as a time of spiritual clarity and uncorrupted communion with nature.

Many years later Sedgwick wrote of the meeting between Opal and Grey in his memoirs: "I have never watched two more delighted and understanding friends than the statesman and the child of the woods talking back and forth of wrens and pewits, of orioles and cuckoos."

Grey of Fallodon wrote his impressions to Sedgwick soon after: "She is even more wonderful than I dared to expect. . . ." He wanted copies of her book when it came out to send to friends in England to get a word-of-mouth campaign going there and offered to contribute money to help finance a home for her "in some congenial country place." Grey went on to describe her as "one of the most remarkable and touching persons, and her sensitive feelings and outpouring about natural things is [*sic*] more than I ever heard." He predicted that she would be a "revelation to many people."

Her diary wasn't out yet, and there is no indication Grey had read any advance material. Yet he was already sold. The marketing of Opal, beginning with her early efforts shipping her photo around rural Oregon for Junior Christian Endeavor events and her first interview with Elbert Bede in the *Cottage Grove Sentinel*, had always been as much about her personality as her work.

Opal wrote David Starr Jordan, Lummis's old friend, at Stanford who had written an introduction to *The Fairyland Around Us*, about the meeting. "The other evening I did meet a wonderful man who has a wonderful love for the out-of-doors. It was the British Ambassador to the United States—Viscount Grey of Fallodon. He loves trees very much, and he told me about his pet squirrels and his other friends. He brought me all of Wordsworth's poems which I so much like and I used to pray for when I was a little girl." Perhaps to illustrate that her childhood was ebbing away, she also reported on a new hairstyle: "I do my hair upon my head now. . . ."

During December, Sedgwick was working on his public relations buildup for Opal. He arranged to have some pages of the diary photographed and wrote a photographer named Stebbins complaining about a publicity shot that "foreshortens her face to a degree that makes it unpleasant." The interest of someone like Grey was clearly a good PR opportunity. "Won't you bring in when you come, what you have written of the interview with Lord Grey so that while this is still fresh in our minds we may see that nothing escapes us?" Sedgwick wrote Opal.

Opal's four-page version of the event was full of Grey's knowledge-able references to her forthcoming diary, which had not yet appeared. She explained, however, that Sedgwick had told the statesman all about her book at lunch and that he was ready with specific questions about the fir tree Michael Angelo Sanzio Raphael, the pig Peter Paul Rubens, the toad Lucian Horace Ovid Virgil, and the crow Lars Porsena of Clusium. He had asked about her altar for Good King Edward I and wanted to know what flowers she had planted in honor of his coronation day. Opal said, "I told him they were pyrola routundifolia." He had also asked about the wood rat Thomas Chatterton. "He had forgotten about the last part of his name being Jupiter Zeus," explained Opal.

They had discussed and compared a slew of Oregon and British species of birds, Opal told him about the habits of wood rats and that toads enjoyed having their backs rubbed, and Grey told her that Handel's *Largo* was inspired by a plane tree. She continued:

> Afterwards we talked of Wordsworth. He too feels in Wordsworth a kindred soul. He spoke of the lines on Tintern Abbey, and of how much they have meant to him. And he said often it is when he is in the city he longs for the garden and the trees. And we talked of the Prelude—and of all that nature holds for one who seeks her friend-ship. He too knows the abiding peace that the trees and the fields do bring to one. And when I told him how I felt that the friendship of the trees and the companionship of all nature takes [*sic*] one back into the years that have been and makes [*sic*] one's life a part of all life that has gone before—he did say "Yes and kindred to all that is to come"—and that it makes one's life a part of all eternal life.

Some modern Opalites have told me that Opal was important be-cause she was ahead of her time, a harbinger of the New Age. In her youth, however, her appeal to people like Lord Grey was nostalgic. To a generation exhausted by worldwide slaughter, she represented lost inno-cence.

After the horrors of the war America faced domestic upheaval. The year 1919 was characterized by ugly strikes, a bloody race riot in

Chicago, and panic about Bolsheviks and terrorists, depicted in popular culture as bearded foreign anarchists wielding smoking orbs, round black bombs. In addition to this, there was concern about modern youth. Young women refused to wear corsets, danced to jazz, smoked and drank, despite the new Prohibition law, and indulged in "petting parties." Parents had lost control, and they knew it. They could only read in horror about what their children were up to.

What could be more soothing than an innocent child-woman like Opal, who, by writing about her prewar childhood, could take America back to a more innocent time? By piecing the diary together, she was pasting together a recent past that seemed to have been destroyed forever.

CHAPTER
Nine

*I*n January 1920, several months before the first diary installment was published, and while she and Sedgwick were still giving the first magazine installment of the diary some editorial tweaks, Opal wrote to her friend Nellie Hemenway: "That which I mention below here please do not speak of to anyone at all—none at all—Please do not mention what I write. Parts of a childhood diary which I kept when I was a very little girl are to be published. In this will come out something which I have never told you, but which you may have guessed. That was that I am not Mrs. and Mr. Whiteley's child. I was put in the care of Mrs. Whiteley in Portland when she was on her way from Washington [State] to the lumber camp in Oregon. Something happened there in Portland which I have never understood . . . something happened to her other little girl."

Opal had been hinting at this idea for years, beginning with a statement to Mrs. Hunt in Eugene that she was adopted, indications to Gertrude Lummis that her parents were Italians, the switched-at-birth story in which her family was French that she gave to the theosophists, and the story that she had appeared "from God knows where" in rural Oregon to McGroarty. Now she was announcing that the diary would reveal her secret past to all.

She went on to say that Mrs. Whiteley had pretended to others that Opal was her own child, but when they were alone, she was "constantly reminding me that I wasn't her own child and if I had been I wouldn't have had this longing to write and the longing for the out-of-doors and books." Opal added that she had been forced to lie about her birthplace, Colton, Washington, and about her origins when Elbert Bede wrote about her in the *Cottage Grove Sentinel* in 1915 after she had been chosen the state superintendent of Junior Christian Endeavor.

She also sent a copy of *The Fairyland Around Us* to Nellie, inscribed "To Nellie Hemenway with loving greetings from the author, Opal Whiteley."

Dear Nellie.

This is my first book. As a first book it speaks of how little knowledge of book making I had—but it was a labor of love. May it bring to you some of the joy of my loved fields and woods.

You loving Friend,

Opal Whiteley

PS There are places in it which read oddly owing to the make up man having changed some of my sentences to make them read with fewer words in order to lock up certain pages, which had too many millimeters of lynotype [sic] *and the make up man changed where I had written "the mother of the father of the mama" to "my grandmother" which made the sense incorrect as she was not my grandmother. These changes were made just before printing.*

O. W.

At about the same time that Nellie received these startling revelations about Opal's life, *Cottage Grove Sentinel* editor Elbert Bede received a similar communication from Opal. In a letter dated January 24, 1920, she enclosed another letter in an envelope. Opal explained that while opening one of the boxes of diary pieces, she had come across an unmailed letter to Bede that she had written in California two years before, on April 2, 1918.

In her cover letter, Opal said she did not want any of this put in the paper, adding, "I wrote you the other letter nearly two years ago because I felt you should know—but I did not feel it was safe to let you know before." The enclosed letter headed "Hollywood, California," and dated April 2, 1918, began, "This letter is concerning the letter you printed from me in May 5, 1915," referring to the publicity she got in the *Cottage Grove Sentinel* when elected Junior Endeavor superintendent.

That letter which you printed is not the letter I wrote in answer to your request that I write of my life. The original letter in which I wrote you of my early childhood days and of my pets and of the cathedral in the woods where I had the services with my pets and of the nature books I was working on, and of the Junior work. This letter was taken from me by Mrs. Whiteley and a tall woman who came with her to Eugene. And I was made to write the one which you received and printed. . . . They made me to write that about "I was born in Whitman county, Washington Dec. 11, 1897." I was not. I don't know just when or where I was born. That birthday and that birthplace are of the other little girl which Mrs. Whiteley lost.

She explained that she had been switched with the real Opal when Mrs. Whiteley was on her way from Colton, Washington, to Wendling, Oregon, and changed trains at Portland. Mrs. Whiteley was to have been paid to raise this new little girl but never was. "There is much of my childhood and girlhood I do not understand."

The letter said that items that might provide clues to her real identity had been taken from her except for two little books that were kept in a box with a secret compartment. "And these two books I learned much from. But when I was about 12 years old, they were taken from the log where I kept them hidden in the woods."

Since the disappearance of these books, the only proof she had of her real identity were some letters that Mrs. Whiteley had written her while she was away working, complaining that she never got the pay she was to have received to raise Opal. Opal also said she had a number of letters from Mrs. Patrick, Ed Whiteley's mother, now deceased, who also knew the secret of her birth. (Actually, in the only known letter from Mrs. Patrick, she addressed Opal as "My Dear Granddaughter," referred to Lizzie and Ed Whiteley as "your Mother and Father," and signed off "Lovingly, Grandma.")

Opal said she had almost told Bede everything when she had lunch at the Bede home "after my voice came back in 1916. Then I thought everyone has her own burdens. I must not burden them with mine."

The 1918 letter came in an envelope with a three-cent stamp. This was an authentic touch. That had been the right postage for 1918, but there had since been a rate change.

Interestingly, on April 2, 1918, the date she had presumably written Bede, she also wrote a letter to Nellie Hemenway, which did get mailed. It described her new life in Hollywood at Mrs. Bales's house in glowing, sunny terms. "I am meeting many wonderful people—poets, musicians, authors, and artists. Carrie Jacobs Bond lives six blocks from the house." Bond was a popular composer of sentimental songs, somewhat passé by 1918. She had had a big hit with "I Love You Truly" in 1901.

If Opal is to be believed, she produced both the fraught letter to Bede about dark conspiracies and a breathless teenage letter to a girlfriend about her proximity to celebrity on the same day, mailing one of them and sealing the other in her box full of diary pieces.

The arrival in a small town of such startling letters, despite Opal's injunctions to the recipients to keep quiet, was bound to get out. Before the first installment of the diary appeared, the gossip had already started.

Ed Whiteley wrote Opal that he had heard she was disclaiming her family. Telling her she knew that what she was saying wasn't true, he expressed fears for her sanity. Sedgwick took a look at Ed Whiteley's letter and dismissed it on the grounds that it was illiterate and later said he didn't give it another thought. For the moment Sedgwick was apparently unaware or unperturbed about what was simmering in Cottage Grove, but he too was thinking about Opal's origins. He was puzzled about the fact that French phrases appeared in the diary of a seven-year-old in Oregon, as well as by the erudition exhibited by the precocious diarist, and to account for it, he had to try to find out just how it had come about.

At first, while the book was being put together, Opal had appeared puzzled by the French words and phrases in it. Sedgwick said she had to be told they were French words. She had no explanation for the awkwardly crayoned phrases such as "The little leaves are calling, come petite Françoise," or "I did sing him un chant des fleurs." Sedgwick did not completely question the French but he was clearly concerned about some of the French references and left many of them out of the diary.

He told Opal she could keep references to herself as "petite Françoise," which was how her Angel Mother and Father and such elements of nature as the wind addressed her.

Examples of French that Sedgwick allowed into the published diary included the names of species. "When I grow up I am going to write a book about the glads of blue—and about the *dauphinelle* and *lin* and *cornette* and *nigelle* and *herbe-de-la-trinite*." (Opal indeed had a chapter titled "Aurelius Evangel in Search of the Joyous Blue" in *The Fairyland Around Us*, in which "the All-Wise Father, perceiving that the Children of Men were having 'blue' days [,] did send a little Wind Fairy, Aurelius Evangel, in search of the Joyous Blue," after which a large group of blue flower and bird species was listed.) French geographic names were also used to describe the creeks and woods of Lane County, Oregon. "On and on I go. To the Orne and Rille I go. . . . Into the woods beyond the rivière—into the forêt de Saint Germaine-en-Laye I go."

In one passage the child Opal was chastised for speaking French by an ignorant schoolteacher. "And teacher did ask me eight things at once. She did ask me what is a pig and a mouse and a baby deer and a duck and a turkey and a fish and a colt and a blackbird. And I did say in a real quick way, 'A pig is a *cochon* and a mouse is a *mulot* and a baby deer is a *daine* and a duck is a *canard* and a turkey is a *dindon* and a fish is a *poisson* and a colt is a *pulain* and a blackbird is a *merle*.' " The teacher insisted she was wrong, and when plucky little Opal insisted she was right, she was kept in at recess for two days.

In a note to a copy editor or typesetter, Opal wrote that Sedgwick "said the french [*sic*] bird and flower songs might go in. I have put two in. The others I left until another edition." Referred to as "chansons," these were presented as songs taught to her by Angel Mother and Father and also revealed a preoccupation with lists. ". . . I did sing to the rivière a song. I sang it *Le chant de Seine, de Havre, et Essonne et Nonette et Roullon et Iton et Darnetal et Ourcq et Rille et Loing et Eure et Audelle et Nonette et Sarc*. I sang it as Angel Father did teach me to, and as he has wrote in the book."

Sedgwick, innocent of Opal's efforts to set the record straight back in her own hometown, simultaneously sent out a brace of letters to people Opal had known in Oregon and California, asking about her mysterious past. To department store heiress Marie Mullen he wrote: "I have become very much interested in Opal Whiteley who is now spending all her days restoring her childhood's diary so that I may print it in the Atlantic. I am naturally eager to get hold of the true facts of her career. The whole story is very puzzling to her and to all who are interested in her. It ought, I think [,] to be possible to find out who her parents actually were and any information you can give me regarding her condition at the time you found her or the names of any of her earlier friends whom you may know I shall be grateful for." He also asked Mrs. King Camp Gillette what she knew about the late Mrs. Whiteley and whether she knew if Mr. Whiteley was still alive.

Other recipients of Sedgwick's letters included teachers, the Protestant minister who had baptized Opal in Cottage Grove, adults associated with her Oregon Junior Endeavor work, Los Angeles society ladies, and David Starr Jordan. Opal had provided Sedgwick with the references. Charles Lummis and Mrs. Bales weren't included.

In due course, the replies trickled in. An Oregon correspondent said that Opal had always been called the Little Nature Study Girl, had always been "peculiar," and that her family had never "fully understood her." Marie Mullen wrote from the Clift Hotel in San Francisco, "Surely she is a genius." David Starr Jordan, president of Stanford, described her as "a charmingly open-eyed and simple-hearted young woman," with "a very attractive personality." He said he could hardly to wait to read her childhood diary and expected more from Opal than from little Daisy Ashford, of bestselling *Young Visiters* fame.

He was right that nothing could be more different from Daisy's diary than Opal's. While Opal's diary was to reveal the frustration of being housebound and away from nature, the adult Daisy later remembered she had hoped for bad weather so she could stay indoors and write. Little Daisy was clearly interested in popular fiction of the day, grown-ups and their little hypocrisies, social class, and the doings of high society, which in her vision included the Prince of Wales wearing "a lovely ermine cloak and a small but costly crown," sipping champagne, eating as much ice cream as he liked, smoking a cigar, and sharing a few world-weary insights. "It upsets me said the prince lapping up his strawberry ice all I want is peace and quiet and a little fun and here I am tied down to this life he said taking off his crown being royal has many painful drawbacks." Her social-climbing protagonist, Mr. Salteena, described himself thus: "I am fond of digging in the garden and I am parshial to ladies if they are nice. I suppose it is my nature. I am not quite a gentleman but you would hardly notice it but can't be helped anyhow." Little everyday justifications were neatly captured: "I shall put some red ruge [*sic*] on my face said Ethel becouse I am very pale owing to the drains in this house."

Jordan clearly had it in for Daisy. Around the same time he also wrote Lummis, sneering at Daisy's phrase "a small but costly crown," which he apparently found not charming and funny but crass and vulgar.

It is rather surprising that Opal gave Sedgwick Willard C. James's name as a reference, inasmuch as she had spurned his geriatric advances, fled from him into the Pacific Ocean, and also owed him $650. James replied to Sedgwick on his son-in-law's letterhead that Opal was "one of the brightest minds" he had ever known.

CHAPTER
Ten

$\mathcal{M}$eanwhile, back in Cottage Grove, mysterious anonymous letters began to arrive at the Whiteleys'. The first one, dated February 3, began: "Burn this letter after you have written out the questions that are in it. It will be wise for you not to keep the letters we will be sending to you." The letter said that *The Atlantic Monthly* had just announced that Opal Whiteley's childhood diary would be published in the next issue. It went on to explain that the real Opal had been switched with "a child whom you now know as your sister. . . . For taking this child and rearing her as her own child, Opal, your mother was to have been paid a sum of money equal to about 10,000 francs." The good news for the Whiteleys was that Mrs. Whiteley had wanted to use this money to buy presents for them, and since the money had now been made available, these presents would now be bought and sent to them.

The letter went on to say that Opal had been followed for years and that while the letter writers had intended she spend the rest of her life in the lumber camps, "she slipped us up on that and got out and continued her studies of the out of doors."

It asked that the Whiteleys get from Opal letters from her mother and her grandmother Mrs. Patrick that she had in her possession that proved her true identity. It also asked them to ask Opal if she had any idea how old she really was and explained that she was near in age but actually some months older.

There were also questions about two books that Opal had had but that had been taken from her. "We have been making a wide search for them but we are afraid someone has gotten them and turned them over to her." It was apparently necessary to get them back because they contained the handwriting of Opal's real parents, her father's in French.

The letter referred to a strange man who seemed to have gotten wind of the substitution and to a governess who knew the secret but had died. Opal's real father, it revealed, had married her real mother in a secret ceremony by a priest unknown to his family. The letter writers said that both of Opal's birth parents were dead but that the letter writers would make sure her remaining relatives never learned of her existence.

The Whiteleys were to "Ask Opal what part of India her father went to" and enjoined to write Opal at once by registered mail. The letter helpfully provided Opal's new address at Mrs. Cabot's, adding, "She is not at Cambridge as you think. She is in the country at 275 Heath Street, Chestnut Hill Mass." The letter ended "B.C.M. All communications to you will be so signed."

More letters soon arrived. They were typed, with lots of mistakes and raggedy margins. Another B.C.M. letter to Ed Whiteley explained that a peddler woman who used to come to the logging camps had been working undercover to spy on Opal. This same agent, dressed differently, had gone with Lizzie Whiteley to Eugene in 1915 to strong-arm Opal into writing a bogus version of her life for Elbert Bede's newspaper.

A letter of February 11 to Ed gave a list of the presents Lizzie had wanted the family to have with the money owing for Opal's care and announced that they would soon be arriving, including "silver table ware which your wife Lizzie wanted Faye and Pearl and Cloe to have." For Ed there was a watch with "a very good movement so we have got a good Swiss movement." He would also get a silver shaving mug. Jewel boxes and glove and handkerchief boxes would be sent to the girls as well as gold-plated penknives with their engraved initials and a gold bracelet for Cloe, centerpieces that Lizzie had wanted them to embroider for their hope chests, music she had wanted Faye to have, silk scarves, and mechanical toys "for the little boy Elwin." By Decoration Day (now Memorial Day) of 1920, the Whiteleys could expect fifty dollars to help buy a tombstone for Lizzie's grave "as she so faithfully took care of this child that was put in her care to bring up as her own child which she did as she agreed to."

The silverware the girls were to receive was described in astonishing detail and came to a total of 273 pieces. Each girl was to receive six knives, forks, tablespoons, teaspoons, orange spoons, soup spoons, salad forks, fruit knives, and iced tea spoons as well as serving pieces, bowls, various ladles, casseroles, and crumb trays and scrapers. The tines of the cold meat forks, as well as the insides of the berry spoons, would be gold-plated. The genteel Lizzie Whiteley, whose domestic agenda had never been satisfactorily addressed, would have been very happy.

The same day the anonymous correspondents wrote this, Opal wrote to a Mrs. Dimm in Portland, refunding the $2.50 down payment she had paid for *The Fairyland Around Us,* Mrs. Dimm apparently not having received the book. Although she got no advance for the diary in book form, Opal did get money for the magazine excerpts on publication and immediately began to pay back people who had loaned her money. *The Atlantic Monthly* staff was helping her settle her debts. Checks and covering letters went out from their offices. Her memo "Debts of Opal Whiteley" included the $650 to Willard C. James, from whom she had presumably hidden in the water underneath the Santa Monica pier. He got a $100 partial payment, and Opal wished him the best of success with "your Little Rock Fruit ranch." The First National Bank of Cottage Grove got its final $100, on her $150 leaving town loan. There were small amounts all over Oregon, such as $2.50 to her old Cottage Grove friend Nellie Hemenway. Her fisherman beau Steve Pearson got a chilly note in the third person referring to "$80.00 in part payment of the two hundred and thirty dollars Miss Whiteley owes you." The University of Oregon scholarship fund and Charles Lummis, to whom she owed back rent, didn't make the list.

In early March the first installment of the diary was published. In "The Contributor's Column" Sedgwick was coy about Opal's origins. "Now, the right way to read the story of Opal is for the delight of it, but if you want to speculate about the author and her education, you may do so to your heart's content. About her past, the editor knows only what she has told him, but about the manuscript, he knows a good deal; during the five months she has passed in piecing it together at his instigation, he has seen her frequently and with some intimacy."

Sedgwick went on to explain how the manuscript had been assembled. Crayon colors and paper type were used as clues to put it together like a picture puzzle. "The method employed is to fit sheets, and later, fragments of episodes together, smoothing out the paper bags on which, for the most part, they are written . . . whenever a small fragment is completed it is typed on a card; and in this way Miss Whiteley has prepared a card system that would do credit to a scientific museum. Finally, the cards are filed in sequence and the manuscript is then typed off just as was first written, except for capitals and punctuation. In the original, the style employed uses all capitals and punctuation—much like inscriptions dug up by archeologists."

In the introduction to the first installment Opal explained that she didn't remember much about her life before she was taken to the logging camp, but she remembered her real mother, who took her for walks in the woods, taught her poetry, and then taught her how to print what she had seen and heard. Angel Mother also gave Opal advice that every high school journalism student gets and that may have appeared in a book Opal read titled *What Editors Want*: "Always to Ask What, Where, When, Why, and How." Opal said she had been attended by servants, and sometimes her father would come back from travels abroad, and she would sit on his knee and ride on his shoulders. This happy time was followed by a boating accident in which Angel Mother and Opal both ended up in the sea, and Angel Mother drowned. Soon Opal was told by a kindly servant or governess that her father too had "gone to heaven while he was away in far lands."

The two of them set out for Opal's paternal grandparents but never got there. Strange, frightening people instead took her on a long journey. "Then it was that they put me with Mrs. Whiteley. The day they put me with her it was a rainy day and I thought she was a little afraid of them too. She took me on the train and in a stage coach to the lumber camp. She called me Opal Whiteley, the same name as that of another little girl who was the same size as I was when her mother lost her."

This story didn't go down well in Oregon, and nobody was buying it. Her maternal grandmother, Mrs. Scott, had seen Opal as a baby when Lizzie had left Ed temporarily and came home and later when she came to the Cottage Grove area to live, around age four, and was certain there had been no substitution in between. People in Cottage Grove pointed out that Opal was the spitting image of her mother and sisters and that she had never made these claims while growing up.

In the *Cottage Grove Sentinel*, Elbert Bede reported: "The opinion here is quite unanimous that the foster-parent theory is a childish fantasy and *Atlantic Monthly* is being quite severely criticized for making not the least investigation as to the authenticity of this statement by the author." Under the subhead "Has Atlantic Monthly Been Spoofed," Bede pointed out politely that he wasn't suggesting that the "staid and respectable old Atlantic" had engaged in deceit. He could understand Sedgwick's failure to check out the story, Bede wrote, because of Opal's "innocently sincere way in which she tells her stories" and her "face to which deceit and hypocrisy would seem strange companions."

Professor Conklin wrote Sedgwick an equally polite but skeptical letter and told him that as part of his foster child fantasy research, he would "attempt a little quiet investigation" in Cottage Grove. He hustled out to interview Grandma Scott, who produced family pictures from an old trunk.

The Oregonian already had a file on Opal. Just before leaving for California, Opal had given the interview quoted earlier, saying, "My dearest girl chum was my mother. In my love of music, art, poetry, biography, the drama, history, she was in close sympathy with me and we had many wonderful twilight hours together." This hardly sounded like the cruel "the mamma" of the diary or like a home devoid of books. When *The Oregonian* pointed out she had referred to Lizzie Whiteley affectionately as her mother, Sedgwick in a letter to the editor said she had been misquoted. He also complained that his own position on Opal's claims hadn't been portrayed accurately, quoting what he himself had written in "The Contributor's Column." "About her past the editor knows only what she has told him."

The Oregonian wasn't going to take this meekly or allow itself to be patronized or contradicted by some Boston Brahmin, who had swallowed a ridiculous story in which a native daughter had snobbishly rejected her Oregon roots. "Not only were Opal's own words quoted in the passage referred to," it replied tartly, but the reporter had read all her quotes to her prior to publication, and she had approved them. It pointed out that Sedgwick was being disingenuous not to mention that inside the magazine, a foreword to Opal's diary, signed with the initials E. S., stated that Opal was not a child of the Whiteleys, that pictures of her real parents were taken from her, that a "foster-sister" tore the diary into pieces, and that she had been substituted for the real Opal, who had died. *The Oregonian* stated firmly, "These statements were published by *The Atlantic* editor not as claims set forth by Opal, but as facts. They are all flatly contradicted by a considerable number of reputable persons in Oregon who say they have known Opal from infancy." Whether *The Oregonian* thought Sedgwick believed Oregon contained any reputable persons is not clear.

The Oregonian didn't come right out and call Opal a liar, but it did republish her Isadora Duncanesque barefoot publicity shot, which had run in 1918 over the caption "Interpreting the Spirit of Nature in the Dance." Now it ran with the headline OPAL WHITELEY IN ONE OF HER POSES, with the cutline "An exemplification of Opal Whiteley's fondness for investing herself with fanciful roles is given in the accompanying picture. Although Opal did not dance, she dressed herself in this costume and had her picture taken to make herself appear as a dancer. Similarly she arrayed herself in other costumes and had photographs made."

Sedgwick wrote several people that he didn't claim to know the truth of Opal's origins, but that he was completely convinced of the authenticity of the diary because he had mentioned it to her first, without prompting from her. Unfortunately that statement was not true.

Sedgwick also said he was completely convinced the diary hadn't been tampered with and characterized the suggestion that Opal had embellished the manuscript as "absurd." Therefore, he said, he had to take the French references seriously and find some way to account for them. He didn't say he'd expunged a large number of those French phrases before publication. He also said that the case was being discussed all over the country and that it was certainly puzzling.

"I am not a particularly credulous man," Sedgwick wrote to Bede, a statement that might have caused snickers back in Cottage Grove. He defended Opal by saying her story was always the same, that "scientists and men of great distinction" had seen her manuscript and talked with her about it, and perhaps most tellingly, that "Indeed, her whole attitude is one of the most complete and simple innocence." He also told Bede he had seen letters from Ed Whiteley and his daughters, commenting, "A greater contrast in education or in natural character I cannot imagine." Sedgwick later said that he was convinced of Opal's claims because it was inconceivable to him she could be related to the Whiteleys, whom he clearly considered backwoods hicks. He had dismissed Ed Whiteley's prepublication letter calling Opal's story a lie because it seemed illiterate. He objected to his use of the expression "this stuff" in reference to the claims she was making. The prose style of the Whiteley sisters, he said, resembled that of "servant girls."

While it is true that Pearl once sent a letter to "Dear Ople," Sedgwick's perceptions of the sensitivities and abilities of working-class westerners clearly colored his judgment. Back in her Junior Endeavor days, Opal had given a newspaper interview in which said she came by her love of nature from her uncle Henry Pearson, a miner. Opal now denied this. Sedgwick said that the idea that "a rough miner" could have taught her a love of nature was "fantastic" and "preposterous." Later he wrote that while he was investigating Opal, he received "letters from persons, many half illiterate, from the rough Northwest." Eastern ignorance of the West was not unusual for the times. An old lady once told me that as a young girl in the 1920s she went to a tea party in New York. Her hostess, upon hearing she was from Seattle, said, "Oh, there's another girl here from the West. She's from Chicago. Perhaps you know her."

Bede sent Sedgwick pictures of Opal and Pearl as children, to show the family resemblance. Sedgwick examined them and returned them without comment. Professor Conklin then wrote Sedgwick that after interviewing the family and friends, he had no doubt that Opal's story was a fantasy. He expressed concern for her health and happiness and said he had decided not to write up the case for a scientific journal out of consideration for the family and Opal's future. He tactfully didn't mention that he also believed the diary itself was a fake.

Besides dealing with western skeptics, Sedgwick was worried about Opal herself. He described her after the diary appeared as "wrought to a high pitch of excitement." She began once again to scream in the night. One of the nurses at Mrs. Cabot's grew so alarmed that she piled encyclopedias in the window lest Opal inadvertently jump out at night.

Sitting on a streetcar, she turned to strangers, announced suddenly that she was Opal Whiteley, and began to talk very excitedly about her diary, in a manner so alarming that it was brought to the attention of the Cabots. A neighbor of the Cabots' declared she would never allow Opal to teach her children because her gaze was insane, and one of the nurses who took care of the insane Mrs. Cabot and had worked in an asylum, said that in her professional opinion, anyone who exhibited such excitement and suspicion as Opal did was bound to go mad.

Opal was acting in a secretive manner, packing a lot of things in a box and hiding it in the cellar. She also began to tell Sedgwick more about her past. Trembling and clearly frightened, she told of having been taken violently from a governess who cared for her after her real parents died and described the horror of seeing the woman's face covered in blood. She also said that her grandmother Mrs. Patrick had heard a deathbed confession in which a mysterious woman gave her clothing originally belonging to Opal as a baby, daintily hand-embroidered, and said she had been part of a conspiracy to bring Opal to the West. (Dainty, hand-embroidered baby clothes are an important clue to establishing the aristocratic birth of a backwoods orphan in *Freckles*, the Gene Stratton-Porter novel Opal had read and liked.)

Sedgwick tried to find employment for her and arranged for Miss Woodward of Miss Woodward's School in Boston to interview Opal. Miss Woodward didn't seem to notice her excitability and described her as "real and very lovely—a rare blending of interpreter, child and early Christian! [exclamation point hers]" Miss Woodward promised to get her set up with nature classes and to work through the Private School Association to get her speaking engagements and classes elsewhere.

Sedgwick, who said he found himself acting "in the capacity of guardian" and referred to Opal habitually as "this child," although she was now twenty-two, warned Miss Woodward that his greatest fear was that "throughout this period of exploitation . . . the young girl be affected by indiscriminate and unconsidered praise."

What was Sedgwick getting at here? Had he noticed that the charming, unspoiled child of the woods and fields who had appeared in his office eight months before seemed to have developed self-aggrandizing tendencies and a hefty ego? Or was he concerned about her mental stability?

He also turned down a speaking engagement for her at the Author's Club. Sedgwick said that he didn't want her regarded as "a curiosity" and said he was taking great pain not to "overpraise her." He also turned down an invitation to tea on her behalf on the grounds that she had too much work to do.

The diary was a huge success. *The Atlantic* attracted new subscribers, the issue sold well, fan mail poured in, and within weeks of the first installment, Sedgwick sold the English and British Empire rights to a seventy-one-thousand-word book version of the diary to G. P. Putnam's London branch for a thousand-dollar advance. Noting that *The Atlantic* was selling "like mad out West," Sedgwick tried to keep the bad publicity in Oregon from getting too much circulation in the East lest it hurt future book sales.

Seven more boxes of material arrived at Mrs. Cabot's house in early April, after the first two installments had been published. Sedgwick was present at the opening of at least five of these boxes, which he said contained "the rest of her diary, torn into countless fragments." He said that among the fragments were "miscellaneous photographs, pictures, and mementoes" as well as more unmailed letters, just like the ones she told Bede she had found in the first shipment. The packing label survives. It says the boxes contained "books and seashells" and had been sent from Los Angeles in January.

Opal wrote back to Ed Whiteley. Addressing him as "Dear Papa," she thanked him for his concern and pointed out that it was the first time he'd shown any since he'd helped her with an arithmetic problem in the fourth grade. She told him that she regretted the annoyance reporters were causing the family and demanded to know about "my own mother and father" and the two books she said had been taken from her.

The happiest person about all these developments was Elbert Bede, enjoying the pursuit of the biggest scoop of his life. A story of national interest had cropped up right there in Cottage Grove. If Opal's claims could be proved or disproved, Bede wanted to be the man to do it.

Elbert Bede ran around interviewing everyone he could and was in frequent communication with both Sedgwick and Professor Conklin, regularly batting out letters to the two of them on his well-worn type-writer with its crooked letters. Reading all this communication today is like reading a barrage of e-mail, but of course it all took longer.

Bede always used a polite tone with Sedgwick while he pumped him for details about Opal and the diary "editor to editor." With Professor Conklin, he was less restrained, keeping him more slangily informed about his investigation and exuding enthusiasm about the chase for the truth. "Mrs. Scott admitted to me that at one time Mrs. Whiteley was very much out of her head," he wrote on one occasion, later writing, "At last I have some dope on Mrs. Whiteley. Mrs. FW Hawkins, who knew her well, says she was most peculiar woman she ever knew."

Bede followed the story wherever it led, including visiting the Oregon State Library. Opal's old enemy Cornelia Marvin had contacted him and, exhibiting a disregard for patron privacy that would appall a modern librarian, said she wanted to show him Opal's library file, both her reading matter throughout her childhood and documentation of her cavalier way with library materials.

From Grandma Scott he got the interesting information that when Opal arrived in Cottage Grove from Colton, Washington, after the switch had supposedly taken place, Opal had asked when her dog Ginger would be arriving and wanted to see a little red chair that was left behind and belonged to Pearl. She also referred to Doug Mustard, the farmer who had rented them land in Colton. If this were true, the idea of a switch in Portland would be impossible, unless a tiny French child had been taught English and had also been briefed on the real Opal's past.

Bede and Conklin sent a recently graduated student of the professor's to check out Colton, Washington. Bede thought it interesting that it had a contingent of French immigrants and was 80 percent Catholic. He thought Opal could have picked up the details of Latin mass that Opal in the diary performed for her animal friends in a cathedral-like forest grove.

The promised-for presents described in the anonymous letters were also arriving. Ed Whiteley, sporting his new watch, came into town, and Bede, much to his delight, ran into him. All efforts to pump him, however, failed. When asked if Opal had written the diary as a child, Ed said she had always been writing. Asked if there was any question about her birth, he was mysteriously vague.

Ed Whiteley had written Opal to ask her why she was saying things that were untrue, but that wasn't the line he took outside the family. He worried that his daughter had gone mad, and he suspected Sedgwick had put her up to some kind of con game. His evasive replies can be explained by the fact he didn't want to say anything that would make her look crazy or crooked, so he said as little as possible. As a Cottage Grove citizen explained to a visiting reporter when asked why Ed wouldn't go on the record and insist Opal was his, "That's easy. He doesn't want people to think she's yarning about it, and he's doing it to protect her reputation."

Somehow, although perhaps in a small town it wasn't too difficult, Bede learned about the anonymous letters the Whiteleys had received. He had been panting to get a look at them and soon learned that Ed Whiteley had turned them over to the Lane County sheriff, Fred Stickels. Bede was a Mason, and so was Stickels. Bede got a look at the letters.

When Bede wrote Sedgwick about the anonymous letters and asked for his reaction, Sedgwick replied that he wanted to see them. Bede told Sedgwick that if he were a Mason, "particularly of the Scottish Rite," and sent "documentary evidence" to prove it, Bede could get him a look at the letters. Sedgwick replied he wasn't a Mason but told Bede he could rely on "my discretion and my recognition of your services."

Bede managed to break down the sheriff anyway. He sent Sedgwick a telegram: "Succeeded getting all you ask in your hands in a few days." Brother Stickels would be sending copies directly to Sedgwick "in the line of duty" as part of his investigation. Bede explained that the complainant in the matter, Ed Whiteley, would not be told of this because he "believes or pretends to believe" that Sedgwick was "in on some scheme to exploit Opal."

Ed Whiteley wasn't talking to Bede or anyone else, but Bede managed to discover that the gifts were arriving in a steady stream. Grandma Scott told him that a box of presents sent to Pearl contained some items that had belonged to Opal before she left Cottage Grove. The family believed the gifts came from Opal.

The anonymous letters down at the sheriff's office were photographed, a costly and cumbersome procedure in the pre–photocopy machine era, and the photographs were sent to Sedgwick, who immediately began to try to determine if Opal had written them. There was some question about whether or not she knew how to type, but he later recalled that she had arrived at Mrs. Cabot's with a rented Remington typewriter. He got his secretary to try to track down the exact machine with the typewriter rental company.

Bede soon received mysterious photographs, mailed from Portland but sent in an envelope from a hotel in Walla Walla, Washington. They were old photographic portraits, and neatly penciled on the back were the words "Opal's grandfather," "Opal's real uncle," and "Opal's real father." Bede checked the hotel register and noted that some guests from Boston were staying there at the time the letters were sent. Not long after, Sedgwick in Boston received more old studio photographs with similar inscriptions. They bore the likeness of mustachioed people from the 1870s and 1880s. The set Sedgwick got had been mailed from Calgary. None of the photographs was ever traced.

Bede followed up on every lead that came his way, even taking seriously a letter with the salutation "Dear Sir!" from a man with a German name, who wrote of Opal: "Her statement that she is the Daughter of Angel parents is correct. Her parents are of the angelic race of people called Germans." The letter went on to say that Opal was the author of *Elisabeth and Her German Garden* and that other clues to her identity were to be found in that perennial favorite of the deranged the Book of Revelation. The letter writer invited Bede to come to the Portland hotel where he lived to discuss the matter further. Whether he made it or not,

Bede did type up a list of questions to ask him and took the trouble to pass the wacky letter on to Sedgwick.

Bede never lost enthusiasm for the story. In the end, he covered Opal Whiteley, starting in 1915 with her Junior Christian Endeavor election, for almost forty years.

Sedgwick described the spring and summer of 1920 as a period of "great excitement" for Opal. In mid-May she had another breakdown. The doctor prescribed bed rest and said she should avoid overwork. She wrote Nellie Hemenway that she was very ill from overwork and was spending seven weeks in bed. It was her third nervous breakdown in four years.

After the breakdown, Opal spent a week with Dr. Richard C. Cabot and his wife, Ella, at their country place in Cohasset, Massachusetts, a scenic coastal village going back to the seventeenth century. Dr. Cabot was a cousin of Sedgwick's wife and a professor of clinical medicine at Harvard. He was also interested in public health issues and social ethics. The visit was no doubt intended to be therapeutic and perhaps to give Sedgwick a second opinion on Opal's mental state. During the visit Opal awoke screaming in the night, but she also was instantly fond of the Cabots, and the visit seemed to calm her down.

She felt that the cultivated, childless, and very wealthy Cabots were kindred spirits. Dr. Cabot had degrees in classics and philosophy as well as his medical degree. He was a Harvard professor, a philanthropist, and the author of many books. Ella, as well connected as her husband and with large fortune of her own, was also committed to, in the phrase of the time, "social betterment." She was an educator, lecturing at the Salem Normal School. An extremely capable woman, she was the author of numerous books on education and managed her own extensive stock portfolio, often curtly dismissing her broker's advice. The couple made music together, he on violin, she on piano.

The Cabots were completely enchanted with their high-strung guest. He wrote to Sedgwick. "She seems to have all the zest and freshness of the ideally vivid child, together with the wide interests and aspirations of the grown up. . . . So either I am wholly wrong or she is one of the loveliest and best creatures the Lord has let me see." He said he and his wife loved her completely.

Opal was now planning to leave the rather gloomy home of Sedgwick's mother-in-law. Sedgwick had arranged for Opal to spend the summer with a Mr. and Mrs. McKean, at Beverly Farms, Massachusetts. The McKeans lived at Willow Tree Farm and had three little girls, ages six, five, and two. The plan was for Opal to take care of the girls from nine to eleven-thirty every morning, for room and board, and to continue piecing together the diary in the afternoons. Soon after her happy visit with Richard and Ella Cabot, she moved in with the McKeans. Opal was pleased with her new surroundings. There was a "tiny" swamp, a duck pond with Canada geese, a flock of white chickens, carrier pigeons, and many trees.

With Opal safely stashed in the country recovering from her breakdown, Sedgwick continued his investigation into her claims. He kept up correspondence with Bede to see what he was up to, and he also got in touch with Nellie Hemenway, offering her twenty-five dollars to poke around Cottage Grove to see if she could substantiate the events in the diary. Sedgwick told her to keep *The Atlantic*'s name out of the investigation.

Nellie agreed but said she couldn't do it immediately. She scrupulously refused to cash Sedgwick's check until she could perform the chore on her vacation. Nellie, who seems always to have behaved honorably, didn't spy on her friend Opal behind her back. Opal knew about this investigation. Earlier she had written Nellie to say Sedgwick might be asking questions about her past and described him as a "wonderful man" with "a lovely wife and four dear children."

Sedgwick also sent out another batch of letters asking more people about their memories of Opal. He hit pay dirt with a letter from Nellie's cousin Ora Almond Hemenway, of Cottage Grove, who said Opal had come to her in tears six years before, because Faye Whiteley had torn up her diary. Mrs. Hemenway also said Opal had had "queer names for her pets." She hedged, however, on the question of Opal's origins, stating only that it was too bad the matter had come up.

Sedgwick arranged for notarized affidavits from Mrs. Hemenway, and from saloonkeeper Mrs. Lou Thompson, who swore that she knew Opal had kept a childhood diary when she was thirteen. He also got one from a schoolteacher who swore Opal had not studied French in Cottage Grove. He arranged for Professor Conklin to send Opal's university transcripts to see if she had studied French there. She hadn't.

Sedgwick also got a letter from the "career advisor" and "character analyst" Jean Morris Ellis, whom Bede referred to as a phrenologist. Mrs. Ellis replied from the Eccles Hotel in Blackfoot, Idaho, that she was appearing at an American Legion convention, scheduled right after a boxing match. It was during the match, waiting to go on, that she took pen in hand to write that Opal had brought out strong protective instincts in her on the two occasions they had met, once in Cottage Grove and once when Opal was at college in Eugene. She said that "to me she seemed like all the rest of earths [*sic*] children ought to be . . . infinitely [*sic*] gentle and tender, crystal clear and pure."

Still, Mrs. Ellis had sensed that things were not quite right with Opal and that "conditions" were not favorable. Despite her rather vaguely expressed misgivings, Mrs. Ellis went on to say: "In any event the fact of her genius remains. . . ."

Sedgwick kept searching for answers. He sent Bede twenty-five dollars for expenses and asked him to research specific events and people in the diary. One assignment was to track down her teacher portrayed in the book as whacking her with a ruler for working on the diary in class. Bede found her. The teacher remembered nothing of the kind and said the diary was a hoax. Sedgwick also tried to get Bede to interview Faye Whiteley about the destruction of the diary and the serial number on Ed Whiteley's new gold watch so it could be traced. Bede was hard at work on the story and even gave up going to the national Shriners' convention to work on the case. (Lane County Sheriff Fred Stickels packed up his fez and went, though.)

Sedgwick's best hope for confirmation of Opal's story came from G.

Evert Baker, the Portland lawyer who knew Opal through church work. He had met Opal in 1911, after he had been elected adult head of the Oregon Christian Endeavor Union. She was then thirteen. He said while he was speaking, he was taken with her alert manner, dark hair, and "big round eyes." Afterward Opal had told him how much she liked his talk and asked him if he would send her a copy of a poem he had quoted. At one point Opal went to the side of the room with some other girls, and the woman who was with her, presumably Mrs. Whiteley, thanked Baker for taking an interest in her as she was "an orphan child." Baker said he subsequently sent the poem to Opal and that Lizzie Whiteley had written him back, again thanking him for helping "a homeless child." He said he was sure he still had the letter somewhere.

Baker was so inspired by Opal that he often referred to her in talks he gave, pointing out that if a plucky orphan could make something of herself, anyone could. Apparently, Opal was often introduced as an orphan working her way through college at Junior Christian Endeavor events. Bede's initial sensationalized 1915 *Oregonian* story about her, saying she had no parents to guide her, could have also contributed to the idea she was an orphan.

Baker said he would produce the letter from Mrs. Whiteley, but despite the efforts of Bede, Sedgwick, and a woman Professor Conklin sent out in person to ask for it, he was unable to find it, although he said it had been on his desk quite recently. He apologized to Opal for losing it.

Meanwhile Bede learned that reporter Fred Lockley of *The Oregon Journal* had found a another reputable witness, Fanny Morse, who told him that Mrs. Whiteley was known to declare to Opal and her other children that they were not her real children when she was frustrated with them. These assertions were attributed to her "mental condition."

Through Sedgwick, Bede also tried to get Opal to produce the letters from her mother and her grandmother Mrs. Patrick that she said would prove she was a foster child. She had referred to them in the letter she claimed she had failed to mail to him in 1918. Opal told Sedgwick she couldn't produce these letters because they had been stolen from her in a mysterious Watergate-style burglary in the San Fernando Building back in Los Angeles. The burglars had taken only the letters, leaving behind the thirty-six dollars in *Fairyland Around Us* money that was also in the desk.

In the spring of 1920 a shadowy figure called Mrs. Duane entered the picture. Caroline Elise Ravenel Duane, the wife of William Duane, a direct descendant of Benjamin Franklin and a professor of physics at Harvard, who had invented an X-ray machine that was supposed to treat cancer, was a dramatic woman who loved intrigue. After reading the first installment of Opal's diary in *The Atlantic*, Mrs. Duane felt she had specialized knowledge that might explain a lot about the French references in the diary. She got in touch with Sedgwick, who was so interested in what she had to say that he went to see her.

She and her husband had lived in France. She pointed out that the names of local streams and roads found in the diary were from a specific area in Chantilly around the ancestral home of the d'Orléans family. The streams and roads were too small to appear on any readily available map. Opal must have come from there and remembered these landmarks. In fact, Mrs. Duane felt quite sure she had actually *seen* the child Opal walking there many years ago with an older woman.

Although this sighting has often been cited it was never investigated. Had it been, it would have come out that the Duanes didn't go to France, where Professor Duane worked with Pierre and Marie Curie at the University of Paris, until 1907, at which point Opal had been living in Lane County, Oregon, for five years. During the period of this supposed sighting, Mrs. Duane lived in Colorado.

Sedgwick must by now must have been feeling rather desperate. *The Atlantic* was a highly respectable upper-middle-class journal of opinion, with a sterling pedigree going back to an 1857 meeting at Boston's Parker House, where a group including Ralph Waldo Emerson, Henry Wadsworth Longfellow, James Russell Lowell, and Oliver Wendell Holmes, made plans for a new magazine. How would it look if it came out that such a venerable institution had been conned by a mere slip of a girl who had grown up in a little logging town in the West?

Sedgwick hoped that Mrs. Duane could solve the mystery of Opal's origins and prove her bona fides. He eagerly turned over unpublished portions of the diary to her with what he referred to as "tell-tale" passages to examine. These were French passages that Sedgwick had cut because he thought would make the diary look phony. Opal never spelled out names in the diary, but there were a score of these clues, which seemed to direct the reader to the d'Orléans family, and indicate that Opal was the daughter of Prince Henri d'Orléans.

The d'Orléans family were descended from the duke of Orléans, the younger brother of Louis XIV. They lived in exile in England between 1848 and 1871, when they were allowed to return to France. In 1867, Henri d'Orléans was born in exile, near Richmond, Surrey, the eldest son of the duke of Chartres whose brother became the pretender to the throne of France after another branch of the family died out in 1880s.

As a result, the pretender (Henri's uncle) and his son (Henri's cousin) were exiled from France again in 1886. Three years later Henri d'Orléans began his career as an explorer, traveling from Siberia to Siam, and writing up his observations, winning a gold medal from the Geographical Society of Paris and the cross of the Legion of Honor. Later he joined his cousin on tiger hunts in India. He died in Saigon in 1901.

Clues in the diary outtakes pointing to Henri d'Orléans as Opal's father included mention of a *rivière* named Irouaddy, the French spelling of a river described by Henri d'Orléans in his book *From Tonkin to India by the Sources of the Irawadi*, an account of an 1895 expedition. There were also references to objects owned by Henri d'Orléans's mother— pearl earrings and a bracelet with family miniatures—and mentions in French of places where he and his family lived, studied, or explored: the forests of Indochina, the château of Neuilly, Morgan House at Ham, and a military school in Turin. There were also direct quotes, in French, from a book by Henri d'Orléans about the astonishing number of tigers he had slain on his trip to India, and references to the fact that his father, "Grandpère," had served with General George McClellan in the American Civil War.

With these clues added to those she had already spotted in the magazine, Mrs. Duane soon made the d'Orléans connection. Sedgwick introduced her to Opal, hoping she could find out more, but he insisted Opal not be told about the new discoveries. His approach throughout was to keep everything from her, so that she couldn't be accused of faking fu-

ture installments of the diary on the basis of the information he provided.

Mrs. Duane duly began to ingratiate herself with Opal. Opal later
complained that while she was socially isolated because Sedgwick kept
her working all the time and turned down invitations on her behalf, he
nevertheless foisted Mrs. Duane on her and that Mrs. Duane then
pumped her "about her family and meanings of references in the diary."
Opal wrote that she saw through her and hated her.

Soon Mrs. Duane wasn't just pumping Opal but was confiding in
her, lamenting that because she was a professor's wife, she had come
down in the world, materially speaking. She had inherited so many
lovely things—twelve barrels of china and two trunks full of silver—
but there was nowhere to put them in their new tiny apartment, which
also required a thorough extermination of cockroaches and silverfish.
Adapting, apparently, to her reduced status, she took it upon herself to
sew her daughter's dress for dancing school and was thankful for at least
having the domestic help of two "raw but faithful Irish girls." Mrs.
Duane echoed Lizzie Whiteley's unhappiness with her domestic infra-
structure.

Around this time Opal also claimed to have received an anonymous
letter to the effect that Sedgwick was not to be trusted, saying "horrible"
things about him. When Sedgwick asked to see the letter, she said she
had burned it. When he protested that because of the season, there were
no fireplaces lit in the house, she said she had gone down to the cellar to
burn it in the furnace. Sedgwick learned that Opal had asked Mrs.
Duane if it was she who had written this letter. Sedgwick felt that his relationship with Opal was beginning to disintegrate.

*B*ack in California, Maud Harwood Bales, Opal's former landlady in Hollywood, read the diary excerpts in *The Atlantic* and sprang into action. She wrote Bede to say that she believed Opal had cooked up the diary while she was living with her.

As evidence, she cited the fact that Opal had asked to borrow a French dictionary, *Hugo's French Simplified*, and, most tellingly, a copy of a book titled *French Self-Taught*, in which the list of animals the Opal of the diary recited to her unfeeling teacher in French was listed in the same order in which the diary recorded it. Mrs. Bales said that Opal had taken many books from her shelves, including a "Catholic Manual," up to her room.

Most damaging of all, she said that Opal worked late into the night in her room writing "sheets of big printing on white typing paper, all big letters without spacing between letters or lines." In addition, Mrs. Bales's brother-in-law, who had helped unpack all her boxes, swore there was no shredded diary among her possessions.

In a later letter she added the information that Opal used to write by hand all day. She was at it when the Baleses went to bed at ten and still at it when Mr. Bales got up at four-thirty for a long commute to a wartime shipyard. Mrs. Bales also took Bede to task personally for giving Opal her first taste of publicity in the *Cottage Grove Sentinel* back in 1915. She claimed "fame and publicity were necessary to Opal as dope to a drug fiend." She fired off a similar blast to Sedgwick, expressing her disappointment with John Steven McGroarty, whom she referred to as "the beloved philosopher of Verdugo Hills," who had written the laudatory story about Opal in the *Los Angeles Times*. She described Opal as a self-obsessed liar and "a new kind of adventuress."

Throughout the nineteenth century, adventuresses were a staple of cheap and not-so-cheap fiction. Becky Sharp in Thackeray's *Vanity Fair* is a classic example. Adventuresses used underhanded means to get ahead, and they pretended to be more respectable and highborn than they were. They were insincere and pushy and out for themselves. According to *The Oxford English Dictionary*, an adventuress is "a woman on the look-out for a position." Mrs. Bales believed that Opal had all the qualities of an adventuress. What struck her as astonishing was that Opal was in it for publicity ("the breath of life to her"), not position.

Mrs. Bales was on to something here. Just as Opal's childhood coincided with the end of the winning of the West and the beginning of its romanticization, so her debut as an adult coincided with the dawn of mass media celebrity.

The first movie star worked uncredited and was known as the Biograph Girl. It hadn't occurred to early producers that movies would spawn movie stars. Eventually Florence Lawrence got screen credit and publicity, and when she arrived in Chicago in 1910, she pulled a bigger crowd than the president of the United States, who had been through town the week before. Within the decade little Opal Whiteley in Eugene, Oregon, was subscribing to *Motion Picture Classics* and getting together a portfolio of pictures of herself to take to Hollywood.

Bede shared Mrs. Bales's letter with Professor Conklin, and both were taken aback at Mrs. Bales's strong feelings, Bede noting that Mrs. Bales sure "had it in" for Opal and Conklin commenting that while Opal may have been hard to live with, the same no doubt applied to Mrs. Bales.

It's pretty clear that Maud Bales was absolutely furious about Opal's success, which she believed was undeserved and had been achieved through ruthlessness, charm, and good looks. She had a Cassandra-like frustration at the inability of others to see what seemed so clear to her. Mrs. Bales, a tall, strapping woman, added, that Opal had exploited her small stature "very cleverly." To both Bede and Sedgwick, she predicted that Opal would end her days in a lunatic asylum.

Mrs. Bales's testimony, perhaps the most damaging about the authenticity of the diary, has been discredited to the satisfaction of those who believe Opal wrote the diary as a child, partly by her vehemence and partly because in his book Benjamin Hoff pointed out that Mrs. Bales said Opal was writing on *white* typing paper when the diary was actually written on *brown* paper bags. Hoff accused Bede of suppressing this fact. Actually it wasn't all written on brown paper bags, and I have seen diary fragments on lighter paper. Sedgwick wrote, "[T]he paper was of all shades, sorts, and sizes: butcher's bags pressed and sliced in two, wrapping-paper, the backs of envelopes—Anything and everything that could hold writing."

Maud Bales's niece Dorothy Randle was told by Mrs. Bales's daughter, Elisa, in the 1970s, that Opal squirreled away every paper bag or bit of butcher paper she could find and kept it in her room and that books on French that they hadn't seen before were also in her room. (The fact that Opal did indeed have French books is corroborated by a letter from Mr. Awbrey in Oakland, California, who wrote Opal in Boston to say he was forwarding the books "on the French language" that she had left behind.)

Sedgwick dismissed Mrs. Bales's accusations, saying she was an "ill-natured" woman. Opal had told him there was "much misunderstanding between them," and Sedgwick wrote Bede, "I think I am quite correct in saying that any jury would remain unaffected by it."

Mrs. Bales also provided background information about the possessions Opal brought from Oregon through to the arrival of the diary in Boston. She said that Opal arrived with unopened boxes a few days after coming to Los Angeles, that they all were opened in front of witnesses, and no diary was seen, and that she left a huge number of boxes in the Baleses' garage when she moved out.

When the Baleses moved from Hollywood to the San Fernando Valley, Opal had already left town. Ruth Gentle, whose father was an attorney in the building in Los Angeles where Opal had office space had come over to their garage, complained about Opal's carelessness, commented that geniuses could be trying, burned most of the material as trash, and packed up the rest to be stored at Marie Mullen's department store.

Ruth Gentle later wrote Sedgwick that she had met Opal in 1919 and helped her with cutting and pasting the nature pictures in the books at the San Fernando Building office. She also helped Opal pack to go to Boston after her hospitalization. Ruth said they were in a hurry and threw things in boxes "rather promiscuously." Opal left before they finished packing, so Ruth packed up the rest of the things and sent them to Mullen & Bluett.

It was the end of September when Ruth went to Mrs. Bales's garage. The boxes there, she said, were sent to Opal in Boston. Ruth claimed to have seen the original manuscript of *The Fairyland Around Us*, but nowhere did she say she had seen the manuscript of the diary or the pieces. It appears that the boxes she sent were the second set, arriving in January 1920. The initial delivery was said to have come in October 1919 to the Misses Salter, and Sedgwick had not been present when it was opened.

Meanwhile at El Alisal, Charles Lummis was poring over the diary in *The Atlantic*. Examining the photograph of a pieced-together diary page in *The Atlantic*, Lummis did some math. "The editor says they have 45,000 words definitely ascribed to her at 6 and 7—and the total Diary about 150,000 words," he wrote. He figured that at seven words to a page that the manuscript would run 5,260 pages. "Which leads one to wonder at quenchless energy of that 'peevish foster sister' who tore up all these 5600 sheets of manila paper 'in a fit of childish rage.'" Sarcastically, he suggested she had done it over her summer vacation.

Lummis may have shared his calculations about page numbers with David Starr Jordan, because when Opal's Boston friends the Forbeses ran into Jordan, he too raised the question of the volume of paper required. Opal wrote Jordon immediately to explain. "The quantity of paper is not nearly so much as people have estimated," she said. "There are two and more things to consider when estimating the quantity used in the diary—1st that the words were nearly all spelled by sound—as sum for some, cum for come, to-da for today. The words being spelled by sound takes up much less room than if they were correctly spelled. As Mr. Sedgwick stated in the introduction it was necessary to correct the spelling—2ndly, there is *never* spacing between words. And because of no spacing between words it was possible to get many words on a page."

Opal added that she realized she looked bad in "the Western papers" but had faith that "the truth will ultimately prevail."

Lummis's estimate of seven words to a page seems low. In reviewing a sample of typed selections in the archives of the Massachusetts Historical Society of the "seven-year period," there appear to be ten words to a page. That still leaves a manuscript of forty-five hundred pages. When Sedgwick sold the English rights to the book, the contract said it was seventy-one thousand words, which pushed it above seven thousand pages.

The pages were all different sizes. The manuscript page duplicated in the original published manuscript contains ninety-six words. But even if all the pages had so many words—and they don't—the shredded diary would still consist of more than seven hundred pages. If there was writing on both sides of every page, these numbers would be cut in half. Sedgwick said there was writing on both sides, and see-through backing paper was used. Of the pages that still exist, some are pasted on this transparent paper, but others must have been one-sided because they are glued on *Atlantic Monthly* letterheads or old pages of the *National Geographic*.

One skeptic, true-crime writer Gregg Olsen, who has investigated the case and believes Ellery Sedgwick knowingly perpetrated a fraud, has examined the pictures of the diary pages stored on a table in Mrs. Cabot's dormer room. He believes that's all there were—just enough for a photo opportunity. There are about two dozen inverted cardboard boxes of various sizes on which the pieces were mounted, enough for maybe fifty diary pages at the very most, some very small. Why, Olsen asks, wouldn't Sedgwick display the entire thing in this photograph, which accompanied the published diary?

The content of the diary also raised some eyebrows. Lummis questioned a scene in which Opal's pet pig, Peter Paul Rubens, was butchered with his head in Opal's lap, blood from its cut throat drenching her clothes. (Afterward the bloody clothes were left to soak in a rain barrel, and Opal was made by her cruel guardians to grind Peter Paul Rubens into sausage.) Others also doubted that a child of six or seven would be permitted to allow a butchered hog to bleed all over her clothes, and Grandma Scott flatly denied the incident had ever happened.

Bede as well was skeptical about some scenes, including one in which Opal took a hike accompanied by two pigs, a lamb, a dog with a crow on its back, and several smaller animals deployed in pockets, a journey that necessitated crossing a foot log. Bede got into his car and clocked the route to come up with the twelve miles, later reduced to ten miles. In Opal's defense, Steve Williamson, the researcher who has been over all the terrain described in the diary, claims the distance was much shorter, and he has worked out a different route.

Bede questioned too an episode in which Opal took it upon herself to ride a horse named William Shakespeare bareback and without a bridle, climbing on a stump to get onto the animal. She then stood on its back on tiptoe to reach a tree branch, from which she swung. When she had finished swinging, the horse had disappeared, but she called to it, it walked backward into position beneath her, and she landed back on its back. Mrs. Scott denied that Opal rode a horse at all, let alone indulged in the trick riding described.

Williamson has thought about this too. "Lots of people have said that is incredible. That couldn't have happened. Horses don't do that no matter how magical the connection. And that is wrong, because there's one breed of horse that does that, and that's the logging horse. Logging horses are trained to go very slow, straight, stop, and back up. They're trained under voice command to back straight up and pull forward. They would do exactly what William Shakespeare is said to have done. You can look that up on any logging Web site."

Bede spent a lot of time going over the diary to put real names to about twenty pseudonyms and checking birthdates and the dates of other events. Some of these he checked with Opal, who provided him with the answers to his questions. Most of the information seems to have panned out correctly in regard to dates but there were a few discrepancies.

Members of the public were also working on finding out the truth. Several products, Bon Ami scouring powder and Mentholatum, a medicinal preparation, were mentioned in the diary. Readers began writing these companies demanding to know when these products had become commercially available. The correct answers were 1892 and 1894 respectively, well before Opal said she wrote the diary.

Another point raised about the authenticity of the diary was a paragraph about Opal's feeding bread and jam to wasps. In the 1990s, when Opalite David Caruso was typing the manuscript of *The Fairyland Around Us* to put it online, he came across this passage. Although Caruso believes *The Story of Opal* is genuine and was written when Opal was seven or eight, his faith seems to have been shaken somewhat when he discovered that essentially the same paragraph appears in both books. Here's how it reads in *Fairyland*:

July 5th—To-day I climbed upon the old rail fence close to their home with a piece and a half of bread and jam—the half piece for them and the piece for myself—But they all wanted to be served at once, so it became necessary to turn over all bread and jam on hand. I broke it into little pieces and they had a royal feast right there on the old fence rail. I wanted my bread and jam—but then Yellowjackets are such interesting fairies, being among the worlds [sic] first paper-makers—and baby Yellowjackets are such chubby youngsters. (Have you seen them in their cells within their paper homes?) Thinking on these things made it a joy to share one's bread and jam with these Wasp fairies.

With the exception of the parenthetical question in the teacher Opal voice, the exact same words are in *The Story of Opal*. Elbert Bede cited this duplication as an indication that the diary was faked, inasmuch as at the time *The Fairyland Around Us* was written in Los Angeles, the diary was supposedly still in pieces stored in a hatbox.

Caruso believes that Opal sneaked this paragraph into the diary when it was being transcribed in Boston, on the ground that she'd worked hard on *The Fairyland Around Us*, which wasn't going to be published while the diary was. Another Opalite take is that although the actual diary was shredded by Faye Whiteley, parts had been copied elsewhere, and it was a copy Opal used as a source for *Fairyland*.

In June 1920, Sedgwick was in the thick of his investigation, including trying to get his hands on the rented typewriter Opal had brought with her to Mrs. Cabot's to compare it with the typing on the anonymous letters sent to Cottage Grove. He then received an additional shock.

Opal wrote to Sedgwick telling him she had hired a lawyer to explain her contract to her. She said that she still had faith in him, but that as he was always too busy to explain to her what she had signed, she had thought it best to consult a lawyer. She was very careful to thank him for all his kindness to her, but she also pointed out that his viewpoint and hers could be different, for he had obligations to the magazine. The letter has a tone that indicates Opal may have had help framing her thoughts.

She also said her lawyer would discuss with Sedgwick the meaning of the French in the diary, although she added, "I abide by your wish that I not know its meaning." She wrote that she was looking forward to learning the truth about her origins eventually.

The next day Sedgwick invited Opal to his house in the country for dinner, and she asked to speak to him alone. They went outside, and she asked him if he knew who her parents were. He replied that there were signs leading toward a specific group of people, but he didn't want to tell her because "subsequent 'proof' taken from the diary would be of less value."

Presumably, as Sedgwick planned at this point to bring out much more of the diary, he wanted to guarantee that she not take this new-found knowledge and embellish the rest of the manuscript with it. This attitude on Sedgwick's part is puzzling and a tacit admission that she *could* make additions to the diary as she pieced it together and wrote out and filed the cards. Yet his public position was that there was no way this could be done. He had called such an assumption "absurd."

He later told his lawyers that at this meeting Opal grew violently excited. He quoted her as saying "Do you mean to say that when I find a reference in the diary to my Angel Grandpère wearing a bracelet with a picture set in jewels—[this] is no evidence?"

Soon afterward Sedgwick complained to Mrs. Duane that Opal had written him "a very singular letter." He said he had always treated Opal with consideration "and I may add, with generosity. . . . She now seems to hold me under suspicion."

Sedgwick thought it might be the result of "mental excitement." He told Mrs. Duane he'd like her to assess the situation when she next saw Opal and said he would also be glad to show Mrs. Duane any documents, such as Opal's contract, to prove that he had been square with her, should Opal mention the matter. He said he was happy he had someone he could confide in.

His confidence was misplaced. Opal later wrote that it was Mrs. Duane who first asked to see her contract, and when Opal told her that Sedgwick wouldn't let her have a copy and kept it at his office so it would be safe, Mrs. Duane "threw her head back and roared with laughter," then suggested Opal go down to Sedgwick's office while he was out of town in New York and ask to look at her contract.

Opal took her advice. With Sedgwick away, Opal went down to the office and asked his secretary, Gertrude Tompson, to show her a copy of her contract. Miss Tompson had trouble finding it and showed her a file of fan letters to look at while she searched. Eventually it was found in the safe, but by then Opal had had a look at the Opal Whiteley correspondence in with the fan mail and discovered that Sedgwick was in correspondence with her old enemy Mrs. Bales and with people who knew the Scotts and Whiteleys. She felt angry and betrayed. When she saw the contract, she said she realized she had signed two "codicils," concerning film rights and foreign rights, which she said she didn't remember signing.

Mrs. Duane got her an appointment with a lawyer, Raymond Oveson. Mrs. Duane also told Opal that Sedgwick was withholding royalties from the sale of the English rights. Sedgwick was unaware she was stabbing him in the back.

Although Mrs. Duane began as Sedgwick's not-so-secret agent, writing to "my dear Miss Whiteley" that it would be wise to take the advice of "Mr. S," she was soon leaking the details she had found on Sedgwick's behalf to Opal. She seemed to have switched her allegiance. By August she was writing to Opal as "my dear little F.," which stood for Françoise, the name Angel Mother and Father called the young diarist. Mrs. Duane said that they spent so much time discussing the mysteries of Opal's origins that they didn't have time to talk about all the other things they had in common, such as Mrs. Duane's interest in butterfly collecting and spider observation. She told Opal she was working with some letters "Mr. S." had provided about her and not to tell Sedgwick she'd mentioned them.

Mrs. Duane had discovered various things in the Boston Public Library, including the memoirs of the duchess of Orléans, in English, which included a copy of her will. In the will, she bequeathed various heirlooms to the mother of Henri d'Orléans, the duchess of Chartres. Heirlooms described in the will were also mentioned in the parts of the diary that had been cut by Sedgwick. Mrs. Duane showed the will to Opal behind Sedgwick's back and enjoined her to "never be afraid to trust me about what you think."

Mrs. Duane's letters to Sedgwick dealt with Opal's claims in a more businesslike manner. She suggested that if Opal had lied about a previous knowledge of French, it was "from anxiety to have her story investigated." Mrs. Duane also eliminated the possibility of insanity, explaining confidently that she was in a position to make a good diagnosis inasmuch as she had had personal experience with various "abnormal mentalities." What really convinced Mrs. Duane was when she ran the names of some châteaux past Opal to see if she had lived there, Opal rejected one château on the basis of its being "a little place," which was correct.

Mrs. Duane was soon so caught up in the mystery of Opal's origins she began to buy into Opal's conspiracy theories. When Opal began to say she was being followed by strange men, one of whom had also stalked her in California, Mrs. Duane said she too had been followed by strange men since her association with Opal. Mrs. Duane began working to arrange for Opal to go to Europe, presumably to get in touch with her real family, but she seemed to think this must be done secretly.

While all this intrigue was going on, in late August, Sedgwick was busying himself with the first, special version of the diary, a limited edition of 650, each of which was to be signed by Opal. Sedgwick also had in hand Lord Grey's glowing introduction for the mass-market edition to follow, in which Lord Grey reiterated his praise of Opal's pure, childlike qualities.

Sedgwick's introduction to the book version of the diary included this information about the author: "Opal Whiteley—so her story runs—was born about twenty-two years ago—where we have no knowledge. Of her parents, whom she lost before her fifth year, she is sure of nothing except that they loved her with a tenacity of affection as strong now as at the time of parting." Sedgwick added that her only link to them had been two notebooks that contained their pictures, "and wherein her mother and father had set down things which they wished their little daughter to learn, both of the world and that older world of legend and history, with which the diarist shows such capricious and entertaining familiarity."

He went on to say the notebooks had been taken from Opal at age twelve "for reasons beyond her knowledge . . . although there is ground for believing they are still in existence." What ground this was, he didn't say.

Clearly pleased that Mrs. Duane had given him persuasive evidence about Opal's claims to the d'Orléans lineage, Sedgwick wrote Elbert Bede. He explained that sketches and "rough pictures" on the back of diary pages spotted by Mrs. Duane, presumably the childhood sketches of Opal, had been thoroughly investigated. They had been identified as buildings in France. One of them was a church close to where diary clues revealed Opal had lived as a child before coming to live with the Whiteleys. The clincher seemed to be that the sketch had been drawn from a vantage point above the church, as if it had been seen from a window in Opal's château.

Things seemed to be looking up for Sedgwick. Thanks to the peculiar Mrs. Duane, he had some ammunition against charges of fraud. Then within days Opal vanished. Strangers had come in an automobile and taken her from Willow Tree Farm, where she was staying with the McKean family at eleven o'clock at night on September 4. No one knew who they were or where they had taken Opal.

Thirteen

A few days after her sudden departure from Boston, a letter signed by Opal but written in someone else's hand, asked the Boston postmaster to redirect all mail to Opal Whiteley at *The Atlantic Monthly* to 58 West Twelfth Street, New York City. Another letter, typed on paper headed "Chapel Farm, Riverdale on Hudson" and also signed by Opal, was sent to Mrs. Henry Cabot, who lived in the family compound with Sedgwick's mother-in-law. Opal was too tired to write, but she was resting in bed for a few days and she was "safe with very kind friends who have brought me from Boston." A PS, in Opal's hand, says, "A great English doctor—London—has just been here going over my back again. He doesn't say when I can be out of bed again."

More typewritten letters were sent out to the mothers of children enrolled in an upcoming nature class, enclosing $1.50 checks for the missed lessons. The word "check" is the British spelling "cheque." Another such letter to Sedgwick demanded that "all letters, papers or other things including *all* the original diary, belonging to me, in your possession, or in the possession of the Atlantic Monthly" be turned over to her lawyer, Raymond Oveson, as promptly as possible.

Before vanishing, Opal had been furious to discover that in the proofs of the mass-market edition of the diary, which included a list of dramatis personae, the character Grandpère was described as Mrs. Whiteley's father, implying that Opal was a Whiteley.

Even though Opal had disappeared, Oveson was still on the job. In the following week he barraged Sedgwick with letters and phone calls, demanding that the books at the bindery include a correction slip making it clear Grandpère was not Mrs. Whiteley's father. Sedgwick said it wasn't a big deal, and Oveson replied that Opal Whiteley's "friends who are assisting her in this matter are as insistent as she is that the necessary legal steps be taken. . . ."

Sedgwick asked Oveson just who these friends were and received no answer. He also hustled up to the bindery and had the plates altered so the second edition now read that Grandpère was the "father of Angel Father." He wrote to Opal asking her to remain his friend and telling her that the book was selling well. He also speculated that she had bolted because she was worried he had discovered she was a fraud, and he reiterated that he was still trying to solve the mystery of her identity. He tried to lure her into the office to show her Nellie Hemenway's report on her Cottage Grove investigation, which had just arrived.

Nellie's report was inconclusive, noting that there were people who had known Opal kept a diary, that the Whiteleys didn't want to talk, and that events in the diary corresponded to some degree with events as remembered by the citizens of Cottage Grove. Nellie was always polite, correct, and scrupulously honest. She was hardly the ideal candidate to sneak around Cottage Grove trying to pump its citizens.

Soon Sedgwick had a new fire to put out. Elbert Bede wrote he'd heard a rumor Opal had confessed she had faked the diary at age nineteen. This false rumor, which eventually appeared in *Vanity Fair*, was traced to a clerk at Houghton Mifflin, the former owners of *The Atlantic Monthly* and a publishing company connected to Sedgwick, which shared office space with the magazine.

Two weeks after her vanishing act, Opal in another typewritten letter to Sedgwick said she was being frank, and frankly she did not trust him, although she was grateful that he had agreed to publish the diary in the first place.

Sedgwick was in an odd position. The book was selling very well. The first mass-market printing of five thousand sold out immediately. Fan letters were pouring in. Sedgwick figured he could sell fifty thousand copies. His author, however, whom he had hoped to promote along with the book, had turned on him, and she was now under the influence of mysterious strangers. Sedgwick kept quiet about the fact that she had fled and pleaded with her to get back in touch.

After she had been gone for twelve days, a few explanations emerged. Opal, again in a typed letter that bore very little resemblance to her usual style, wrote to Mrs. Henry Cabot that she had been all ready for bed on the Sunday she vanished when "these dear friends who had been very worried about me" arrived at the McKeans' at 11:00 P.M.

After quickly dressing, Opal had gone with them to the Copley Plaza in Boston, where she slept in until noon the next day, then went by car to New York, sleeping most of the way. Opal said a terrible crisis had been coming since the previous winter and had come to a head during spring and summer, "and God in my great need sent loving friends just when I needed them most . . . a great peace has come into my soul."

Of all the eccentrics with whom Opal fell in over her life, her four "loving friends" were the weirdest. The phrase "What a crew!" comes to mind. When she threw in her lot with them, Opal had known her new friends for about two weeks.

First, she had received a fan letter from Emma Achelis Miller of New York City, who told her how enthusiastic she was about the diary and how anxious she was to meet Opal. Opal, feeling vulnerable and betrayed, having just discovered the error in the dramatis personae and sensing a plot against her, was pleased to get such a supportive letter. Mrs. Miller had also decided that Opal would be a good influence on her thirteen-year-old daughter, Hope. She asked whether she "dare hope" that her daughter might "come in touch with you personally." In a follow-up letter, she explained that Opal's influence on Hope could be "a great blessing for her." Mrs. Miller's eleven-year-old son, Gardiner, was at "a Chapel School," but Hope was being home schooled and having a difficult time.

Mrs. Miller was worried about her daughter and had found solace in Opal's childhood as described in the diary, in which God had taken care of her by sending angels to be her guardians. The diary had become an important part of her family's life, and she urged Opal to come to New York and meet the family in their "dear little old-fashioned house in Washington Square." She asked Opal to get in touch.

Opal phoned as Mrs. Miller had requested, and Mrs. Miller came to

Boston to meet her. While there, she told Opal about the chapel she attended in New York and about her friend Genevieve Griscom, who was also involved with this chapel.

From her room at the Copley Plaza Hotel, in front of Opal, she called Mrs. Griscom to announce that Opal was everything they had hoped for. Mrs. Griscom got on the line and invited Opal to spend the weekend with her at Chapel Farm, Riverdale on the Hudson, a religious retreat she described in glowing terms. Opal later said that she was not attracted to Mrs. Miller, but she was dying to meet Mrs. Griscom and visit Chapel Farm. She called the McKeans and said she would be staying with friends in New York for the weekend.

In New York, Opal and Mrs. Miller were met by Ernest Temple Hargrove, a fiftyish English bachelor, who took her to visit the chapel at 10 Horatio Street in Greenwich Village. Opal, who had already announced that she was Catholic to her theosophist friends in California over a year before, thought it was a Catholic church and was delighted with it. They then proceeded to Chapel Farm and met Mrs. Griscom, a very rich widow in her fifties, whom Opal later described as coquettish and very pretty. She had pale eyes and white hair. Mrs. Griscom and Mr. Hargrove, who was styled as Mrs. Griscom's "business manager," asked Opal about her life and origins. Mrs. Griscom said she had lost a child, Joyce, who had burned to death before her very eyes, and that Opal had been sent to lighten her burden. (Joyce, born in 1898, would have been about Opal's age had she lived. Her dress had caught fire from a stove when a nursemaid left her alone. In a biography of the distinguished ornithologist Ludlow Griscom, Genevieve Griscom's son, Mrs. Griscom is quoted as having told people in later years that she had warned Joyce about the dangers of the stove, adding, "She was always a very willful child." Little Joyce was three years old at the time of the tragedy.) Mrs. Griscom said she would be henceforth be Opal's fairy godmother. The atmosphere became very personal very quickly. Hargrove would be her fairy godfather.

Over the weekend Hargrove and Mrs. Griscom planned Opal's life for the near future. Mrs. Griscom said she would make sure Opal got to France to be reunited with her birth family by Easter. Mrs. Griscom had some connection with the d'Orléans family, for the duchess of Chartres, Henri d'Orléans mother, had stayed with Mrs. Griscom's aunt and uncle during the Civil War. Mrs. Griscom also said that she had been great friends with a sister of Lord Grey, with whom she had been involved in religious work.

Meanwhile, they all thought Opal should forget about piecing together more of the diary and should devote herself to teaching Hope Miller and children at Chapel School, which Gardiner attended and which was presumably affiliated with Mr. Hargrove's church.

Working on the diary, they believed, would only create a nervous strain. On Sunday evening Mrs. Griscom handed Opal an envelope with a check for a thousand dollars. They wanted her to come and be with them at Chapel Farm and to be free of debt. She could repay them with royalties when they came in from the book and by fees for teaching Hope Miller. They asked for her exclusive services. Opal would give up the diary and give up teaching children outside their circle.

Who exactly were these people, and what did they want from Opal?

They were, like Dr. Turnbull, with whom Opal had communed with fairies in city parks of Los Angeles, theosophists. And they weren't just any theosophists. Genevieve Ludlow Griscom, Ernest Temple Hargrove, and even the doctor who treated Opal, Archibald Keightley, an old pal of Madame Blavatsky's, had been leading lights of the movement in the latter decades of the nineteenth century.

By the time Opal fell in with them, however, they were well past their prime, and had split from the movement in a nasty schism instigated by Hargrove at the 1898 Chicago convention of the American Theosophical Society. Hargrove, characterized in mainstream theosophical history as pontifical, arrogant, and full of assurances that his spiritual communications from the masters were on the money, was the second son of a distinguished English solicitor.

He went to Harrow, where he claimed he spent most of his time reading books, and his conversion to theosophy came quite suddenly. Simply seeing the word in print caused "his whole inner and outer life" to change. He first cut a swath in theosophy writing articles under the name Chew-Yew Tsâng.

Pseudonyms were characteristic of theosophists, partly to create the impression on their publications' mastheads that there were more people on staff than there were, partly as a reflection of their belief in reincarnation and the idea of souls wandering through time. The circumflex over the *a* in Tsang is another wacky period touch, beloved also by Opal's contemporary, the occultist and dope fiend Sax Rohmer, author of the Fu Manchu books. Other theosophists loved Hargrove's stuff and some decided he must be an "Adept," or highly tuned spiritual being.

Hargrove came to the United States in the 1890s and was president of the American Theosophical Society until he formed his own group representing about 5 percent of the membership, a number that diminished over time. According to a 1925 history of theosophy, by the 1920s his little offshoot had become "a mild and respectable Theosophical Episcopalianism," with an emphasis on "the Master Jesus, the 'theosophy' of the saints, and Catholic history." It dwindled eventually to about eight members.

The chapel Opal had visited, which she had assumed was Roman Catholic, was actually an establishment built by Mr. Hargrove and run according to his own brand of theology—outwardly Episcopal and drawing on direct inspiration from theosophical hidden masters. Like a shopkeeper, Hargrove lived in an apartment over the church.

Genevieve Griscom was a Philadelphia blueblood who traced her lineage back to the Magna Carta, the widow of an heir to a shipping fortune, and wealthy in her own right, the daughter of a distinguished general, considered by the theosophists of her day to have been one of the intellectual heavyweights of the movement. Under the pen name Cavé, she wrote many articles and several beautifully designed and bound books, published by the theosophical press that Hargrove controlled.

Her fraught prose, addressing the reader as "disciple" or "seeker after immortality," includes such phrases as "Lo, Master, what is it thou showest me?" and is full of imagery of souls in torment and their "sharp shrieks and curses." Her work also described personal visions and cosmic messages, often of an unpleasant nature. " 'Appalling is the work!' I cried aghast."

She seemed particularly keen on pain, calling it "our best teacher."

"Pain is Joy," she announced, reveling in the conviction demonstrated by saints, prophets, and martyrs that enabled man to "rise above slow torture and rejoice in it."

She was, however, aware of the spiritual pitfalls, warning that "the delight of sacrifice" could be so great that seekers should be "carefully kept from it, lest they come to do it for the pleasure they find in it . . . and so grow in vice rather than virtue."

A contemporary neighbor of Chapel Farm, a lovely wooded area in the Bronx that locals are trying to save from developers, told me that she had heard that Mrs. Griscom built a mansion on the property for the return of Christ in 2000. He was expected to return to her farm because it was the highest point in New York, presumably the most sinful place in the world. The farm was headquarters for the cult she ran with Hargrove, the Order of the Living Christ, and adherents lived in spartan cottages, portable dwellings without water or electricity. One of the adherents was a professor of mathematics at Columbia, who lived on the grounds. Reincarnation was part of the spiritual mix, and Mrs. Griscom and her late husband had a huge collection of books about Joan of Arc and Napoleon, whom they may have believed they had been in past lives.

Opal fell in love with the farm immediately. She was told that everyone on the property was an Episcopalian, but this wasn't exactly the church staunch Episcopalian Elbert Bede would have recognized. It contained, however, lots of monastic trappings of an Anglo-Catholic nature, including bells ringing five times a day to call the devotees to prayer, a practice Opal found charming.

What she did not fully understand, however, was that her new friends believed that it was their job to guide her spiritual development and mold her into something better, just as the Millers planned to do with their daughter, Hope. They promised to reunite Opal with her real family in France; in exchange, they wanted her soul, or at the very least, they wanted to improve it along their own lines. Theosophy has a strong streak of what Maoists called criticism and self-criticism, long, brutally frank discussions of the faults and weaknesses of others in order that they may improve.

Besides her preoccupation with pain, Cavé's published works had a lot to say about obedience and the relationship between spiritual masters and pupils: "Training and struggle along the path . . . these have an interest profound." Their training methods seem to have been to carry on at great length about their affection for her and concern for her well-being, coupled with harsh criticism, cataloging her faults, telling her what to do, expressing disappointment with her progress, and encouraging her to surrender her will. It's a formula that appeared designed to foster dependence. Initially, Opal seems to have accepted the program, referring to it as "learning."

It is clear that when she met these people, Opal was feeling exploited and hurt and ready for a change, and to her, these nice, generous friends who appealed to her religious feelings and were prepared to come right out and believe she was a d'Orléans were a refreshing contrast with Sedgwick, who kept stalling her when she asked who she was and hooked her up with child care jobs rather than giving her large checks.

She had been unhappy too because Boston had proved to be less socially fluid than Los Angeles. Here she was on her way to becoming a famous author, and she was still treated like the help. She later remembered that the Henry Cabots had lots of parties for young people but never invited Opal. Once they invited her to a children's party, she wrote bitterly. She was twenty-one. Her friend Marie Mullen, who had come to Boston for a visit that spring had told her that in the eyes of these Boston Brahmins she was just a governess and that she shouldn't expect to be accepted by them as a social equal because she was probably illegitimate, which would all come out when the mystery of her birth was resolved.

Opal's exclusion from social events for people her age could have been because the Henry Cabots snobbishly found her "not our kind." In the Cabots' defense, however, it must be said that Opal's friends at the time, a couple called the Nickersons and the Forbeses, who invited her to the theater and parties, Richard and Ella Cabot, and Mrs. Duane, all were much older than she was, as were most of the people in Los Angeles and Boston who were taken with her.

As a child she'd spent her time with younger children. Opal was almost always out of sync with people her age. F. Scott Fitzgerald was just a year older than Opal, but they hardly seem to be from the same generation. His *This Side of Paradise* was accepted by Scribner's the same week Opal went to meet Sedgwick for the first time, but her work didn't speak to her contemporaries as his did. His college novel talks about booze, sex, war weariness, and socialism. In contrast, Opal's world was an idealization of childhood, appealing to the middle-aged, nostalgic for an innocent prewar world.

It is significant that one exception to the broad enthusiasm for the diary came from a group of people about Opal's age who were perhaps less sentimental about children; precisely the crowd of young people she would have met at the Henry Cabots' parties for young people had she been included.

The Harvard University humor magazine produced a snickering send-up, *Isette Likely*. In a parody of Sedgwick's introduction to her work, the student satirists wrote, "We can safely say that not since Darwin's 'Evolution of Man' has a book so full of observation of Nature appeared, or one which proves so clearly a near relationship to the animals. All through this remarkable composition runs a charming naïveté remarkable in one so young; her appreciation of the World and its Creatures is inspiring, her joy in mere existence profound."

Any lack of popularity with her peers aside, Opal was also undeniably eccentric, screaming in the night, acting manic, and worrying that strange, sinister people were following her. It is perhaps not surprising she didn't get invitations to social events.

Opal had also grown unhappy at the McKeans'. Opal described Mrs. McKean as well intentioned but unable to manage either the servants, who were always quarreling, or the three little girls, who had "no discipline." Opal later wrote that the atmosphere around the McKeans was a little risqué, marred by drinking and racy talk. Mrs. McKean's brother, she had noted, was a roué who was having an affair with the wife of a friend.

Opal's New York friends offered a more wholesome and holy atmosphere. After that first weekend, Opal planned to return to Massachusetts, finish teaching some nature lessons and rejoin her new Fairy Godmother at Chapel Farm just as soon as she could. As souvenirs of her first visit, Mrs. Griscom gave Opal images of the Sacred Heart of Jesus and various holy medals as well as pictures of Chapel Farm, where an outdoor crucifix was a prominent garden ornament.

A cultish recruitment campaign began after her return to the McKeans'. A letter from the Millers' eleven-year-old son survives. Written on his own elegant art deco monogrammed notepaper, completely in the style of the diary, it gave the impression of having been dictated by an adult and designed to lure Opal into the bosom of her new spiritual family. Addressing her as "Dear Little Sister," he said he was looking forward with "the joy feels" to their next meeting. Gardiner told her that he had a pet that he thought might be a reincarnation of the Brave Horatius, a dog in Opal's diary. He signed off "Affectionately, Gardiner Hope Miller, Jr." Mr. Hargrove got into the act too. He seemed to be worrying that Opal wouldn't come join them. She had apparently expressed to Mrs. Griscom and Mrs. Miller the fear that Sedgwick wouldn't like it.

Hargrove wrote Opal a letter that asserted Sedgwick was "unchristian and inhuman" for not allowing her to mention her Angel Father and Angel Mother and for getting it into his "silly head" that their "union had not been regular." Hargrove felt that the worst-case scenario was that Opal's mother was perhaps not noble but "a very good governess." Sounding creepily vindictive, Hargrove went on to say that Sedgwick had put his head in a noose. "He does not feel the noose, and the time to has not come to make him feel it."

Mrs. Griscom wrote Opal that she had missed her so much and couldn't wait for her to come back permanently. She told Opal they would read and pray together and that Opal must tell her all her hopes and feelings. She also said she would work hard to determine who Opal really was, in conjunction with Mrs. Duane, and gave her very specific instructions on how to avoid Sedgwick. Mrs. Griscom seemed to think Sedgwick was keeping the truth from Opal in a sinister way. "You, dear child, are coming home, to the home the dear master has prepared for you." Opal's new friends were operating at a fevered pitch on very slight acquaintance.

Three days later Mr. and Mrs. Miller and Mr. Hargrove drove up to the McKeans' and fetched Opal for the second visit. When it came time to go home, she was told she was not well enough and needed two or three weeks in bed. Her new friends told her they had already gone to the McKeans' to get her things. It was intended to be another short visit, before her final move in, but Opal never came back. Instead, she disappeared. Hargrove then began composing the typed letters that Opal had signed.

Fourteen

*T*hree weeks after her disappearance Opal wrote Dr. Richard Cabot and his wife, Ella, in her own hand that she would spend the year in New York. "I am very happily situated with a dear family who very much love the things I so love," she explained. She said the Millers' children, Hope and Gardiner, were delightful. Both played the violin, and Hope and her mother played the piano, providing happy hours of family musicales. There was family worship first thing in the morning and the last thing at night and lots of culturally uplifting conversation.

"God is so wonderful," wrote Opal. "He sent me this whole dear family just when my heart was most breaking with loneliness. The little girl is my little sister and the little boy is my little brother and their mother and father are my dear Big Sister and Big Brother. Then there is the dear fairy godmother who lives close by. She has snow white hair and a heart and voice full of love." She seemed oblivious to the fact that her book had recently appeared and she was beginning a legal battle with Sedgwick.

At the beginning of Opal's stay, Hargrove came to see her often at the Millers', where she lived for several months, but usually only for a few minutes. In November, Opal was taken to the Marlton Hotel in Greenwich Village and put in the care of Mr. Hargrove's sister Norah, who lived in Sloane Square in London. Opal was instructed to address her as Tante. When a friend wrote Opal at the hotel, she received a reply from Hargrove's secretary explaining that Opal was not able to read or write at the present.

Hargrove showered Opal with notes and letters full of spiritual directions. In one, he recommended the equivalent of "six months in a Carmelite convent . . . rest, silence, stillness, quietude—with as much solitude as you can endure." Hargrove told Opal he had bought three opera tickets, so Opal could accompany her fairy godparents to the opera, but Mrs. Griscom had been horrified and nixed the idea. It would be much too exciting for Opal. He agreed, and added that any pleasurable excitement would be terrible for her nerves. She must also avoid reading exciting books and read only literature of a "sedative" nature. Hargrove repeated again and again that it was a miracle she hadn't snapped completely.

Although Opal was a young woman of twenty-three, Hargrove wrote to her as if she were seven or eight, the age of Opal in the diary. He mailed all her outgoing letters, reading them first and letting her know if they were suitable. He referred to her in his letters as "dear child." Mrs. Griscom called her "little girl." At first, Opal completely accepted the domination of her new friends and tried to ingratiate herself with them by sending them little gifts. When she offered to plant some flowers around Hargrove's "cabin" at the farm, he said it was sweet of her but explained that it was not her place to "make plans of any kind which might involve me or my cabin." Hargrove often seemed to be too busy for her, dashing off letters and signing off "In haste." Time and again, as Opal tried to get Fairy Godmother and Fairy Godfather interested in her, they fobbed her off on the less interesting Millers, who fobbed her off on their children.

Blowing hot and cold, Hargrove occasionally allowed her to do something nice for him. When she suggested knitting a tie for him for his birthday, a rare domestic urge on her part, he wrote back, "What a nice letter from the Fairies. I think you must be their Queen."

As far as formal instruction went, Hargrove offered to get her a theosophical glossary, presumably so she could figure out what he was talking about when he instructed her, and the Apocrypha. He urged her to "Seek the Master," his theosophical term for Christ. Good works were not enough. Opal had to "Seek His Will in each moment and about the smallest task." Hargrove's fanatical religious demands could be met only by a saint or a mystic. Opal was being set up for spiritual failure.

While he didn't seem to want to spend too much time with Opal personally, Hargrove was very busy on her behalf for the next few months, wrangling with Sedgwick via his lawyers. A month after she had gone to New York, her Boston lawyer, Mr. Oveson, wrote to say that no publicity about her could be issued without her permission and that Sedgwick had better not sell the movie rights. Oveson also arranged for *Vanity Fair* to publish a retraction of the rumor that Opal had confessed to have written the diary as a nineteen-year-old.

A month after that Oveson was fired, and a typed letter over Opal's signature told Sedgwick he would hearing from the new legal team, Messrs. Beekman, Menken, and Griscom, presumably a relative of Fairy Godmother, in short order.

The next day Sedgwick's lawyers wrote the new firm. They asked for an affidavit from Opal swearing to the authenticity of the diary to protect the reputation of *The Atlantic Monthly*.

Sedgwick confessed to Elbert Bede that Opal had fled and had been "taken up by a number of very rich people." Sedgwick said that although she was being treated kindly, she had turned on her old Boston friends "with a degree of insanity that is hard to understand."

Bede wrote back that he wasn't entirely surprised at this development, inasmuch as Opal had already shown a tendency to turn on people who had helped her, including Mrs. Bales, a tendency he attributed to "a complete lack on Opal's part of understanding of moral responsibility." Bede couldn't understand why Ed Whiteley, who was still stonewalling Bede, "shows no resentment of this treatment." Bede told Sedgwick that the family was very sensitive about the subject of Lizzie Whiteley's mental state for some time before her death, "and there is no question that while under mental delusions she frequently told Opal and others of the children that they did not belong to her."

This letter apparently gave Sedgwick pause. He immediately set up an appointment with Mrs. Duane. He wanted to go over the books in the public library that Mrs. Duane believed bolstered Opal's claim to royal parentage. A more cynical observer might come to the conclusion that because there were passages from these books in the diary and Opal could easily have had access to them in the Boston Public Library, they might actually indicate fraud. What Sedgwick didn't know was that the slippery Mrs. Duane had been in touch with Opal after her flight to New York, had met Opal's new friends, and had since written her there, asking to be remembered to the Millers and Mr. Hargrove. No doubt the genteel Mrs. Duane, forced to live in a cockroach-infested apartment, was delighted to be entertained by the fabulously wealthy Genevieve Griscom.

Hargrove wanted to find out about Opal's antecedents, and inspired perhaps by both Opal and Mrs. Duane, who had already worked themselves into a hysterical state, he had a bee in his bonnet about some conspiracy. Mrs. Duane, who had already thought she was being followed by mysterious strangers for learning too much of the truth of Opal's origins, was summoned for this visit by Hargrove's long-distance phone call, and although she wanted to see her brother on the same trip, it was felt this was unwise and some kind of breach of security.

Opal's new lawyer high-handedly demanded Sedgwick's presence immediately in New York. Not only did Sedgwick resent this peremptory summons, but he was serving as a jury foreman and couldn't leave Boston. Sedgwick's lawyer told the New York lawyer if he was so interested in talking to him, he should come up to Boston. The very strong reply said in part, "You do not realize the intensity of feeling on the part of Miss Whiteley's advisors in New York. I do not think that you realize the seriousness of this situation and I cannot impress upon you too strongly the absolute necessity for immediate action."

At the end of the month Sedgwick did go to New York to talk to Opal's lawyer. There he met Hargrove, who ranted at him for hours. "He talked all day and deep into the night," wrote Sedgwick, "accusing me of almost every crime in the calendar."

Sedgwick charitably decided that Hargrove was a sincere man who "has simply become crazy concerning the story of a fancied wrong." He later wrote to Opal's English publisher, the American Constant Huntington, in London, giving him a little heads-up about Hargrove. Sedgwick said that Fairy Godfather had carried on for twelve to fourteen hours at their meeting in New York and described him as paying for her legal bills and "inciting her to a belligerent attitude." Sedgwick's conclusion: "He was evidently ripe for adventure, and Opal's cause made a knight errant out of him." Hargrove seemed to think that if Opal's true parentage were known, she would be in physical danger, and that there was some kind of conspiracy afoot. Opal herself, Sedgwick believed, was never allowed to be alone, day or night, and was treated "*en princesse*."

Sedgwick was further taken aback by the news that back in Los Angeles, before coming to Boston, Opal had sent a card to the Library of Congress to secure a copyright for *The Fairyland Around Us*. The name she used was Opal de Vere Gabrielle Bourbon de la Tremville Stanley Whiteley. Sedgwick wrote his lawyer that Opal had repeatedly told him and others that she did not know her own real name and that this claim now seemed "questionable." He was poring over those volumes from the Boston Public Library, including, besides the memoirs of the duchess of Orléans with its inventory of heirlooms mentioned by Opal in the diary outtakes; *Du Tonkin aux Indes* by Prince Henri d'Orléans; *Across Thibet* by G. Bonvalot, who had accompanied d'Orléans; *Six Mois aux Indes* by Henri d'Orléans, which contained complete passages about Henri's bloody tiger-hunting adventures that had appeared in the diary pages; and the explorer's *L'Ame du voyage*. Sedgwick also learned from the Los Angeles Public Library that Opal had arrived there after she received letters with blurbs for her first book, seeking translations from French of some of the replies she had received to her celebrity mailing for *The Fairyland Around Us*.

This would place it after January 1919. The staff, with the same candor about their patron's activities exhibited by Cornelia Marvin, Oregon state librarian, said that Opal then spent several weeks at the library checking books of quotations, magazine articles, general reference books, and encyclopedias. Someone in Sedgwick's office underlined the word "after" in the phrase "after the production of her first book." What *had* she been working on? Could it have been the childhood diary?

Interestingly, at the same time she had access to books at El Alisal. Lummis's library included, among other reference books, the 1911 *Encyclopaedia Britannica* and the *Century Dictionary and Cyclopedia*. The latter included a volume devoted to proper names and contained most of the famous names referred to in her diary and their dates. The Lummis library also had a book made up entirely of acrostics, *Acrostic Dictionary* by Rabbi Isidore Myers, and acrostics were eventually discovered in the diary.

Lummis also owned an inscribed copy of a book titled *Recent European History*, by George Emory Fellows. When I opened Lummis's copy, it fell open to where its spine had been cracked, on a genealogical chart of the d'Orléans family. I wondered if it had lain there facedown, as was Opal's practice with books, in her room or in Quimu's den strewn among her books and papers.

Meanwhile Bede had managed to get a look at seventeen notebooks Opal had left behind in Eugene. These notebooks were in the care of the university librarian, Mr. Douglass, who maintained they were Opal's property and shouldn't be handed over to Bede or anyone else for examination.

Somehow the persistent Bede got a quick look, but he didn't have time to copy anything down. The notebooks had been written when Opal was a college student in Eugene, and one of the notebooks listed childhood events "to be written out." Some of these subjects appeared in the diary, such as "The Cathedral in the Woods," "The Shepherd and His Flock," and "My First Errand." Bede noted that her intention to write about these events in the future cast some doubt on the authenticity of the childhood diary.

The notebooks also referred to the Whiteleys and Scotts as parents and grandparents. At one point Ed Whiteley was called "Dear Old Dad." There was also a list of childhood pets, which Bede found damaging, in that the names bore no resemblance to the elaborate names in the diary. They were more pedestrian pet names, including Gyp, Shep, and Ginger.

Sedgwick wired that he wanted photocopies of the notebooks. Initially Sedgwick had looked for proof that Opal was genuine and dismissed anything to the contrary, such as Ed Whiteley's and Mrs. Bales's letters. Now that he and Opal were in an adversarial position, he seemed more eager to get something he could use against her.

Bede wrote the librarian Douglass frantic pleas and went over his head to the president of the university, characterizing the notebooks as abandoned property, all to no avail. After several tries, asking what Opal wanted done with her notebooks, Mr. Douglass finally got a reply from her and shipped the notebooks off to her post office box in New York, at the same station where Hargrove's Theosophical Press kept a post office box.

The notebooks were opened in Opal's lawyer's office, in Hargrove's presence. Opal's lawyer wrote Sedgwick that they didn't contain a shred of evidence about "the subject matter concerning which we are all interested." They were described as regular college notebooks with notes on chemistry, biology, geology, "and other kindred subjects." The lawyer went on to say that whoever had told Sedgwick they held any clues to the mystery of Opal was entirely misinformed.

Sedgwick now confided in Bede that Opal's lawyer was all over him, and that the main complaint seemed to be the English rights, which Sedgwick maintained had been his to sell, with the fifty-fifty royalty split between author and publisher standard practice. Sedgwick wrote Bede all the legal details and warned him that her aggressive lawyer might soon be pumping him. He expressed his confidence in Bede's good faith and asked him not to be too forthcoming.

That same week Sedgwick's investigation into the mysterious typed letters that had arrived at the Whiteleys' bore fruit. Opal had earlier said the typewriter had been rented by someone else and she had taken possession of it while it was still under a rental contract. That turned out not to be true. According to the company records, Opal had rented the typewriter herself and paid for it by the month. It had been delivered at her request to Mrs. Cabot's house, and the company produced a signed receipt with the serial number of the typewriter. Sedgwick made arrangements to get his hands on that typewriter. If he could prove Opal had sent those mysterious letters, he could discredit her and perhaps get her lawyer off his back. Opal's new friends had very deep pockets indeed and were making life unpleasant, and presumably expensive.

In the midst of all this, Sedgwick, knowing nothing of Charles Lummis's connection to Opal, turned down a poem that Lummis had submitted to *The Atlantic Monthly*, saying, "We are sorry to return

Lizzie Whiteley's
wedding picture.

*University of Oregon
Library Special
Collections*

Opal as a baby
before the alleged switch.

*University of Oregon Library
Special Collections*

Above: Opal (right) with her sister Pearl.

University of Oregon Library
Special Collections

Left: From left to right, Pearl, Opal, and Faye Whiteley.
Courtesy Alan Klein

Below: Opal, third from front at right, in school, 1907.
University of Oregon Library
Special Collections

This picture, captioned "Lumber Camp Folk" appeared in the published diary.

A Lane County, Oregon, covered bridge during the time of Opal's childhood.

University of Oregon Library Special Collections

Right: "A path to 'explores' in the far woods," reproduced in Opal's published diary.

Opal, fourth from left, at Dorena High School next to her teacher Lily Black, third from left. *University of Oregon Library Special Collections*

Below: Opal at graduation from Cottage Grove High School. *University of Oregon Library Special Collections*

MISS OPAL WHITELEY

Above: Opal in 1915, newly-elected state chairman of Junior Christian Endeavor. *University of Oregon Library Special Collections*

1916 publicity shot of Opal as the "Sunshine Fairy."
Courtesy Binfords & Mort

Above: Opal used this photo on posters promoting her nature lectures.

University of London Library

Left: A waifish Opal.

Massachusetts Historical Society

Right: Opal in prayerful pose.
Massachusetts Historical Society

Below: Opal as a seated ballerina.
University of Oregon Library
Special Collections

Above: Opal at nineteen or twenty.
University of Oregon Library Special
Collections

Left: Opal as a Native American.
She is said to have made the outfit
and caught the fish.
University of Oregon Library
Special Collections

Charles Fletcher Lummis
Southwest Museum, Los Angeles

Jordan "Quimu" Lummis in
military school uniform, 1918.
Southwest Museum, Los Angeles

Maude McDonald
University of London Library

Opal's author portrait from
The Fairyland Around Us.
Courtesy R.L. Nassif

Ellery Sedgwick with his wife
Mabel Cabot Sedgwick at
their Beverly, Massachusetts,
home, Long Hill.

Copyright The Trustees of
Reservations / Long Hill, Beverly, MA

Manuscript page of the diary written on a paper bag, with examples of Opal's biblical phrasing such as "near unto the log," and "the wind doth blow."

A PAGE OF THE DIARY WITH KEY

TODATHEFOA	Today the folks
KSRGONAW	are gone away
AFRUMTHEH	from the
OWSEWEDO	house we do
LIVINTHARG	live in. They are
ONALITULWAA	gone a little way a-
WATOTHERAN	way to the ranch
CHHOWSEWH	house wh[ich,]

The page of Opal Whiteley's diary, taken at random from the strange manuscript and reproduced herewith, gives a faithful idea of its physical character in general. Crayons of many colors besides green were used, and since there was a thrifty employment of both sides of the paper, the piecing together of the pages was thereby somewhat facilitated. After some experiment in this direction with pins, a transparent paste and paper were used with excellent results.

A page of Opal's manuscript, and the translation page that appeared alongside it in the original published diary.

Opal at work piecing
together her diary at the
home of Ellery Sedgwick's
mother-in-law.
Photo by Bachrach

Edward Grey, First Viscount Grey of Fallodon, in a portrait by John Singer Sargent.

By courtesy of National Portrait Gallery, London

Above: Elbert Bede
Courtesy Elise Bede Swan

Left: Ernest Temple Hargrove, the "Fairy Godfather."
Archives, Theosophical Society, Pasadena, California

Opal with one of her "dog friends" in Washington, D.C., 1923.
University of London Library

Above: Opal's "Angel Father," Prince Henri d'Orléans, by caricaturist Jean Baptiste Guth.
By courtesy of National Portrait Gallery, London

Right: Dr. Richard C. Cabot
Harvard University Archives

Above: Murari Lal—Swami
Duetanand—snapped by Opal
during their travels.
University of London Library

Right: Maharana Fateh Singh
Courtesy of Shriji Arvind Singh Mewar

Opal in London, 1929.
By permission of The British Library/
Queen *magazine, Nov. 27, 1929, pg. 41*

Below: George Palmer Putnam with
his wife, Amelia Earhart.
Purdue University Libraries Special Collections

Opal in 1960, photographed by
Carlisle Moore.
*University of Oregon Library
Special Collections*

Playwright and composer Robert Lindsey Nassif visiting Opal at Napsbury.
Copyright R.L. Nassif

verses of real emotional quality." Lummis wrote his family bitterly that *The Atlantic* had clearly "modernized . . . it even has Opal."

On Christmas Eve, Bede, still yearning for a national scoop, wrote Sedgwick saying that at Sedgwick's request he had not published the strange photographs that had arrived in his mail the previous spring, and he asked, perhaps in return, to see any repressed parts of the diary. He added that he thought there might well be a skeleton in the family closet. "I have often thought it possible that Opal is not a Whiteley but a very close relative."

Back in the office after Christmas, Sedgwick discovered he had received another letter from Oregon, and it summed up the position about Opal's credibility he eventually took and stuck with for the rest of his life. It was from the man who had been principal of Cottage Grove High School when Opal had gone there to finish her senior year so she could get into the University of Oregon.

The man, James E. Dutton, had been as bowled over by Opal as Sedgwick had. He began by saying she had a made a big impression on him as soon as she "flitted" into his office. He mentioned her smallness, her darkness, and her animation. He described her as very ambitious but also thoughtful and considerate, ready to believe only in the good of others, a sweet, unspoiled child. And he was astounded at her knowledge and ability to name thousands of species by common and Latin names and arranged for her to house her collection of nature specimens in a spare schoolroom, an exhibit eventually visited by twelve hundred people.

Mr. Dutton said he had read the diary in *The Atlantic*, and he knew her and imagined that she must have written it when she said she did. This was the official position Sedgwick later staked out. The diary was genuine.

However, Mr. Dutton said he didn't approve of the "opening statements concerning her parenthood." He "had not the slightest doubt" that she was the Whiteleys' child, pointing out that she was the spitting image of Faye. In a more sympathetic variation of Mrs. Bales's theory that Opal was a publicity fiend, Dutton says that he believed the diary was an expression "of her own genius" but that she perhaps used the device of her mysterious birth to "make a simple story more interesting to a sensation seeking public."

Sedgwick too came to the conclusion that she had embellished the diary with the references to the d'Orléans family. From then on he said the diary was authentic except for the French bits, which had been added later.

Opal's year-end royalty statement was due, and with it she received a check for $3,209. Her New York lawyer said she wouldn't cash the check if it would prejudice her rights, still to be negotiated. They said Opal wanted to get Sedgwick out of the picture entirely and to take the printing plates and the rights to any future editions elsewhere. It was a drastic and highly unusual move. Sedgwick's lawyers told him royalty checks were for work done and she could cash them or not as she wished. They also drafted a letter directly to Hargrove, presumably in reply to one from him, that said they were still waiting for an affidavit from her swearing the work was genuine and therefore felt free to answer any questions about the diary with frankness, hinting that they now possessed information detrimental to Opal.

Which they did indeed, thanks to Bede and his lodge brother Fred Stickels. The missing rented typewriter had been found, and a sample typed on it compared to the photocopies of weird anonymous letters to the Whiteleys leaked by the Lane County sheriff. They had been written on the same typewriter. To the lawyers, this new information served simply as a bargaining tool to get Opal to back off.

The fact she wrote them revealed something about the workings of her mind. Opal, as the eldest daughter, would have been expected to take over the Whiteley household on the death of her mother, but she had bailed out and left Pearl to become the surrogate mother. She later wrote Nellie Hemenway, acknowledging that others would be critical of her for this lapse and explaining that her failure to do so was based on the fact she wasn't actually a Whiteley. The wacky B.C.M. letters and the barrage of genteel middle-class gifts for the hope chests of the Whiteley girls seem to have been her pathetic attempt to make amends and to do what Lizzie would have wanted while disassociating herself from the Whiteleys. It appears to be the only instance in Opal's adult life of remorse and an attempt to make amends.

Sedgwick's lawyers now had Hargrove exactly where they wanted him. They wrote him that after three months of discussing baseless charges with "Miss Opal Whiteley's friends," and incurring expense and inconvenience in the process, *The Atlantic Monthly* had decided that there was no reason for doing so further. The lawyers said their many requests for an affidavit from Opal that the diary wasn't a hoax had been refused, that they no longer cared why, that they no longer requested an affidavit and felt free to go public with whatever information they had.

Sedgwick immediately got on to Opal's publisher in England, Constant Huntington, at Putnam's. He explained that while he had intended to publish more volumes of the diary, he didn't think this would ever happen. He suggested that Putnam's, which had English and American branches, should feel free to take on any sequels. He'd heard Opal was now at work on a book "of an imaginative character, not based directly on her diary." He also reported that the original diary had been sent to her in New York. "She demanded it and received it."

By now Sedgwick was pretty disillusioned with Opal. He wrote to Bede and laid out the Henri d'Orléans story that Mrs. Duane had pried out of the material, writing that there was no doubt that "consciously or unconsciously" it all pointed to the French explorer. He said he thought that the story was "about to burst" but that he feared a libel action if he went public with allegations of fraud. Enclosing a check for $150, he begged Bede to nail Opal, getting information on the silverware and other gifts. Now that he had her on the typewriter, he could prove she had tried to cook up the whole story. Couldn't Bede go interview the girls or Mrs. Scott? Ed Whiteley, Sedgwick now believed, had been bought off and was evasive in return for his new watch and silverware and perhaps more. Sedgwick's motivation is not entirely clear. He may simply have wanted to know the truth about Opal.

Hargrove meanwhile had sent agents to Paris and to Oregon to investigate Opal's claims and prove them. He appears to have believed this was important because he was a snob who associated finer feeling and spiritual sensitivity with gentle birth and had taken Opal on as a soul to be molded along the lines of his own wacky theology. Sedgwick told Bede he didn't know what Hargrove's Oregon agent was doing, but he assured Bede, "I think we may safely match your wits against his." Bede later wrote that "strangers sneaked furtively into and out of Cottage Grove, but they scrupulously avoided me and my editorial office."

Reporter Bede, now Secret Agent Bede, replied that he planned to drive to Portland and interview Opal's sisters Pearl and Faye, who were attending business college there. He also planned to grill their cousin Merle Scott, a friend of his daughter Ruth's, and he had enlisted his wife Olive's help to pump any relative whom she might run across.

Bede hustled up to Portland and waylaid Faye Whiteley. Her big sister Pearl was out, which was to his advantage. Pearl, who had taken over as mother of the family, was protective of the Whiteley name and thought the press had hounded the family. Faye was cagey enough. She would only say the postmarks on the gift packages appeared to have been semiobliterated, suggesting collusion from postal authorities but there had been one clear one, from nowhere near where Opal was at present. When Bede asked her to be more specific, she wouldn't even say if the packages came from North America. Bede was frustrated by the whole interview and said he "couldn't get a clear picture."

In his report to Sedgwick he said that poor Faye, "a sweet and lovable little miss," had been asked by some friends to join a girls' athletic club but had been afraid to apply. She asked Bede if he thought the talk about Opal would cause her to be blackballed and looked up at him in a way that made him think of "a bird with a broken wing."

Bede also went over to Grandma Scott's and got a picture of Faye to give to Sedgwick. It showed a remarkable resemblance to Opal. Grandma Scott told Bede for the first time that Opal had always been a liar, despite her religious nature, and confirmed that the silver and watch had arrived. Even little Elwin, who Bede estimated to be about eight, chimed up that he had seen it too, evidence Bede took seriously. Mysteriously, the family now seemed to think that perhaps the silver had not come from Opal.

At this point, Grandma Scott and Ed Whiteley were somewhat at odds. Whiteley, always enigmatic, said to some people in the family "How do you know Opal was not an orphan?," at which point Mrs. Scott quickly shut him up. Mrs. Scott attributed his attitude to defensiveness. Opal had been his favorite, and she believed he couldn't bring himself to say she was a liar. Mrs. Scott also wondered to Bede how Ed

Whiteley kept his three daughters so well dressed and going to school in Portland on his income and hinted that he might have been bought off by someone.

Bede was excited about his detective work. He was impatient to start publishing some of it. Sedgwick kept asking him to hold back, on the grounds that Hargrove was working hard to prove Opal's true parentage and if he came up with the goods, he would sue Sedgwick for casting doubt on the story. Bede wrote at one point, "I trust the time is not far off when I may be able to publish the greatest story, from a news standpoint, which it has ever been my pleasure to handle."

Sedgwick and Bede had reversed roles. At first Sedgwick had been on the defensive while Bede grilled him on what proof he had. Now he wanted the goods on Opal and was irritated Bede couldn't connect Opal directly to the silver and other gifts. He insisted that she must have sent them, as she had faked the letters, but he couldn't figure out where she had got the money to buy them. When the gifts were mailed, he had been keeping her bankbook in his office and was familiar with its contents. All the deposits came from his payments to her. There were no big outgoings by the time she left. Who was helping her? Had she arrived in Boston with a huge stash of cash? She had told him she was down to forty dollars. He assumed that now she was being supported by her new friends, but the expensive gifts had arrived in Cottage Grove before she met them.

In another bizarre development, in February 1921, alert reader Edward Cozens-Smith wrote Sedgwick from Exeter College, Oxford, that he had been so fascinated by the diary and that he felt "emboldened" to write. Cozens-Smith was convinced that Opal was part of the d'Orléans family. He had discovered acrostics embedded in the diary. The diary included the sentence, "I sang it *Le chant de Seine, de Havre, et Essonne et Nonette et Roullon et Iton et Darnetal et Ourcq et Rille et Loing et Eure et Audelle et Nonette et Sarc.* I sang it as Angel Father did teach me to, and as he has wrote it in the book." The first letters of the list of rivers and streams beginning with "Havre" spells out the name Henri d'Orléans.

Another entry read, "Angel Father did teach me to sing of birds of *oncle* what did have going away, of *roitelet, ortolan, bruant, épervier, rousserolle, tourterelle, farlouse, ramier, aigle, nonnette, chardonneret, orfraie, ibis, rossignol, loriot, ortolan, ibis, sansonnet, pinson, hirondelle, ibis, lanier, ibis, pic, pivoine, épeiche, faisan, étourneau, roitelet, draine, ibis, nonnette, aigle niverolle, durbec, aigle, roitelet, ibis, étourneau, draine, ortolan, roitelet, loriot, émerillon, aigle, niverolle, sarçelle.*" The list of birds is an acrostic for Robert Francoi Lois Philippe Ferdinand Arie d'Orléans, close enough, despite some missing letters, to the name of a brother of Henri d'Orléans's.

Elsewhere was a passage that read, "Today I did sing him *un chant des fleurs de fête d'oncle* [a song of flowers of Uncle's birthday]; of *souci et eglantine et pensée et tulipe et quintefeuille et ulmaire et apalachine et tournesol et romarin et éclaire,* which spells out "Sept Quatre," or September 4, the birthday of Robert d'Orléans (and also of Pearl Whiteley). In another scene she named a horse Savonarola because she met him on "the going away day of Girolama Savonarola" and then sang him "a song of *Fleurs de tante* of *myosatis et anemone et romarin et iris et éclaire,* the list of flowers spelling out "Mariè," a sister of Henri d'Orléans's. Henri's parents, referred to as Grandmère and Grandpère, also had their names spelled out in acrostics, as was Grandpère's birthday, November 9. Another sister, Marguerite, also appeared.

Sedgwick had kept many d'Orléans clues he had spotted out of the published diaries but had allowed these little songs to go in. Had Opal composed them as a way to get around him? Or had Henri d'Orléans taught her these chants so she could prove her bona fides later in life?

Sedgwick believed it was the former. He told Cozens-Smith that the acrostics were news to him, that he wished the book could be taken seriously for its literary merit, and that he thought the story of the d'Orléans family was the result of "dual personality or some obsession dating back to childhood."

Bede held back his story. When he wrote to Professor Conklin, who was still investigating Opal for his paper on foster parent fantasies, about the typewriter Sedgwick had found, he asked Conklin to keep it "strictly on the q.t." Why he didn't go ahead and publish is not entirely clear. He was now freelancing as a researcher for Sedgwick and perhaps felt it was a matter of honor. And he seems to have been afraid of libel and wanted Sedgwick to speak out first. Still, he was obsessed enough with the possibility of a big national scoop to tell Sedgwick the story was one reason he was stalling accepting a lucrative offer to edit another paper "with salary and other inducements to knock me off my feet."

Sedgwick kindly wrote back that "entirely apart from my own interests in having you on the spot, I shall be sorry when you leave. There are few enough individual papers of character in the United States and it has always seemed to me a peculiarly satisfactory career to conduct one."

Opal was engendering a great amount of activity for Bede, Sedgwick, Hargrove, and various attorneys. But she herself was silent. What was she doing all this time?

*I*n December, Opal left the hotel where she had been under the care of Hargrove's sister Norah, aka Tante, and went to live at the Millers' house in town at 58 West Twelfth Street. Her room was full of crucifixes and religious pictures and books about Chantilly, home of the d'Orléans family.

Opal wanted to spend more time at the farm and with her idol, Mrs. Griscom. But as had been the case in Boston, it appeared that she was to be shunted off to governess duties. Mrs. Griscom, who had initially told her they'd be spending a lot of quality time together, didn't have time for her. When Opal complained, she was told that she was selfish and that it was part of her spiritual development to teach Hope and Gardiner.

Mrs. Miller was feeling guilty about Hope, whom she feared she had neglected until the age of eight, allowing her to develop an "ugly soul." She believed the child had been born with a "perfect heart" but had become corrupted. The fact that Hope was thirteen may have explained why her mother thought she wasn't the sweet child she once had been.

Mrs. Miller's rigorous home-schooling program, included instruction in religion, dancing, embroidery, music, and literature. The aim of all this cultural enrichment was to give Hope back the "beautiful heart" that had been destroyed by bad parenting. Opal was to teach Hope about nature, but with absolutely no reference to how plants and animals reproduced. "Her mother allowed nothing of the beautiful things of parenthood among the birds and flowers to be mentioned," Opal wrote later. Hope, however, had already noticed. When Opal pointed out some lovely trees from the window of the Millers' car as it was chauffeured from Manhattan to Chapel Farm, Hope was more interested in the sex of dogs she saw. Hope also engaged in theosophical ruminations, postulating that the ages between seventeen and twenty-five were the most trying on one's lower nature. Opal was apparently expected to do anything Hope wanted, and she grew to resent her. Mrs. Miller encouraged Hope to create her own childhood diary, with Opal's assistance, for hours at a time. When Opal complained, she was told not to be so selfish and to think of giving happiness to Hope. It didn't help that Opal was also told by Fairy Godmother that Mrs. Miller's concerns about Hope aside, Hope and Gardiner had been brought up perfectly and that Opal needed a lot of improvement and could learn from her young charges.

Opal wrote Mrs. Griscom reminding her she had said they would spend time together. Mrs. Griscom replied that after she had seen Opal twice, she knew all she had to know about her, although she had sadly underestimated her willingness to learn. She admitted she had planned to spend an hour a week with her, but Opal's lack of progress had made that impossible. Opal was not spiritually advanced enough to be in her presence.

Mrs. Griscom wrote Opal pages and pages of critical letters, knocking her for vanity, disobedience, insincerity, and poor personal hygiene. Even when Opal tried, it was never good enough for Fairy Godmother. "You are not trying to be considerate. You are trying to appear considerate." And when Opal confessed her faults, Mrs. Griscom jumped on her for that too.

Mrs. Miller lacked the cruel finesse of Mrs. Griscom and took a whinier approach, but she operated along the same lines, cataloging sins and faults, demanding obedience, and specializing in I'm-telling-you-this-because-I-love-you guilt tripping. She accused Opal of acting very sweet to her face, then trashing her to Fairy Godmother and Fairy Godfather behind her back. She told Opal that she must become the person Fairy Godmother and Godfather wanted her to be.

Hargrove and Griscom, by dint of their highly tuned spiritual natures, were in charge not just of Opal's life but of those of the Millers as well. It was apparently Opal's spiritual task to surrender her will completely and do everything they said. Hargrove told Opal that the child of the diary had been "overlaid" and that these bad new layers had to go. She needed to pray for guidance and light. She should also be working on her faults. At one point he demanded she tell him the six biggest lies she had ever told. He told her that she had to stop lying, which, he pointed out, she had done when she denied she had gone to Hollywood to try to get into the movies.

Why did she put up with it?

At first she genuinely seemed to believe these people could help her. Their brand of theosophy, with its trappings of Catholicism—crucifixes, sacred hearts of Jesus, and so forth—appealed to her. A vulnerable young woman, she was responsive to the hot and cold cult techniques designed to get her to knuckle under and cooperate. In addition, they had promised to get her to France and to find her family. Hargrove actually had a man in France on the job. They also arranged for her to have French lessons, and they gave her money—about five thousand dollars in all, which they invested in bonds for her under a new name they gave her, Françoise Claudel. On the other hand, they prevented her from spending the money she earned from her books, on the grounds she would squander it.

By May Sedgwick had severed all his business ties to Opal. He was relieved that another publisher would take over her contract, "lock, stock, and barrel." When *The Oregonian* wired him "Reported you have evidence Opal Whiteley descended from Bourbons that grandmother admits she was substituted and that diary was written since college. Would appreciate detailed wire reply," he didn't even bother with a denial, he simply gave them the address of Opal's post office box in New York.

Mrs. Scott had said no such thing. She told an old Cottage Grove acquaintance she met on the train that Opal had meant to come back home from California to Cottage Grove until she got in with a set of "mind readers," presumably the theosophists under the leadership of Coulson Turnbull. She also said that someone else was "managing" Opal and that she believed that ultimately her "trickery" would be exposed. Grandma Scott also said Opal had never written a diary until she was fourteen.

Two days later a telegram arrived at Sedgwick's office from a frantic Bede, who certainly didn't want to get scooped by *The Oregonian*: "Rumors getting thick. Some hitting close to facts. When can I release information I now have without liable [*sic*] danger. Papers demanding something. When information your end released."

The Oregonian had printed a sensational story full of carefully labeled rumors, including the assertion that Grandma Scott had provided Sedgwick with a signed admission saying Opal wasn't a Whiteley. RUMOR MAKES OPAL BOURBON OF FRANCE, read the headline. STORY LINKS MISS WHITELEY WITH ROYAL FAMILY. DIARY CONTAINS CLEW. WAR NURSE IDENTIFIES CHATEAU OF PRINCE PHILIP IN GIRLISH REFERENCE TO FAIRY HOME.

Mrs. Duane, the professor's wife, had been romantically transmogrified into an American nurse serving in France during the world war. Henri d'Orléans had become Philip. The story also cited a rumor that private detectives had managed to get a copy of a receipt the Whiteleys had signed for compensation for raising Opal and delivered it to Sedgwick. *The Oregonian* also said that Opal had been invited to become a member of the household of Lord Grey of Fallodon. "He would not be interested in a child prodigy, it is said, but would be in a Bourbon."

Bede, whose information was a lot more thorough and accurate, knew what *The Oregonian* didn't. Opal had typed anonymous letters full of strange stories about her origins and mysterious strangers spying on her from afar and had probably sent anonymous gifts to the family. But for some reason, he was waiting for permission from Sedgwick to go ahead and publish the results of his investigations.

Sedgwick was no longer interested. He told Bede he wanted nothing more to do with Opal, didn't want to be quoted, and was very worried about two of his children who were ill. He said he was determined never to comment further on Opal and her claims. Should the matter arise, he was forearmed. He had purchased the rental typewriter she had used to write the anonymous letters. It was a smoking gun, ready to be taken out and used to discredit her if need be.

Bede was aggressive in pursuit of a scoop, but he also knew when it was proper to back off. He replied that he hoped the children were "on their way to renewed health," adding, "Having three of my own [his youngest was not yet born] I know what a father's feelings are under the circumstances you relate and how hard it is to attend to trivial business affairs. . . . I will in this letter only express concern for the welfare of the members of your family and the hope that your forced detention from your office will not be for long."

In the saga of Opal, Sedgwick is usually presented as a gentlemanly, literary, blue-blooded Bostonian, with impeccable credentials. He was all those things, but he was more complex than that.

Ellery Sedgwick was also a self-made man and he always referred to himself as a "man of business," not of literature. His family money was gone by the time he graduated from Harvard and left Boston for New York to make his fortune. He wrote in his memoir, *The Happy Profession*, "I laugh as I see myself clenching my fist and shaking it at the big bank opposite, muttering to himself [*sic*]: 'Damn you, New York. I will wring a living out of you yet.'"

Sedgwick got himself hired at a failing tabloid, *Frank Leslie's Popular Monthly*. He pulled the business and editorial sides of the house together and eventually got financial control of the publication. He later wrote, "Yellow journalism has no law. It lives by two simple rules: first, when there is news, transform it; second, when there isn't, make it. There was no news so I made it."

After explaining that there is a difference between a stunt and a hoax and insisting that he acted perfectly correctly, he explained in a jocular way how he had commissioned an article about cat-size horses discovered on a tropical island and currently being bred on an American farm. It included a story of a horse thief running off with a stallion under one arm and a mare under the other, and was illustrated with doctored photographs of the animals. In his memoir he assured the reader that he meant it all as a joke and was astounded that the public actually bought it.

By the time he met Opal, Sedgwick had presumably left these cheap stunts behind him. After increasing the value of the tabloid, he sold it and went home to Boston, where in 1909 he could afford to buy *The Atlantic Monthly*.

The story of the tiny horses is interesting in light of future developments. "I have spoken of the gullibility of the public," Sedgwick wrote in his memoir. "The American mouth is always open. The monstrosities it gulps down outstrip the confines of credulity." At least one Opal researcher told me he believes the tiny horse episode indicates that Sedgwick colluded with Opal in consciously perpetrating a fraud.

His correspondence with Bede seems to indicate otherwise. While Sedgwick was not truthful about all aspects of the case, he seems to have been sincere, perhaps overcome by enthusiasm. His dramatic account of Opal's bursting into tears in his office after he asked her if she kept a diary is not supported by the facts. Despite his assertion in his introduction that no changes were made to the manuscript, this was not true; he personally edited out many French bits. And he was not believable when he said that Opal was watched the whole time at Mrs. Cabot's and couldn't have added anything to the diary. He later speculated that she had done just that. Still, his evasions do not necessarily indicate fraud, just a desire to make the story more credible, perhaps to himself.

After his break with Opal, Sedgwick made his feelings known in a letter to Mrs. Duane, who he still hadn't realized was not his friend. Referring to further volumes of the diary then planned for publication by another publisher, he wrote her: "The whole affair of Opal Whiteley, which began so auspiciously, has ended in a rather revolting disillusionment. I hope that Opal's new book may be full of the charm of the diary without venturing into the foolish and unstable ground of hints to an ancestry as that which is apparently in the background of her mind."

What is clearly true is that Sedgwick was charmed by Opal. His picture of her as "something very young and eager and fluttering, like a bird in a thicket," sums up her appeal nicely.

Apparently, she never lost her charm for him either, despite all she put him through. Sedgwick's son Cabot Sedgwick, who knows very little about the whole story, remembers Opal herself and how his father felt about her. Cabot was about seven when the diary came out. He said that Opal was charming, pretty, and captivating, full of animation, and that when she came to visit, she played with him, initiating games and delighting him. He said too that his father always spoke of her fondly and thought highly of her. Whatever Sedgwick's role was, it appears that if he didn't completely believe in the authenticity of the diary, he wanted to. He may have believed because he wanted to. He may also have believed and not believed simultaneously. This is not an uncommon phenomenon when charm as powerful as Opal's and the facts are tangled up together.

Sixteen

When she first fell into the clutches of the Griscom and Hargrove cult, Opal was told not to piece together any more of the diary for Sedgwick to publish as volume two, because it wouldn't be good for her nerves. Instead she was to devote herself to spiritual development. After Hargrove's lawyers had bullied Sedgwick out of the picture, however, and were firmly in control of Opal, the little cult reversed its position. In May 1921 it arranged to sell a second volume of the diary, featuring Opal at an older age, to another publisher, and she was told to get back to work piecing together more diary scraps. Opal signed a contract with G. P. Putnam's Sons for a fifty-thousand-word continuation of the diary. Mr. Miller witnessed her signature.

Opal signed two contracts with Putnam's at the Millers' house that day. The other one transferred the American rights to republish the first volume of the diary from *The Atlantic Monthly* press to Putnam's. It is difficult to know if the Millers or Hargrove were after her money. They certainly seemed to have plenty of it already, and Mrs. Griscom was very rich indeed. Whatever their motives, they seemed bent on controlling every aspect of her life, including her business affairs.

Opal's new editor was George Palmer Putnam, later famous as the widower of Amelia Earhart. Putnam came from the family that bore the firm's name, but he had also had an adventurous youth, including a stint in Bend, Oregon, where he, like Bede, ran a small-town paper, the *Bend Bulletin*, and later became mayor. Putnam appeared to believe Opal's royal parentage would soon be revealed and he would have a hot property on his hands. No doubt Hargrove and Miller, with whom he negotiated the contract, assured him of the truth of her noble pedigree. They certainly believed it, and he seems to have bought it.

Elbert Bede, still on the case, wrote to Putnam asking about the next volume of the diary. Putnam's reply hinted heavily that the story was about to break. "It seems likely that there will be some extremely interesting developments in the near future concerning Miss Whiteley," he said, whetting Bede's appetite for more.

Always a publicist, Putnam later successfully promoted his future wife, Amelia Earhart, after first going out and searching for a marketable aviatrix, "a Lady Lindy." He wanted her to be the first woman to fly across the Atlantic, then write a book about it. He interviewed the Kansas-born social worker for the job and chose her over other candidates partly because of her physical resemblance to another of his personality authors, Charles Lindbergh. Earhart went as a passenger on a transatlantic flight, not as a pilot, and Putnam kept her name in the papers and publicized her book about her experience as the first female passenger to fly across the Atlantic, booked her personal appearances around the country on the lecture circuit, and arranged for her to endorse a line of luggage and a collection of tomboyish sportswear. (She later did pilot across the Atlantic.)

The fact that Putnam was also interested in Opal as a marketable personality is evident from the contract she signed for the continuation of the diary. It contained a clause which gave Putnam's the exclusive right to any material in any print form from Opal relating to the diary or "relative to her parentage and past history." George Palmer Putnam was buying a personality and a sensational story. If Opal wrote about her life for a magazine, for example, Putnam's would get paid.

Although she signed the contracts, Opal had been feeling the stirrings of rebellion. She asked if she could send out uncensored letters. Hargrove was having none of it and told her to continue to submit them to him.

In a long letter in April, Big Sister, Mrs. Miller, accused Opal of attempting to turn Hargrove against her. She also responded to Opal's assertion that she had been "trying hard" to be a better person: "No dear, not so very hard. You are trying some, yes." Opal was told she was trying to *look* as if she were trying. Mrs. Miller also reminded Opal that Fairy Godmother and Fairy Godfather knew "what is right and true."

Things were getting nastier. Opal, in her own rant, attributed Big Sister's autocratic and cruel behavior to her German blood.

It was typical of the little self-obsessed cult that Opal and Mrs. Miller were living in the same house but writing long, unpleasant letters to each other.

Opal, irritated at being relegated to governess duties and long hours of piecing together the diary, had tried to flee Sedgwick's control. Now she was living through the same Cinderella scenario. Hargrove insisted on controlling her every move as well as reviewing all of her outside correspondence. The Millers didn't think she was working hard enough and threatened to kick her out if she didn't repent and get cracking on volume two of the diary, which they had just sold to Putnam's. They told her that if she didn't shape up, they would give her fair notice, so she could find another home or "proper chaperonage" on the ground that she could not possibly live alone in New York. Not only was she on probation with the Millers, but Hargrove, and possibly Fairy Godmother as well, gave up on her spiritual development at this point and dropped her. Hargrove declared he had never seen in one person such an unpleasant combination of "envy, jealousy and malice," but the Millers decided to give her a second chance. Exiled, she tried to speak to Hargrove and Mrs. Griscom at a church bazaar, presumably at Hargrove's oddball Greenwich Village theosophical-Episcopal chapel, but they snubbed her. Hargrove told the Millers she was "hopeless."

In her thirties, Opal wrote about this period of her life. The story fell spectacularly apart when she got to the autumn of 1921. Until this point her version of her time with Hargrove, Griscom, and the Millers was coherent and corroborated by many documents. After October 1921, the story got wild, with Opal being kept in a secret room at the Millers', a room built just to keep her prisoner. Through her grilled window, she signaled with colored handkerchiefs to Alice, an old family retainer of the d'Orléans family who had appeared to help her and whom she met at times in a bramble patch next to a hospital for the insane.

She was asked by French priests to signal to them from her barred window with crucifixes and candles when she was in danger. She was told by her mysterious allies that the police would not rescue her from captivity because of the wealth and reputation of the "Hargrove-Griscom-Miller colony." The Millers fed her properly and took care of her but treated her as insane and "an imbecile."

These stories sound delusional, but perhaps there was some core of truth in them: the hospital for the insane, the accusations of insanity, the grilled window. She might have had a mental breakdown at the time and been hospitalized. In fact Elbert Bede wrote Conklin in October 1921 that he had heard a rumor that Opal had been living it up with the "swells" in New York and was now in a "home for the nervously diseased." There might have been an attempt to keep a hospitalization secret. Two separate documents that cover this period, once in Opal's possession and later in private hands, have missing pages covering precisely this time.

By Christmas 1921, however, two months later, she can definitely be placed at the Millers'. According to a letter to Nellie Hemenway, undoubtedly approved of by Hargrove, she was working away at volume two of the diary, six months after signing the contract for it. The letter to Nellie contained no word about the poisonous atmosphere in which she was living. Another letter to Dr. and Mrs. Cabot was also strictly according to the party line. Opal described a quiet peaceful life, rising at six-thirty and getting to bed by nine. She appeared to have had a mandatory bedtime. She praised the Millers and said that they had provided her with the refinement and exposure to culture she missed because her Angel Mother had died.

When the end came, in February 1922, Opal left her new friends with bad feelings as usual. She "ran away," in Hargrove's words, leaving behind a note that she'd found somewhere else to live and would come get her things later. Her habit of leaving a trail of possessions behind her was now well established.

Opal wrote Hargrove a scathing letter, accusing him of brainwashing her and controlling her. In his reply, written pointedly "To Miss Opal Whiteley," although the little group had been calling her Françoise, he referred to her use of the term "hypnotism" and her allegations that the Millers had destroyed her letters. Hargrove defended Mr. Miller by saying that he destroyed, with Opal's knowledge and consent, only two book catalogs that contained "immoral books." He pointed out that when she had arrived in September 1920, a year and a half earlier, poor and ill, the Millers offered her refuge, a home, and money.

None of this peculiar set was ever mealymouthed. Even when they told Opal how much they loved her, they had been insulting and harsh. In his final letter Hargrove accused her of slandering them and signed off with "It would be difficult to say how completely I am disgusted. You must understand that I do not intend to have anything whatever to do with you again."

In later years Opal took to going over old letters and writing her own setting-the-record-straight comments. Perhaps they were messages to any future researchers. On this letter she wrote: "I was not penniless. I wanted to go to stay at a convent. I was decoyed here. . . . I was supposed to go France and Jerusalem for Easter 1921. I escaped from 58 W 12th street February 22, 1922. I was not allowed to go to Mass, nor to see friends. I was an unwilling guest. They were constantly abusive."

After Opal left the Millers', she went to 1224 Union Avenue in the Bronx, where she stayed a few months with a Dorothy Rohrbeck, whom Opal later called "a kindly nurse." As soon as she left the Millers' and was installed with Dorothy, Opal was approached by her old friend, Sedgwick's wife's cousin, Dr. Richard C. Cabot, who visited her in New York. Cabot had a long talk with her about, among other things, her time at the Millers' and her finances. She still had several thousand dollars and some bonds. Richard and Ella Cabot invited her to come see them in Boston soon and expressed their support for her.

After the meeting Opal wrote a friendly letter to the Sedgwicks, remarking on how nice Dr. Cabot had been and saying, "I was a very silly little girl to have come away from Beverly Farms with those people that night in September, 1920." She said she had intended to come back but hadn't even been allowed to write. She said her New York friends had told her lies about him. To Sedgwick's secretary, Gertrude Tompson, she sent a note with her new Bronx address for forwarding letters and told her that under no circumstance should she give out her present address to Mrs. Miller, who had already written to ask for it.

Opal began to call herself Opal Whiteley again. Françoise seemed to have been forgotten. And she was now under the care of Dr. Frederick Peterson. "I have been very ill. Not in bed—but a nervous reaction after those months at the Miller house," she wrote. Dr. Peterson was an excellent choice for a patient like Opal. A top specialist in what were then called nervous diseases, he was the first professor of psychiatry at Columbia University and an advocate for the mentally ill. He was also a poet and patron of the arts who wrote about the relationship between madness and the arts.

It seems likely that the Millers or Hargrove and Mrs. Griscom, who never bought anything less than the best, had got this top specialist on the case. Especially if she had indeed been hospitalized in October 1921, they would have had to find some sort of doctor for her. He may have given her the courage to flee the Millers and arranged for her to stay with Dorothy Rohrbeck, the kindly nurse. Opal was delighted with Peterson and said that he was very "kindly" and that she was recovering rapidly from her latest breakdown.

Under his care, Opal also seemed to have gained some insight into her mental instability. She wrote Richard Cabot that she thought she needed a guardian to help her make life decisions and she wanted him to fill that role. She made it very clear she wasn't asking for any financial support but said that under the arrangement she proposed, "before I do anything important—make plans—or go somewhere," she would discuss it with him. Repeating what she had written to Sedgwick, "It was very silly—my coming away from Beverly Farms that night," she added, "and I feel if I had a guardian it would not have happened . . . the guardian would not have been so fascinated by the 'Fairy Godfather' as I was."

She had been badly frightened by her impulsiveness and its result, a year and a half of mental abuse and creepy mind games. She wrote Dr. Cabot that it had been "such a time of disallusion [*sic*]—so many dreams I had about people had been knocked all to pieces."

She spent Easter with Richard and Ella Cabot, and left a furry toy bunny for Sedgwick's son, Cabot, with them. (Sedgwick said he was too ill to see her.) The couple took her under their wing, telling her they would be glad to advise her in the future and monitor her progress and would keep in close touch. She would report on her activities to them, including whether or not she was consuming enough calories and sleep-ing properly. She told Dr. Cabot he could discuss her case with Dr. Peterson, and the two men subsequently corresponded about her con-dition. While today Opal might be on medication, the medical advice she received was to avoid getting run-down or overworked. She may also have been told to avoid morbid thoughts and obsessing about her Angel Parents.

After the visit she was supposed to go straight back to New York, where the "kindly nurse" would be looking after her, but instead she proceeded immediately to Washington, D.C., to try to establish herself as a teacher of nature classes. Bouncing back after being ground down by her theosophist friends, a newly confident Opal embraced the chal-lenge of "meeting people all alone without any references or letters of introduction, picking out names from the newspaper to write."

Using the social bravado and networking skills that had worked so well for her in Los Angeles, Opal took on Washington. She was back in top form, and her celebrity as the author of the diary must certainly have helped. Within weeks she had been taken up by two cabinet wives, Mrs. Charles Evans Hughes, wife of the secretary of state, later chief justice of the United States, and future first lady Mrs. Herbert Hoover, whose husband was then secretary of commerce. She also lined up a speaking engagement with a group of congressional wives and gave talks at a private schools.

"Last week I didn't know anyone here and now I do," she wrote the Cabots, going on to describe several nature lectures she gave to chil-dren, as well as a brace of ladies' teas and other social engagements she had attended. She wrote that she was recovering nicely from her nervous breakdown and said the presence in her life of children, from whom she had been isolated for almost two years at the Millers', had helped her mental health improve.

Soon she was attending functions around town, including a demon-stration of new recipes at the Agriculture Department, where she min-gled with more power wives, including the wives of the vice president, Calvin Coolidge, and of the secretary of agriculture, Henry C. Wallace, and a military review at Fort Myer, complete with cavalry charge, followed by a reception at the home of a Colonel Rivers, where she was delighted to find herself "among the cabinet and diplomatic people." Madame Mabel S. Grouitch, the wife of the Serbian ambassador, had her to tea.

He entrée to this set was through its children, whom she taught about nature, but she was accepted socially by the mothers as well, giving her a great deal of satisfaction. She was earning money too, delivering many nature-talks and receiving a two-dollar honorarium for a graduation address at a girls' school. She soon became a part-time nature teacher at the posh Cathedral School.

Opal checked into the luxurious Wardman Park Hotel, perhaps spending some of the money the Hargrove-Griscom-Miller cartel had left her with. She enjoyed walks in its bosky surroundings and on an outing to Maryland admired catbirds, thrushes, wrens, and cardinals. She wrote about the babies and dogs at the hotel, noting she was making many "dog friends," and she said she was very happy. At the hotel, which served as a home for out-of-town politicians and diplomats, a coterie of older women, including one cabinet wife and several congressmen's wives, began to mother her. The hotel also had a number of diplomats in residence, including some daughters of members of the Chilean legation across the hall from Opal. The ladies, children, and young people visited Opal in her room, where they sat in a row on the bed.

Opal was determined to make a fresh start and avoid another nervous breakdown. She wrote the Cabots that she would be discussing her fall plans with them and would provide them with reports on her health. "We will see how it comes out—my being entirely upon my own responsibility and managing myself," she wrote bravely. She was also learning to dance and began to take an interest in romance, taking note of how married couples had met. For the first time in her life she was socializing with friends her own age. In a letter to the Cabots, the twenty-five-year-old Opal wrote, "I am meeting young people. It has been delightful. I so longed to meet them that spring in Boston but Mr. Sedgwick was so busy he didn't not have thought [sic] of how much [I] might enjoy meeting the young people and going to picnics and parties with them." Opal said that at first she had been shy around people her own age, but that to her relief she found them easy to talk to. She had a rendezvous near the tennis courts with a sporty young man named Linton

Cox, she made friends among schoolteachers at the private girls' school where she gave lectures and nature classes, and she became part of a set of younger members of the diplomatic corps.

One of her older woman friends wrote a letter to tell her that while it may have been romantic to have been rescued from drowning at a swimming party when the Chilean girls pulled her under, "Sousa is not your man." Instead she wanted to fix up Opal with a nice Yale graduate, badly wounded in the war and off to Oxford for his Ph.D., who is "crazy to meet you."

A young diplomat, possibly the Sousa mentioned above, dumped her after a serious summer fling. A campy letter from someone named Cecil, addressing her as "Dear Chica," consoled her with the thought her suitor may have been recalled suddenly to his home country, although Cecil agreed that after she had been "so frank" with him, it was surprising he hadn't phoned or written. He suggested she get out and flirt and "enjoy the brilliant company of a few of the young diplomats. . . . You can never tell when the fairies will come in on the evening breeze with a real gallant knight—true and really appreciative of your delicious self." He agreed with her plan to go ahead and have "young Meronowich" over for tea, told her she owed no loyalty to the departed cad, and advised her to wear her hair up on her head and to try "a bit of powder."

This setback aside, Opal loved her new life and was especially excited about meeting a wide variety of interesting people. She enjoyed asking the foreign diplomats about their home countries.

Some of what she saw surprised her. She noted that Mrs. Coolidge "moves her legs and head in not a lady born way" and was shocked to hear a naval officer announce that he had just made a hundred quarts of beer. Opal, who had once plastered Lane Country, Oregon, with "Oregon Dry" posters and had later learned to sip cheap red wine with Lummis, observed that a lot of people in the government were circumventing Prohibition.

Opal became more friendly with Madame Grouitch, the well-respected American-born wife of the Serbian ambassador and a devout Catholic, who was involved in postwar aid to Europe. It seems that it was through her Opal met an Irish-American woman named Katherine Sullivan and her husband, Jack. Marie Mullen wrote that she was delighted to hear Opal was hanging out with good Catholics. Opal still enjoyed having her picture taken and was photographed by a fancy downtown photo studio in a contemplative pose in front of a Madonna. Although she had ditched the "Françoise" and was Opal Whiteley once again, her Catholicism remained.

Enjoying some financial security and a decent social life for the first time in her life, Opal was full of plans. She wrote David Starr Jordan, saying she would be coming out to California, and at one point arranged to attend Wellesley under the patronage of a Miss Cooke but vacillated about accepting the offer. Opal was also bursting with maternal instinct. The sight of a pair of baby shoes in a shopwindow filled her with happy images of baby feet, and she imagined that children she saw on the street were her own.

She was also working on a book for Putnam's. Although she had originally signed up for a further volume of the childhood diary, she was now at work on what sounds like more of a memoir, with other elements as well. Opal described it as including flowers, animals, and children and said her head was filled with ideas about it, so it was clearly something she was writing in the present. There was no more talk of "piecing" the diary.

D r. Cabot and his wife were in friendly and frequent correspondence and repeatedly invited her to visit at their expense during the summer of 1922. They also wrote Opal advice, warning her that the Miss Cooke at Wellesley who wanted to put her through college had a strong interest in séances and spiritualism. They presumably didn't want a repeat of the theosophical fiasco. As well as monitoring her well-being, the Cabots expressed a strong interest in Opal's diary. Part of the diary itself was now in their hands. They were reading the pages that had been prepared for publication as volume two for George Palmer Putnam while Opal was still at the Millers'. Ella Cabot commented that there were a lot more French words than in the earlier volume, suggesting to Opal that as Opal was older and could read better when this part of the diary was written, she must have been getting more out of the secret books given to her by Angel Mother and Father.

The Cabots advised Opal that it would not be good for anything about her royal origins to be published. Opal agreed, and told them that she thought that in volume two of the diary she should stick to the animals. "I feel I want to stand on my own feet so it would be wrong and injurious to print anything that arouses curiosity as to where I came from. The manuscript as you have it [is] as I was made to send it into Mr. Putnam without any parts taken out. I wished to take all parts referring to Angel Mother & father out—but Millers and then Mrs. Griscom wouldn't allow it."

During this period it is not entirely clear whether Opal still believed in Angel Mother and Father. In any case, she seemed to be trying not to dwell on them, in the interests of her mental health. She referred to herself only as Opal Whiteley, never referred to Angel Mother and Angel Father, and once reported "a longing for mother and father," to the Cabots as if it were a symptom and a part of her mental health report.

Opal said she had already told George Palmer Putnam she wanted the French references out of the continuation of the dairy, and she said she trusted he would be "gentleman enough" to accede to her wishes. This could not have been good news for Putnam, who had signed her up initially to exploit her story of a sensational past.

Sounding defensive, Opal explained to Mrs. Cabot that there actually wasn't more French in the proposed second volume than in the published first volume. She said there had been just as much in the first volume too, "but when Mr. Sedgwick took those little parts and would not let me know what they meant I became frightened and all the pieces with strange words I put way. There are pages and pages & pages of strange words but they are locked away." She said they would remain locked away forever.

In August, Opal moved from the hotel to an apartment on Calvert Street near Rock Creek Park that she shared with her friends Katherine and Jack Sullivan. She took lots of walks and appreciated her natural surroundings. She continued to report to the Cabots on her weight and sleep habits and spent time writing. She had abandoned the idea of another volume of the diary and was writing poems.

She sent a lot of the poems to Sedgwick for his opinion. He was corresponding with her but always had some excuse for not seeing her when she came to visit the Cabots in Boston. Opal expressed the hope that the poems would fulfill the youthful promise demonstrated by the child diarist. Eventually she decided to publish the poetry herself, just as she had done with *The Fairyland Around Us*. Whether Putnam, who had a contract with her for volume two of the diary, knew or cared about this venture is not known. She borrowed money on a bond that hadn't yet come due to pay the printer. The copyright was in the name of her friend Katherine Sullivan, and the book was called *The Flower of Stars*. It was published under the name Opal Whiteley.

The poems, which everyone, even the staunchest Opalites, agree are not very good, have many images from nature and a lot about God. There is a great deal of imagery involving jewels—sapphires and pearls—and much about flowers and stars. They also reveal a knowledge of classical music, something that came out of her time with the musical Millers. There is one rather sweet little love poem. If the poems show anything about her state of mind, it might be that there is a streak of depression throughout them, with many references to loneliness and grayness. There is also a great deal about mothers and children and a clear yearning for children.

Her new marketing approach was even more audacious than her preselling of *The Fairyland Around Us*. She simply sent copies of the book to people whose names she got from various sources, including Dr. Cabot's copy of *Who's Who*, asking for either $1.50 and a dime for postage and handling or the book back. Reactions to her direct-mail marketing pitch were varied, but they reflect a more courteous time than ours.

Poet Amy Lowell returned the book, saying she was too busy to read it as she was working on a life of Keats. Clement Studebaker, Jr., wrote that he was sure the book was charming but that just now he wasn't adding to his collection. A bank president in Fort Wayne, Indiana, politely explained, "I have suffered a stroke of apoplexy . . . and it is difficult for me to concentrate upon works of this kind." Mrs. Herbert Hoover bought nine copies, and Opal even sent a copy to Mrs. Griscom, who sent back a gracious thank-you letter and five dollars for two copies, one for her and one for Mr. Hargrove. Mrs. Griscom said she wished Opal well, and so did Mr. Hargrove. Opal had been emboldened by the fact that Dr. Cabot had been to New York, where he had met with the Millers and Hargrove and Griscom, presumably to discuss Opal.

Of the remaining replies, only an associate justice of the Supreme Court of Colorado wrote back indignantly that he didn't approve of her sending unsolicited material for sale. She got some other letters she described as "scoldy," but Opal was generally pleased with the early results, writing the Cabots that she had received cash and checks for a total of $121.50, which she characterized as "pretty good." On another occasion she reported coming home after a few days away to find twenty-six checks waiting for her.

Opal shot off a copy to Nellie Hemenway with a letter explaining that she had to have the $1.60 by return mail. The amenable Nellie sent the money. She sent one to Sedgwick, but his office replied that he was in South America.

Just as in *The Fairyland Around Us*, Opal included in the book an ambitious list of upcoming volumes. *The Flower of Stars*, dated January 28, 1923 (it actually appeared in February), was to be followed by *In God's Garden* on March 25 and *The Bride's Girdle* on May 25. After these volumes, at unspecified dates, readers could expect *The Books of the Words*, *The New Little Boy*, *The Road of the Winds*, and finally *The Mirror of Hell*. Actually, some of these titles are of poems already in *The Flower of Stars*, the same quirky pattern she had established with *Fairyland*, which also promoted upcoming books with chapter titles from the present volume.

Opal was feeling cheerful about her book of poetry, though she was sorry it wasn't reviewed. For her next project, she was plotting a novel titled *The Impossible Man*, set in a rough lumber community in Oregon "before the reformation of the camps as to better living conditions." She hoped that George Palmer Putnam would take it instead of volume two of the diary.

The planned novel was full of rough western characters with Runyonesque names like Tooth Pick Tim, Bohemia Sharp, and Allegory Jinks. The plot had some of the same elements as the childhood diary. The protagonist, Richard Livermore, working as a tree feller in Lost Lake Valley, Oregon, was really rich, aristocratic New Yorker Richard Vanderlip. He has worked in a bank at his guardian's insistence, then has served as a diplomat following his uncle's desires, but is now living incognito among the working class in a small Oregon lumber town, not unlike petite Françoise of the diary.

The novel, which was outlined but never written, was to describe two years in the Oregon valley and feature colorful characters, including a half-witted dwarf and a bevy of prostitutes. The central plot was a love story between Richard Livermore and Susan, the sweet schoolmarm who reforms him and encourages him to become an engineer.

For the first time since *The Fairyland Around Us*, Opal portrayed the West where she grew up positively. Protagonist Richard Livermore finds himself in this more egalitarian environment, far away from the controlling eastern aristocrats who have run his life, and he embraces a practical profession then, as now, more associated with enterprising western and midwestern farm boys than with the Ivy League. Unlike the little Opal of the diary, who was oppressed by the West and wanted to flee it, Richard Livermore finds happiness there, as did the young Opal of *The Fairyland Around Us*.

During this period of relative stability and happiness in Opal's life, she changed dramatically. Gone was her complete obsession with herself. She was taking an interest in other people to an extent she never had before, expressing delight in the wide variety of people she was meeting and showing an interest in them, not simply in impressing them. She even became interested in public policy and began reading *The New Republic*.

For the first time she was reaching out and making real friends, instead of simply ingratiating herself with older people who could help with money and professional backing. It is significant that her planned novel, *The Impossible Man*, and her book of poetry are the only literary projects she ever attempted that didn't feature Opal Whiteley as a central element of the work.

After she had been in Washington for a while, her friends the Cabots began a vigorous campaign to keep volume two of the diary from ever appearing. At one point, perhaps when Opal asked for the diary back, Ella Cabot wrote, "I'm afraid the diary went astray. . . . Uncle Richard thinks you mustn't publish the diary now. You are not pledged to it." This was not true. Opal had a contract with Putnam's to publish it. Why did the Cabots have the diary, and why did they not want it published? And how could they have been so careless as to lose it?

What happened to this second volume of the diary has long been a mystery, and the solution is rather astonishing. A few typed pages of it remain, complete with professional-looking copy-editing marks. At the top of one page, in Opal's hand is written "About 9 years." It began: "It is the time of goldenrod and the way is bordered with plumes of gold." Gone was the idiosyncratic English of "joy feels." It still contained fancifully named pets; Aristotle, once a bat, is now "that beautiful toad with jewel eyes" and rides in her apron pocket. There is the same cathedral service routine, with Opal kneeling at the forest altar. There is a scene of her being misunderstood by a schoolteacher and embarrassment at a poorly blackened shoe and a stocking with a hole in it. And it appears to be in diary form, as the passage ended "And now I think I better go to bed." There is no French in it.

Not only was none of this ever published, despite months of "piecing" at the Millers', but Putnam's got out of the project in 1923 through an agreement that seemed designed to ensure another volume of Opal's diary would never see the light of day. This agreement set aside the contract Opal had signed under Hargrove's supervision, selling Putnam's the second volume of the diary, and it amended the contract that had sold Putnam's the reprint rights to volume one, *The Story of Opal*. It prohibited Opal from offering the diary material to any other publisher. It further stipulated that Putnam's could publish it only after her death, a rather startling provision, as she was then twenty-five.

Stranger still, under the agreement, Opal was to turn over to Dr. Richard C. Cabot all the diary material, which would be held by him. (In fact he already had at least some of it, and his wife had said lamely that it had gone astray.) Putnam's was allowed to retain its carbon copy of certain of the diary material that had been prepared in its office "from the original notes and manuscripts of Miss Whiteley."

What did Miss Whiteley get out of this deal? Nothing. In fact, she *waived* royalties already credited to her of $145.80 on the first volume, *The Story of Opal*. She also waived royalties on the 1,178 copies of *The Story of Opal* that Putnam's had on hand as part of its deal with *The Atlantic Monthly*. And she gave up the possibility of future income from a sequel to a book that had received lots of attention.

What did Richard C. Cabot get? He got a legal hold on the diary pages he already had, and he could take possession of more of it. And presumably, he had avoided potential for scandal for his family. His cousin-in-law Ellery Sedgwick, who had been avoiding Opal, already had the typewriter that proved Opal had been deceptive. Now the manuscript itself could never be examined. Nor was it likely that any more text, apparently full of lots more French that hadn't made it into the typed version at Putnam's, would be analyzed.

What did Putnam's get beyond the $145.80 and royalties on 1,178 books? Perhaps it was put to George Palmer Putnam that by disassociating himself from the project, he too would avoid possible charges of fraud or gullibility.

Opal, Putnam, and Dr. Cabot signed the document in Putnam's New York office, and G. P. Putnam's chose not to publish additional copies of the first volume, which it had bought. (It had, however, already published a British edition with the Lord Grey preface, but with Sedgwick's conspicuously absent.) This agreement—suppressing the sequel and turning over the manuscript to an in-law of the man who had sold it to Putnam's in the first place—was unknown to Elbert Bede. Putnam, after his initial tantalizing hints of forthcoming big news about Opal, wouldn't answer Bede's letters asking about the continuation of the diary. Later, when writing his book in the early 1950s, after George Palmer Putnam's death, Bede tried again to discover what had happened to the second volume of the diary. The firm reported there was no sign of any manuscript by Opal or any contract with her in its files. It does not appear that Dr. Cabot kept his part of the bargain, which was to hold the diary pages until after her death. After his own death in 1939, his papers went to Harvard. There is an Opal Whiteley file among the papers, but it does not contain the diary, which has vanished. The file contains only her letters and a typed outline of her proposed novel. It seems likely that the diary was destroyed.

While in New York conducting business with Opal and Putnam, Dr. Cabot also had a long chat with the Millers about Opal. The purpose of this meeting is unclear. Perhaps he was asking for any diary pages she might have left behind. Opal seemed to think he went there to discuss her mental health.

After he returned to Boston, Opal wrote him that she wanted to know how he felt after his talk with the New York theosophists. "Do you feel I was or am a bad girl—also after the talk did you feel I have been ungrateful? It would help me so much to know how you felt after you had talked with them." In a postscript she thanked him profusely for getting her off the hook with Putnam's. "It is just a great big load taken off."

The Cabots had convinced her it would be a bad thing to publish the diary. Had they told her it would be bad for her mental health, which she was counting on them to help her hold on to? Was that why they were so anxious to get hold of it? Or were they trying to hide evidence of what they believed to be fraud? Richard Cabot replied that he felt the Millers had "meant kindly" during her time with them and that Hargrove and Mrs. Griscom "still love" her. In the same letter he asked her for any parts of the diary she still might have.

Opal originally addressed the couple as Dr. and Mrs. Cabot, but since they had taken an important role in her life, this had changed to Aunt Ella and Uncle Richard. In this letter, the first since she signed the contract giving him the diary, Uncle Richard forgot to sign himself that way, and it worried Opal. She asked him if he had done this on purpose. She also said that she hadn't known she was supposed to give him the rest of the diary immediately. She had thought it was to go to him after her death, an absurd idea seeing as Dr. Cabot was thirty years older, but she dutifully said she would gather up what she had and send it to him.

Opal had grown dependent on the Cabots and saw them as safe-guarding her sanity. She told them how grateful she was for their love. She seemed nervous about alienating them or behaving in any way that might offend them. She willingly did whatever they suggested, including signing a ridiculous contract that was not in her best interest. If Cabot had simply wanted to get her out of having to deliver a book she didn't want to do, his agreement was a very peculiar way to do it.

Opal was right to be anxious about her relationship with the Cabots. Once they had the whole diary, their interest in her did diminish, but for now they just wanted more of that diary. Opal said it was scattered all over, and parts seemed to be missing but that she would send it to them that weekend. She sent them several chunks. "A lot of it goes by express today," she wrote in April. "It is inside a suitbox." At the end of May, Opal was coming to Boston to give a lecture. The Cabots told her they were sorry, but the room she usually stayed in had another guest in it, and she'd have to make other arrangements. Although Ella Cabot still wrote affectionately, Uncle Richard stopped writing her, despite her begging for a letter from him.

At the same time as the Cabots were disassociating themselves from her, her life in Washington grew increasingly unstable. She had been living with Jack and Katherine Sullivan, but Jack died suddenly and she had to find somewhere else to live. Opal's finances were rocky once again. In June she tried to sell old copies of *The Atlantic Monthly* back to the magazine to raise cash. It thanked her for thinking of it but said it was amply provided with the issues in question.

In late August Opal wrote the Cabots that she had heard nothing from them since June and hoped to hear from them in September. Both Cabots wrote her in November, and she replied with a wry little chart showing she hadn't received a letter from Uncle Richard for the previous seven months, ever since she'd handed over the diary.

For a while Opal began to fall apart. She became temporarily homeless, getting her mail at general delivery, and sold household items to raise cash. She asked her old friend Marie Mullen for a loan. Miss Mullen, as usual, came through. Opal's projects became more scattered. She was working simultaneously on a nature book and some short stories but didn't seem to produce anything.

By the following spring, however, Opal seemed to be winning the battle with her demons. She was getting her mail at the same Washington, D.C., address used by Miss Cooke, her Wellesley patroness, and she planned to go to college and become a professionally trained educator. She was happy again. In March 1924 she wrote that the previous winter had been the "most healthy" she had ever had. "I have been so well—and I may also add [have had] the happiest year of my life."

After leaving the Millers', Opal had hoped that with the care of Dr. Peterson, and the support of the Cabots, she could stay sane, or "healthy," as she put it. It seems to have worked for a while. There was no time in her adult life when she was as happy and successful as in Washington. After years of being treated like a child by Sedgwick and her New York friends, she was finally leading the normal life of a young woman interested both in her career and in young men and babies. However, after they got their hands on the diary, the Cabots' role diminished dramatically. It is quite likely that if the Cabots hadn't faded out of the picture, Opal's life wouldn't have been any different. But it is also true that when their support system was gone, her life took a radical turn.

After that happy report of a sane Opal in March 1924, there was no trace of her for the next six months. When her trail turned up again, she had become someone else entirely. The Miss Whiteley of Washington, D.C., was gone forever. In fact she never used the name Opal Whiteley again. For the next couple of years very few people knew where Opal was. (An exception was Marie Mullen, whose checks always came in handy.)

Opal later said she had gone straight from Putnam's office, where she signed the agreement giving the diary to Dr. Cabot, to the office of "one of the greatest lawyers in America and he said at once that the whole thing was quite illegal. He also concluded that it was far wiser for me to get home to France at once and I went soon after." This isn't true. She was in Washington for another year, happy and planning for college, before she fled.

Opal told University of Oregon English Professor Carlisle Moore when he interviewed her in the early 1960s that she sailed for France under the name Françoise White. Opal said she went to France to establish herself as a member of the d'Orléans family. It was here she said she met her grandmother, the duchess of Chartres. Opal's acceptance by the duchess as her long-lost granddaughter has become part of the canon, and if it is true, it is the strongest evidence that Opal had any claim to the d'Orléans name. It does not, however, appear to be true.

The only link to this lady is an undated draft letter to her in Opal's hand. Across the top it read "Madame, la Duchesse de Chartres." The salutation was "Madame of the Rose Garden." It began, "Many happy thoughts come to me when I wake up in the morning thinking of you and your rose garden. I'm just thrilled to find how you love the forest— and it makes you more yet to me beside [*sic*] your being the mother of the voyager, whom I hold in reverent esteem because of the honor due to him." In this letter Opal referred twice to Angel Father, Henri d'Orléans, as "the voyager" and said she was writing a book about him. Opal wrote that she felt as if the duchess were a longtime friend because of their common interests: "your preferences for the wilderness of the forest, your desire to search about for rare wild flowers, your love of the companionship of books, your sympathy for horses and dogs, your friendship with birds and your love of flowers."

Opal was apparently in France; there was an unclear, partially crossed-out reference to a library for the blind at 9, rue Duroc. She said she was "so *happy* here in my little room with its dormer window near the sky." Opal used a few Frenchified words, indicating she could well have been living in France. "I have the habitude of . . ."; "I comprehend now." She spelled Tibet, "which she said she and the duchess discussed while eating cherries and which Henri d'Orléans explored, as "Thibet," in the French way.

It is clear that if the meeting described in the letter took place, English was the language they spoke. The duchess of Chartres had lived in exile in England for many years. "I was right glad to hear you use the word 'grub' the other day," wrote Opal ever so genteelly. "I have previously somewhat hesitated; but it so exactly expresses what one does when one is just hunting about for rare wild things." The letter was undated, but she used the American spelling of the word "honor." Opal switched to British spelling in 1928, so it very likely was written before that date, and it supports the idea that such a meeting did indeed take place. Opal told playwright Rob Nassif that she met the duchess on June 23, 1924, when indeed, the roses would have been in bloom and the cherries would have been ripe.

I believe it is likely that they did meet. Nowhere in this draft letter, however, did it appear she was presenting herself as other than a fan of the old woman's dead son, an author who was writing a book about him. She coyly used the fanciful names "Madame of the Rose Garden" and "the voyager" rather than real names or titles. As a published author, with her extensive knowledge of Henri d'Orléans's career and her apparent devotion to him, and with a solid track record of fearlessly making new friends in high places, she could easily have got the appointment with the duchess on the ground she would write a book praising her son.

Interestingly, a page of this draft letter is missing from the copy I examined. Elizabeth Bradburne Lawrence, an English author who wrote a book on Opal in 1962, quoted the now-missing page: "The thought comes to me that for the cover of the book the painting which you showed to me on the wall—the one of Monseigneur Henri seated on those steps in the Orient—would be excellent for the cover paper with the name of the book.

"While continuing my research at the Bibliothèque Nationale I have noticed a number of photographs appearing at the time of his death which were not among those we were looking over that day."

Mrs. Lawrence's book said it was "well authenticated" that Opal was accepted by the duchess as her granddaughter. She got it from Elbert Bede. A 1960 letter to her from Bede said, "My authority for the statement that Opal met the Duchess of Chartres and was accepted as a granddaughter is Ellery Sedgwick. He may have gotten it from Earl [*sic*] Grey." (Bede, with understandable American ignorance of English titles, seemed to have mixed Lord Grey up with a kind of tea.)

Actually, Sedgwick got this from Opal herself, not from Lord Grey. No letters from the duchess were ever found among Opal's papers, and it seems likely that if there had been any, Opal would have kept them. Why she left Washington—where she appeared to be happy—where she was, and what she was doing are unknown. This draft letter offers a tantalizing hint.

Her next documented appearance was in September 1924, a full six months after she was last known to be in Washington. She was calling on Major Pritchard, the British resident in Udaipur, India.

Eighteen

*I*n 1962 an old India hand, Captain Chevenix Trench, wrote a letter to the editor of a British newspaper with a ripping yarn of his memories of Opal in Udaipur. "Opal turned up one day in the capital, the beauty spot of India, with nothing but the clothes she was wearing." He said that the local English ladies loaned her clothes to wear. "She was lodged in a marble pavilion in the palace and given a bodyguard with six aboriginal Bheels." He went on to say she got mixed up in the Indian independence movement and was kicked out of Udaipur after he gave her a stern talking-to. "I hardened up my heart and bluffed. 'Look here, my girl,' I said, 'the game is up and you will leave Udaipur within 24 hours and disappear. The alternative is the internment camp of Bengali terrorists in Nasirabad.' On this she wept exuberantly but her tears were soon dried and she agreed to any proposal I might suggest. She was, in fact, up to the neck in every form of sedition."

In 1995 British documentary filmmaker Ian Taylor, following up on this lead, discovered that the official report of Opal's activities in India was in the British Library Oriental and India Office collection cataloged as R/2/144/A87. The 1924 report had once been secret but was now declassified. The expression "red tape" comes from the ribbons used to tie up bundles of government documents. When Ian Taylor undid the red tape on Opal's 110-page file, it had faded to pink and had left white stripes on browned pages. He was the first person to read it since it had been sealed up years before.

This report told a different and rather shabbier story than that of

Chevenix Trench. In conjunction with Opal's letters and other documents only recently cataloged and made available, it is now possible to find out just what Opal was up to Udaipur, and her problems weren't so much political as sexual.

On arrival, Opal, who had never been shy about introducing herself to powerful people, presented herself to the highest-ranking British civil servant in the place, Major Pritchard. She told him that she was the same person as the Opal Whiteley who had written *The Story of Opal* but that she was really Mademoiselle Françoise D'Orlé [*sic*], with a very un-French capital D., and a French national. Despite a strong American accent and, by all accounts, very bad and limited French—Chevenix Trench described it as "vile"—Pritchard took her story at face value. Whether any of the local British colony had read the British edition of the diary is not known. It had, however, created quite a stir when it appeared in 1921 in London, where it received mixed reviews, ranging from high praise, as a remarkable document of childhood, to scorn and incredulity and one comment that saccharine material went over rather better in America than in Britain, as well as getting satirical coverage in *Punch*.

Opal had been interested in India since childhood. As a little girl she had wanted to go to India as a missionary, and had collected pictures of India. Among the possessions she left behind in Eugene when she went off to Hollywood was a photograph of the Taj Mahal. While at the Millers' she had read Indian sacred texts. And Henri d'Orléans had traveled in and written about India.

Opal told Major Pritchard she had come for three months to gather material for a history of the region of Rajputana but had very little money and planned to live on three rupees a day and get her food from "the stalls" in the bazaar. Pritchard found it appalling that a European should live in poverty in Udaipur and told her that "such an arrangement was out of the question." Opal impressed him with her knowledge of the area, gleaned, he gathered, from libraries in London, New York, and Paris, and he decided that since she was a visiting scholar, she should become a state guest.

The legend of Opal aside, she was not in fact, at first at least, a guest of the royal family. The British took her in to avoid the spectacle of an unrespectable European. For both the Indians and the British, Udaipur was a caste-bound society. Raffish exceptions just weren't on. Opal was put up at the Udaipur Hotel at state expense.

The Rajputana region, a group of native or princely states, was not part of British India. Instead it was ruled under an ambiguous concept known as paramountcy, the result of British treaties with the various kings going back to 1817. In 1858 these kings had been demoted to princes by the British, who also at that time decreed that they should be addressed as highnesses. In Udaipur, His Highness the Maharana of Mewar still ruled. Sort of. (Other princely states were ruled by maharajas; the title of the ruler of Mewar, of which Udaipur was the capital, was maharana). Officially, Britain was in charge of all foreign policy and also had some supervision of domestic matters, on the ground that Britain was protecting the native states of the region from domestic enemies.

The resident was the political officer in charge of keeping an eye out for any domestic enemies and for any activities having to do with the independence movement. Residents were allowed to get involved in issues of succession and often took an interest in the education of those in line to the throne, but they operated behind the scenes to an extent. It was an arrangement that fostered intrigue.

According to *Maharana: The Story of the Rulers of Udaipur* by Brian Masters, the Maharana Fateh Singh had been on the throne since 1885 when Opal arrived. A very religious man with a forked white beard, he had had a simple upbringing in the country and little formal education. He was also a proud man, who resisted any attempts to lower the dignity of the house of Mewar, which traced itself back to A.D. 566. He believed that his power came not from the British crown but from the fact that his family were servants of the sun-god Eklingja. He is said to have loved nature and got up at dawn every morning and prayed for an hour. While other princes lived luxuriously, he kept his life simple. Whereas they had many wives, he had only two and had remarried only after the death of his first wife.

He was said to have had exquisite manners and to have been a man of sterling character and moral authority who enjoyed the loyalty of his people. The British therefore had to handle him gingerly, even though they considered him anti-British. He was often irritating to them in symbolic ways. He called in sick when the Prince of Wales arrived in town, on the ground that because the heir to the British throne wasn't a king and he was, only a crown prince should go down to the railway station to welcome the British prince. The British found out Fateh Singh wasn't really ill and were shocked.

The seventy-six-year-old maharana met Opal and took a liking to her. It is easy to see that their common interest in religion and nature would have drawn them together. She later said he treated her like a granddaughter, and when he died, she wrote the *Times* of London that he called her "my little sister of the birds and flowers."

Chevenix Trench speculated that the maharana might also have been solicitous because of the Henri d'Orléans connection. Henri d'Orléans, despite having grown up in exile in England, was well known to be anti-British, and his books contained snide references to British imperialism side by side with suggestions that the French should do a better job of empire building in Asia. The entry for Henri d'Orléans in the 1911 *Encyclopaedia Britannica,* the edition that Opal consulted at Lummis's house in Los Angeles, described him as "an Anglophobe" and referred to his "violent diatribes" against Great Britain.

Opal was never shy about asking for invitations, and the scrupulously polite house of Mewar always responded hospitably. Surviving letters reveal that when she asked to be invited to the maharana's birthday party, she was told to come around to the palace at eight and that an elephant fight was scheduled. When she asked to go on a tiger hunt, she was told there was a cot ready for her at camp, and a car would come for her and a tiffin box of non-Indian food prepared by the hotel. She was particularly interested in tiger hunts, no doubt because of Henri d'Orléans's *Six Mois aux Indes*, which is primarily concerned with tiger hunting, both on foot and from the back of an elephant.

Animal-loving Opal always maintained she didn't shoot at any tigers herself, although Henri d'Orléans once killed over twenty-one in a single expedition and later wrote that the cut throat of a slain tiger was a beautiful sight. A list of belongings she had with her includes "Daddy's book." She was now following in his footsteps.

The maharana's son Bhopal Singh was the crown prince. Known as Bapji, he had been doing the actual governing of Udaipur since 1921, when the British had decided the maharana wasn't vigilant enough about unrest and, perhaps after his snub of the Prince of Wales, that he wasn't pro-British enough. Aware of the old man's status with the people, Bapji too had to handle the maharana gingerly.

Bapji was less keen on Opal, although in the tradition of his family and of the region, he was unfailingly courteous and invited her to cultural events for her book research and acquiesced to numerous interview requests. He was confined to a wheelchair, a childhood bout with tuberculosis having left him with a curved spine.

Opal besieged him with demands. She borrowed books from him. She asked for a carriage to come take her to an appointment. She asked him to send a man to get a trunk she had left somewhere. In one letter she asked him to write a note to the public library allowing her to check out reference materials and take them home, and at one point she also requested a large table and a couple of dressers that she said she would return later.

Opal had abandoned "sincerely" in her correspondence. As Frenchwoman Françoise D'Orlé, she had switched to an English translation of a French signoff, "I pray you to receive the expression of distinguished sentiments," and had taken to addressing Englishmen as "monsieur." In another letter from this period, to the British resident, she apologized for her English, an odd touch for someone purporting to be writing a book in that language. There is nothing in the letter that could have startled Pritchard, other than perhaps her consistently American spelling.

From Major Pritchard's point of view, Opal was an immediate cause for concern. English ladies took her aside and gave her friendly advice, warning her against "her daily custom" of entertaining presumably male Indians in her hotel room with her clothing strewn about. (Opal was never tidy.) She paid no attention to this advice. Pritchard thought her behavior would upset the nobility and gentry of Udaipur, whose own women lived behind the walls of their own homes and did not socialize.

Opal had thrown herself with her characteristic enthusiasm into her work. She arranged to view the city walls, she was taken around the palace art collection, and she made plans to visit a sanitarium. Her correspondence from this period reveals she was peppering everyone with questions and planned to visit homes for lepers, various missionaries, and any ceremony she could. Pritchard lined up contacts for her, including the director general of archaeology, the head of the Geological Survey of India, and the inspector general of forests, as well as the superintendent of the Rajputana museum. She also learned how to ride from an aide-de-camp to the maharana, who claimed she learned in two months what most men took a year to learn, and had a specific horse from the royal stables assigned to her. And she made visits to the zenana, the part of the palace where the ladies of the court lived in strict purdah.

Besides making many valuable contacts and securing the cooperation of the court, Opal was also taken up enthusiastically by the wives of the British civil servants in Udaipur, who were no doubt delighted to have some new blood in town and viewed her as somewhat of a celebrity. Many people saw her heavily annotated copy of the *Story of Opal* and knew she had written it. They seemed not to have heard of the scandal surrounding its authorship.

The residency surgeon, Lieutenant Colonel Hunt, and his wife found her zest and enthusiasm enchanting. She also became friends with Nora Mitchell, Major Pritchard's son's governess, who visited her on her afternoons off. Opal wasn't a governess anymore. All her time was her own. She went to tennis parties at the residency and to official events. While she was referred to as Mademoiselle D'Orlé, her nickname around town seems to have been "petite Françoise." Opal was now, to all appearances, a full-time writer who, thanks to Major Pritchard, had most of her expenses taken care of by the state. No longer was she required to seek out mothers and little children and teach nature classes.

In October, a month after her arrival, Opal met a man and fell in love. While doing research in the Udaipur public library, a young Indian introduced himself to her and said he heard she was writing a book. He too was embarked on research about Udaipur. He told Opal he was a scholar of the Vedas. Opal later said they talked about Hindu music, astronomy, and botany. He began to call on her at the hotel, and the discussions on many intellectual subjects continued.

A police report later described him as five feet six inches, or about six inches taller than Opal, with a "wheat-colored" complexion, small eyes, spectacles, bare feet, and a white cloak, though he sometimes wore English clothes. He was somewhere around twenty-two, about five years younger than Opal. He was a holy man, Swami Duetanand. A picture that is almost certainly the swami shows him bare-chested and barefoot, with the white cloak tied around his waist and reaching to his calves. Despite the unprepossessing description by the police, he exudes a certain animal vitality and has a nice smile.

Soon he was writing Opal letters with phrases like "I kiss your lips, rosy cheeks." And "Dearest, I have no words for all my love." He included poems, some with Indian nationalist themes, that appear to have been written by others, for the English is much more polished than his prose. Eventually he suggested marriage but was concerned his father would not give him permission. Opal confided in her friend Nora Mitchell, the Pritchards' governess, and said she was seriously considering it. Nora urged to go ahead and accept, writing, "This will be the end of all your loneliness and you will have someone to look after you."

Major Pritchard had also noted Swami Duetanand's arrival and his "abominable appearance." He warned Opal not to get too chummy with him. Pritchard had already been informed by local police that the swami was a suspicious character who spoke French and Russian and was a guest of the maharana, about whose loyalty the British were always nervous.

Pritchard immediately asked the national railway police what they knew about him, and local surveillance also began. A Mr. Chatterji, an official at the court, had a long conversation with the swami, who claimed to be in town studying Mewar history. Mr. Chatterji in a report to Pritchard concluded, "In my humble opinion he is a typical type of wreckless [*sic*] young man with shallow education who for want of some substantial means has placed himself as an instrument in the hands of deep political intriguers and is now being made an instrument by the mischief makers here and has been introduced here to influence people in the garb of a Sannyasi, for which class people have got regard and respect. I did not find him as a man of high calibre." Chatterji noted that on his calling card, "[h]e writes himself as Swami Duetanand, M.A. (Madras) Ph.D. (Cantab) D.D. Leipzig F.R.A.S. (London) etc. Research scholar of Vedic Sociology, but I have grave doubts about such academical qualifications of his."

The swami caused more suspicion when he flashed a letter that he said had been written by the British viceroy of India to the maharana. The person who saw it glimpsed the viceroy's crest on the letterhead. When this got back to the British, they wondered why the maharana was giving his mail to the swami. They suspected the swami was an anti-British political intriguer who was cozying up to the maharana with the promise of helping him get back his powers.

On December 16, 1924, Pritchard was instructed by his superior, Wingate, at the Rajputana Agency in Ajmer, to warn His Highness the maharana and the crown prince that they had information proving the swami to be an impostor and a swindler. There was also some thought that the swami had a pistol.

On December 19 a police report got back to Pritchard saying that Swami Duetanand, accompanied by "an English Miss," had been seen shopping in Ajmer. Handing his calling card with its brace of degrees around, Swami Duetanand had checked into room 3 in the Hindu Hotel with the "English Miss" under the name Dr. K. D. Ranga. While previously he had been seen in "bhagwan clothes" he was now in Western dress. The informant had tried to find out who the English miss was. She was said to be a tourist.

Pritchard soon learned that it was Opal and that she had traveled with Duetanand to Jaipur and Jodhpur as well. Pritchard found this very disturbing news indeed. It was clear where his duty lay. It was his job to protect the reputation of a European woman in his jurisdiction and by extension the reputation of all Europeans. Shacking up with the natives in hotel rooms was completely beyond the pale.

When Opal returned, he confronted her with his knowledge of her trip and the fact that she and the swami had spent time together in hotel rooms. Opal's explanation was that this was not what it appeared to be. Two elderly American tourists, the Misses Parry, were supposed to go with them on a tour of the region but hadn't shown up at the railway station. The swami felt ill, and she had to bring food and water to his room. She had felt sorry for him, and he had threatened to commit suicide, so she had to spend the night in his hotel room on suicide watch.

Opal renounced the swami and said she was sorry she'd ever been kind to him. She prepared a report for Pritchard, disavowing any romantic interest in the swami, and said she would give up his friendship, as it jeopardized Pritchard's support (in the form of free room and board at the Udaipur Hotel), which she needed to write her book.

Pritchard told the twenty-seven-year-old Opal to go home. She was simply too young to be on her own. She had begun to complain that drunken Indians, who assumed she was fast, called on her at her hotel. She now accused the swami of stalking her and pressing her with unwanted attentions. She told Pritchard about "a degrading scene" with the swami at the public library. Pritchard had the impression they'd had an affair that had fizzled and the swami wasn't going quietly, an impression backed up by letters from him that Opal kept for the rest of her life. "You know how ardently I love you. And it is decided fact without you I can't live for a few minutes. In other words you are my soul you are my breathings. . . . To quench the thirst of passion man becomes mad." He told her that her coldness and treachery were driving him crazy. In January 1925 he wrote, after not getting a letter from her, "O how great and terrible pain it is. But girls never realize it."

In February, after Opal had promised Pritchard she'd have nothing more to do with him, the swami spent some time with her in her hotel room right there in Udaipur. Perhaps having learned by now that spies were everywhere, Opal wrote a groveling preemptive note to Pritchard, explaining that the young man had come into her hotel room, but as she had been ill and lying down, and as he was no doubt crazy, she had been afraid to eject him. She told Pritchard she had forbidden him to come back, because it would impede her ability to write her book "for my father's sake."

Opal said she had been afraid to be too firm with him because he was not only crazy but possibly armed. She said she wouldn't let suicide threats and pity soften her up as before. "Notwithstanding the brilliancy of his mind, it is quite an unbalanced one." She told Major Pritchard that she had concluded that the natives had no code of honor "as we have at home." She said she felt the swami could be "a dangerous enemy with his brilliant, unsettled mind."

After receiving this alarming letter, Pritchard had to leave town and report to headquarters in Ajmer. He asked Captain Chevenix Trench to keep an eye on Opal. While Pritchard was away, he received a letter from Chevenix Trench that began, "La petite Françoise is making a lot of trouble here." She had come over to his house to work on her book, and the swami sent in his card. The captain said he had told him to "clear off the premises, and if he showed his face in my compound again I would thrash the hide off him," and the swami then "vanished, shrieking that he would file a civil suit."

When Chevenix Trench went back inside, he learned that Opal had broken down and confessed to his wife, Margaret, that she was afraid of the swami because while comforting him during his suicidal period, she had written him at least one "sentimental" letter, "in the character of his dead wife," which she wanted to get back but which he refused to give her.

The captain wrote ominously, "[T]he inference any Indian would draw from such a letter is obvious." He told Pritchard that her fear of the swami's committing suicide was "all rubbish." Opal had had an affair with him, the letter no doubt contained pretty hot stuff, and she was being blackmailed. The swami had indeed written Opal threatening her reputation. "These aristocratic people of Rajputa to make the chastity of a girl in ashes it is the task of the left hand for them."

In Pritchard's absence, Chevenix Trench had got on to the Indian authorities and suggested the swami be arrested and deported from Rajputana. "It is intolerable that he should come nosing around the hotel and my house after a white girl," he wrote to Pritchard. However, the religious maharana wouldn't eject the swami, a holy man, without a good reason, and the British would lose face if they explained he had seduced one of their own. Chevenix Trench hoped they could get rid of him "with no inquiry or publicity." The alternative he proposed was "that the lady be asked to leave the state before her good name is irretrievably spoiled." He was disgusted that after the scene with the swami at his home and after he had escorted her back to her hotel, despite her weepy promises to be more discreet, she was seen chatting with the swami and another man on the top veranda.

Warning of the potential for a huge scandal, the captain wrote, "The lady works here daily but I won't have her driving out with my family.

She complains of a want of sympathy from the . . . white residents here, but we have all done our best and now she ought to go."

Finally, Opal herself figured out how to get rid of the swami without letting the world know they'd spent time on the road together. She arranged for the maharana to read the love letters the swami had sent her. They revealed him not to be a holy man, and the maharana agreed to kick him out of Udaipur. He was on the night train out of town.

Pritchard wanted Opal out of town too and suggested she leave. In a letter to "Monsieur," she expressed relief that the maharana had ejected the swami, but she explained she was staying. "It doesn't seem possible for you to understand but I have to remain in India for a time, that is for a year or a year and a half." She needed time to write her book. She hinted that if she did return to Europe, she would be caught up in some political intrigue the details of which she was not free to reveal. She said she couldn't return before some family estate was settled. She also said she was too tired to go to another Indian city and develop contacts and get the confidence of the people so she could attend their ceremonies. She said she'd stop being a burden to the state and live as she had planned at first on three rupees a day, just as she had in Paris. She had to stay in Udaipur and keep it as her headquarters. She promised that when she traveled on research trips, she would stay with Catholic nuns.

In response to rumors she planned to marry the swami, she gave Pritchard a lengthy explanation of why this could never be. Perhaps referring to the young man who had jilted her in Washington, D.C., she wrote that as the only man she could ever love was in the diplomatic service and as she was not interested in being a diplomatic wife, she would never marry. She loved this diplomat too much to allow him to lunch with other women as he would have to do in the line of duty. She added, "I certainly would not want to dance with a lot of those diplomats." Some of them, she explained to Major Pritchard with the cruelty of youth, are like "old lizards." She went on for several pages about moral depravity in the diplomatic corps, ending with the fact that she would always love this mysterious diplomat and her heart could never be given to another.

The swami wanted her to leave Udaipur too. He wrote to warn her that there were conspiracies against them, that her room was probably being searched, that she must lock up his photos and letters. In a PS he said someone had tried to poison him; he gave some scraps of food to a dog first, and it died. He took this as a warning and encouraged Opal to leave the city "immediately."

Getting her out of town seemed to be a group effort. A Captain Handcock put down a deposit on a second-class one-way passage to Marseilles in the name of F. M. D'Orlé, but Opal did not sail. She canceled the reservation, and the Peninsular & Oriental Steamship Navigation Company sent her, rather than Captain Handcock, the check returning his deposit.

When Lieutenant Colonel Hunt's wife pleaded with her to leave, Opal refused and then said she had a secret reason for not doing so. After Mrs. Hunt heard her story, she asked her permission to reveal it to Pritchard. Pritchard said he would keep it secret unless it conflicted with his official duties.

Pritchard had believed Opal when she had initially told him she was Françoise D'Orlé and that Opal Whiteley was some sort of pen name. Now he learned of a third identity. In his report, Pritchard wrote, "Mrs. Hunt then told me that Mdlle D'Orlé had informed her that she was Princess Françoise Marguerite of Orléans and the daughter of Prince Henri (It may have been Louis) Philippe of Orléans." The rest of the story gives some insight into the extent to which Opal's story had taken on much new lurid detail.

The Opal Whiteley of Washington, D.C., who had struggled to stay sane and not dwell on Angel Mother and Angel Father, now said, according to Pritchard, "that she had papers in France of the highest historical value as well as priceless lace which belonged to Marie Antoinette, and jewelry of great value; that the Communist party in France were intent on gaining possession of her historic documents, and that, if she returned to France, she would be got at and put to infinite annoyance."

Pritchard summoned Opal and asked her if she had told anyone else this story. She replied that she had confided only in her friend Pritchard's son's governess, Nora Mitchell, and in the swami. Pritchard pointed out that in that case the secret wouldn't remain a secret much longer. Opal then said the swami had seen through her incognito and told her himself who she was. This had led her to believe, on grounds which remain obscure, that he was a Communist agent.

Pritchard conferred with several colleagues. Although he initially believed her story of being incognito royalty, no one else did. It now came out that the maharana had heard her story of royal birth too and that American tourists at the hotel, with their characteristic American fascination with royalty, "were paying her marked deference." Opal had also been showing a photograph of Henri d'Orléans around town. Pritchard demanded to see some proof of her identity. She refused, saying her passport was in order so she needn't show it to him. Later she wrote him that she had a passport in two names, Mademoiselle Françoise Marguerite D'Orlé "and with the additional name under which my books were issued in America, 'Opal Whiteley' for use in case of need in connection with past literary work as issued by the French police, in August 1924 and vized [*sic*] by the Paris office from the vize [*sic*] issued by the London office." When Pritchard asked why D'Orlé, supposedly an assumed name, would appear on her passport, she replied that it didn't matter, because D'Orlé was part of the name d'Orléans.

Pritchard then asked her for a birth certificate, but she said it had been taken from her and that her parents had been married over the objections of both families, causing her many problems. Pritchard reported that she made a big point of maintaining that her parents were legally married. She also said there was much she could not tell him as she had taken certain vows not to. After hearing this bizarre story, Pritchard wrote, "My belief in her received a severe shaking."

The next day Opal wrote Pritchard that she would seek protection from someone other than him, and she upbraided him for what she perceived as his rudeness to her. After years of exhibiting a childlike demeanor, referring to herself as a little girl well into her twenties, she now took on an imperious tone that never left her. Mademoiselle D'Orlé was quite different from the petite Françoise of the diary and the Opal Whiteley of Washington, D.C.

Her new plan was to leave the hotel where she was living as a state guest and live in a small house provided by the maharana, with a police guard around it, presumably to keep out any more boyfriends. The house was duly provided, including a cook and a long list of appointments for which she signed, from furniture right down to butter knives, teacups, and towels. For a professional houseguest, a sort of Kato Kaelin of the twenties and thirties, this was as good as it got and a far cry from living with the demented old Mrs. Cabot and her servants, pulling governess duty at the McKeans', or being mentally abused at the Millers'. There were some loyal servants and a peacock that swept around the garden, as well as a tiny pet deer and two black cocker spaniel puppies, Narcissus and Taugur.

Pritchard thought this move was not a good idea because "the girl is so utterly wanting in all experience, dignity and reserve that she will be the cause of further scandal." He also noted that Bapji, the crown prince, had suggested she should be invited to leave Udaipur even before the scandal with the swami broke because he was afraid she was mixing into local politics, which presumably meant the power struggles between himself and his father, the maharana.

Pritchard had two concerns about Opal. One was that by her scandalous behavior, which would be gossiped about for as long as she stayed, she would make Europeans look bad. "She has let the white woman down badly," he explained. Secondly, whoever she was, she would drag the d'Orléans family, "members of which are related to the King" into association with the sleazy Swami Duetanand's name. He asked his superiors if discovering she was a fake would provide sufficient grounds for "taking steps to get her out of Udaipur." After all this, Pritchard, who seems to have a had a soft spot for her, added, "There is no doubt that Mdlle D'Orlé is shrouded in some mystery. She was an orphan at the age of about seven and was brought up for some years in a lumber camp in America. That is her story and I believe it is true. She speaks English with a strong American accent, is practically unable to converse in French but writes it, probably very badly." After referring to Lord Grey's having written the introduction to her book, the gallant major stated, "I should like to make it clear that I feel certain the girl is absolutely virtuous."

Meanwhile the swami had been arrested for attempted suicide in Baroda and sentenced to five days. Among his papers the authorities found a diary indicating that he had married Opal in January on a trip to Lucknow, that they had honeymooned at the Lucknow Hotel, later rented and moved into a house there, and that Opal had gone back to Udaipur three weeks later. The attempted suicide was said to be motivated by the fact he had married Opal against his father's wishes.

At the request of the extremely thorough British authorities in India, who wanted to know exactly with whom they were dealing, Scotland Yard in London prepared a report about the mysterious woman in Udaipur. Detectives called on Putnam's London office, startling the staff there with questions about its author, but the report appears to have been based almost entirely on a reading of the American version of *The Story of Opal*. The anonymous detective reviewer said the book "contains the records of and by Mademoiselle d'Orlé when she was between the ages of 6 and 7 years. Viewed from the standpoint of an adult, the records are nonsensical. But being compiled by a child they are wisdom and the jottings of a precocious person. Her theme is that of a naturalist, and her characters are animals, birds and insects." Scotland Yard said that it had been unable to establish if the subject had ever been in England, and that it thought the introduction to her book was Lord Grey's "only connection to her."

While Captain Chevenix Trench may have been disgusted with Opal, his wife still found her charming. She wrote her a little note explaining that although her husband didn't want his family to be seen with her around town, this didn't mean she couldn't come over to the house, and it had been a while since she had come by.

In June 1925, after people had been trying to get her to leave Udaipur for at least three months, Chevenix Trench was startled to hear loud sobs coming from his drawing room. Opal, accompanied by a slightly rattled French priest described as a Normandy peasant, was collapsed in an armchair in tears. The manager of the Udaipur Hotel, where she had recently lived, had just been fired. Perhaps he suspected that Opal had something to do with it. Whatever his motive, he had written to Bapji accusing her of "misconduct" with the swami in the hotel and sent a copy to a local French priest, apparently not the one with her in the Chevenix Trench drawing room, but his superior.

Chevenix Trench told Opal she should leave town to protect her reputation. The priest agreed. She told Chevenix Trench she didn't have the money. The priest chimed in that she had only a stipend of two hundred rupees a month from the D'Orlé family, whom Opal had already said didn't really exist. The stipend may have come from Los Angeles department store heiress Marie Mullen. It is not clear where Opal's income did come from, beyond the room and board that were provided by Major Pritchard in his capacity as a representative of the British government.

An unsympathetic Chevenix Trench, writing to Pritchard, claimed she pulled out all the stops. "Her father's secret marriage, family against her, hence a stoppage of funds, all her cash spent on books, very lonely, hopes that an English gentleman would help her with comfort and advice etc. etc. I have just got rid of her."

Within two weeks Opal left Udaipur. Pritchard didn't know for sure, but he believed the maharana had asked her to leave. The hotel manager, presumably creeping around the corridor spying on the guests, as managers of respectable hotels were expected to do in America as well during this period, had managed to do what the highly motivated forces of the British Empire and the crown prince had been unable to do for months and got rid of Opal.

Once again Opal left under unhappy circumstances. It had been just ten months since Pritchard had welcomed her with open arms and made her a state guest and the ladies of the place had loaned her clothes to wear.

Opal went to Bombay, moved into the YWCA, and plotted to get back to Udaipur. Hearing that Pritchard was to be replaced as resident, she wrote the incoming official a four-page letter, saying she had heard such wonderful things about him from the people of Mewar and had heard that he was a true English gentleman. When he asked his staff who she was, he was told that she was a "pure adventuress," that everyone in town had been nice to her at first because they wanted a "puff" in her book, but that they all, from the maharana down, had soon tired of her. Opal also wrote the palace and hinted at coming back. The palace conferred with the British, saying it would suggest she not do so, and the British advised the crown prince that it would take a lot more than a suggestion to discourage her. Apparently the maharana had given her some hope that after Pritchard was replaced, she might get back in.

Opal was closely watched in Bombay by authorities who kept an eye out for any political activity or signs of a sex life. They reported, "She is engrossed in her work and entirely free from objection on political or moral grounds." In September she planned to hit the road. Her itinerary was to take her through the Sind, now in Pakistan, up to the Afghan border and along the Khyber Pass, back over to Delhi, and in November back to Udaipur, where she planned to spend the cold months. She agreed to submit her writing to censorship from all the local authorities where she traveled. She later wrote that during her time in India she had covered nearly nine thousand miles by train, oxen, camel, horse, and elephant.

As a teenager in Cottage Grove, Opal had become Elnora Comstock, the heroine of *Girl of the Limberlost*, the nature girl collecting butterflies in the forest. Now she had transformed herself into Henri d'Orléans. "Daddy's book," which she had with her, may well have been his *From Tonkin to India by the Sources of the Irawadi*. His journey had taken him from Hanoi to Calcutta, and like Opal, he had taken an interest in everything.

His book includes descriptions of women's headdresses and earrings, samples of written languages, and explanations of customs and ceremonies of every sort. He also brought back a collection of specimens, including sixty mammals, two hundred birds, and scores of butterflies and plants, as well as thirty vocabularies from various tribes. Both Opal and Henri d'Orléans were interested in long lists of specimens, and although her travels were not as systematic as his, she took pictures of everything, as did the prince, who later endorsed Kodak cameras in American advertisements.

Opal's devotion to Henri d'Orléans never wavered. She believed that many of her traits that she felt the Whiteleys did not possess were inherited from him. Steve Williamson, the Oregon Opal researcher, is also a mental health worker who once worked with schizophrenics. He looked for clues to where Opal may have gotten her ideas. Pointing out that the mentally ill often base their thoughts on "ear rhymes," he noted that her uncle Henry Pearson, the miner whom she initially said in press interviews and in *The Fairyland Around Us* had inspired her interest in nature, was actually named Henry D. Pearson. He speculated that in her mind she might have made the connection from "Henry D." to "Henri d'."

While she was on the road, Opal learned that Swami Duetanand was in legal trouble again. He was sentenced to two years for fraud, trying to get money in a scam in which he impersonated the son of an official. At the time of his arrest it was discovered that he had at least eleven aliases. It was eventually established that his real name was Murari Lal (his father identified him), that he had indeed dabbled in the politics of independence and been involved in Gandhi's organization, but that he was primarily a confidence man who told grandiose stories about himself. Friends wrote Opal and told her about it.

A few months later Opal received a letter from England. It was from an American tourist she had met in India, one of the Misses Parry who had mysteriously not appeared at the station when Opal set out on an unchaperoned tour of the region with the swami. Miss Parry wrote they'd had trouble finding Opal's husband's relatives when they went through Madras and signed off "God bless you and your noble husband." Many years later Opal wrote on this letter, "Strange. I never was married. That swindling swami. This is terrible. She was taken in by Major Pritchard's intrigues."

Murari Lal, aka Swami Duetanand, wrote her from prison in November, although he claimed he was on a pilgrimage and asked her to write him back care of his relatives. He wanted to know if they could be friends, rambled on in a near-delusional way about various adventures he had had, spouted simplistic philosophy, and reiterated that he was desolated by the loss of her love. Whereas Major Pritchard and Chevenix Trench clearly saw him as a cold-blooded confidence man who had set out to seduce, compromise, and blackmail Opal for financial gain, the letter sounds more like the work of a crazy, mixed-up kid who in his own mind really had been in love and was now heartbroken. Opal and the swami actually had a lot in common, including histories of multiple names and identities.

Opal was now trying to sell the book she was working on sight unseen. In December 1925 she received a telegram in Bombay from George Palmer Putnam, "Examination Manuscript Essential, Writing." Her draft reply said, "I shall await your letter. Meanwhile I am working on the manuscript."

Opal left the Lady Willingdon Hostel in Bombay, and the manager saw her off in January or February 1926, when she sailed for Italy. Before leaving, apparently incensed at the allegations about her affair with the swami, Opal aimed a parting shot at the British authorities in Bombay, providing them with a medical certificate of virginity from a local doctor. This information was duly passed on to Udaipur, where it was added to the secret file on Mlle. D'Orlé.

Nineteen

Opal arrived in Rome, which she now claimed as her birthplace. Her friend Marie Mullen, who had been sending her money in India, wrote how relieved she was that Opal was "safe" in the care of nuns of the Monastery of the Sacred Heart, where she was a paying guest.

Opal opened an account at the Banco di Roma in the name of Principessa Francesca Henriette Marguerite d'Orléans. The account was constantly overdrawn. After the receipt of polite letters addressed to "Signora Principessa" and mentioning her overdrafts, Opal would stanch the flow of red ink with deposits from American friends for amounts ranging from twenty to two hundred dollars. These supporters, including rich ladies from Los Angeles with whom she was in correspondence, appear to have been Opal's sole source of income while she was in Rome. One of the women sent packets of ten-dollar bills.

One correspondent said she didn't dare sign her letter, as it wasn't safe. Some of these people believed that there was some dark conspiracy against Opal, perhaps along the lines of the one she outlined to Pritchard in which the Communists were after both her and Marie Antoinette's lace. Opal was now living a bizarre existence in which she believed she was in danger from some intrigue surrounding the pretenders to the throne of France.

Opal wrote her friend Maude MacDonald, the preacher's wife in Oregon, that she had worked very hard on her book about India for two years, but there was some kind of conspiracy to make sure it never got put before the public.

Opal was getting most of her mail through someone named Hilda Barnard in New York, of whom nothing is known. She said that it wasn't safe for people to know where she was. On her outgoing letters she listed "Somewhere in Fairyland" or "Somewhere in Fairyland Among the Flowers" as the return address. Those who sent money, however, knew her actual whereabouts.

A fervent letter found among Opal's effects began, "I had two other visitors today," and it went on, "I see that in Italy you are not safe. So do *exactly* what I tell you for it is in your own interest. Leave Rome exactly on Friday and go right out of Italy. When you are in Austria, let me know your exact address so that I can let you know what happens as it is important for you. Except for your papers you must keep your incognito Loraine [sic]. D'O . . . is not safe. As soon as you are in Austria I will write and explain you all about it. Now I cannot do so. Do not return here now. It would not be safe. Later on we shall see. Happy journey on Friday. Tear up this note."

It is not clear who wrote this letter, addressed to "Dear Child," signed "M. S. Salm," and sent from the Monastery of the Sacred Heart in Rome, but it is reminiscent, with its injunction to destroy the note, of the B.C.M. letters Sedgwick had traced to Opal's rented typewriter. Perhaps the letter writer was someone in Rome equally as desperate as Major Pritchard had been to get rid of an unwelcome guest. In any case, Opal seems to have taken the advice in the note and left town in a hurry.

A chest and suitcase were rounded up from several locations in Rome and sent on to Vienna, care of someone named Giovanni Rossi, of whom, like Hilda Barnard, nothing is known. Opal also spent some time in the Lord Jesus Student Home there, although she was now nearly thirty. She later said that during this period she lived in what she called an "imperial convent," perhaps because it was near a palace of the Hapsburgs, planning eventually to take her vows. The convent was run not by the former Austro-Hungarian Empire but by the Sisters of the Visitation of Mary, a contemplative order founded by St. Francis de Sales with a strict vow of poverty.

Opal continued to have worldly interests, however, such as trying to sell her book on India to George Palmer Putnam. She told him the photographs were fabulous, and she had some great tiger shots. She had also received permission from the Rome Zoo to photograph its tigers. She may have been trying to enhance the photo collection for the book. All the tigers in her India pictures were dead.

Opal now showed some interest in getting back in touch with her past. She wrote Nellie Hemenway, back in Oregon, telling her to write care of the mysterious Hilda Barnard. "This part of the letter is secret," she wrote of her accommodation address. "Later I will tell you where I am." Opal also asked Nellie, who was now the wife of Carl Price, whom she had met as a young army officer during the war, and the mother of a little boy, Thomas, to find out what she could about the Whiteley girls. "Particularly I am anxious to hear about Chloe as she was born to them while I lived with them at Walden and I had the care of her when a baby. . . . I had much affection for her and would like to hear from her." It isn't known if Nellie tracked down the Whiteley girls, now living under an assumed name because of the scandal Opal had created years before.

Opal also got back in touch with Ella Cabot, and explained that "since the war many of my dear Angel Mother's family live in poverty so we are scattered everywhere." She told her that she had forgiven the cruel Millers as Jesus wanted her to. She also let the Cabots know that they had also caused her pain because of their attitude to Angel Mother and Father. Presumably they did not believe they existed. Her name, she told them firmly, was Françoise. She also made arrangements for a Mrs. Mark Potter to go into a safe-deposit box at the Riggs National Bank in Washington, D.C., remove some lace from it, and send it to her in Europe by registered mail. Was this the lace said to have belonged to Marie Antoinette that she had told Pritchard about? What was it doing in Washington?

At the convent Opal lived in a room full of research materials and notes. By her own count there were forty-two shoeboxes and twenty-two large cartons. There was also a stuffed kingfisher, which she said had belonged to Henri d'Orléans. The mother superior was apparently taken rather aback by the collection but allowed her to keep it because it was orderly. Opal said she was working on her "nature work," studying crickets among other things, as well as spending much time at prayer.

In her books about Opal, Elizabeth Bradburne Lawrence quoted from a letter to Putnam's English publisher, Constant Huntington, in which Opal wrote that in Vienna she met some "kind people" she had known as a child and referred to "a dear historic house we lived in, it was filled with the shadows of the past, memories of the whole Empire." Up to this point Opal had never been clear about who Angel Mother was, but from this time on it seems she believed her to be an Austrian archduchess. There is no record of Henri d'Orléans's marrying an archduchess or anyone else.

By May 1928 Putnam had rejected her Indian manuscript, *River of Romance*, about the Indus River, on the ground that it was "not sufficiently interesting" and that it was also "frankly, just a bit unintelligible." A month later she left the convent and went to England.

Opal later explained her departure from the convent by saying she had been told by the nuns that her place was in the world. She left some boxes of manuscripts and books behind, and she owed Sister Françoise de Sales forty-seven schillings and eighty-eight groschen. She eventually repaid this, and she asked the nuns to sell the books she had left behind and send her the proceeds. For some years afterward she received affectionate letters from Sister Françoise, who wrote her in French, calling her "Ma Chica chérie," "Petit choux," and "chère petite Princesse" and referring to herself as "Petite Maman." Sister Françoise was a rightwing Frenchwoman of a royalist bent interested in *"la vrai France"* and the nationalist symbol, Joan of Arc.

Up until this time Opal's affection for "Daddy," Prince Henri d'Orléans, was connected primarily to what she claimed to remember of him from childhood and his books and his reputation as a scientist and explorer, sharing her love of nature and "going on explores." Now, in the conservative milieu of a Catholic convent, she began to add the political views of the d'Orléans family to her eclectic portfolio of beliefs.

In February 1898, when Opal was a baby, in Paris, novelist Émile Zola was on trial for libel for writing "J'accuse," a courageous statement in support of Captain Alfred Dreyfus, the Jewish Frenchman falsely accused by anti-Semitic military brass of selling secrets to the Germans.

The accusation was supported by forged documents. While Dreyfus languished in chains on Devil's Island, sentenced to life, the real culprit, Major Ferdinand Esterhazy, went free. The affair caught the attention of the world and polarized France.

Henri d'Orléans's cousin and old tiger-hunting buddy the duke of Orléans was pretender to the throne of France. He hoped the wave of nationalism and antirepublicanism, which was enmeshed with conservative Catholicism, militarism, and anti-Semitism, would result in the overthrow of the republic and the restoration of the monarchy.

The duke of Orléans had been rather a joke figure up until then, little more than the subject of society gossip, but the Dreyfus affair and the resulting nationalistic fervor had given new life to his ambitions to regain the throne. He provided a regular subsidy from the family fortune to the frankly named Anti-Semitic League, with branches all over France. The Anti-Semitic League was led by Jules Guérin, publisher of a newspaper titled just as blatantly *L'Anti-Juif*, or the Anti-Jew. The hysteria included allegations that a murky "syndicate," a secret conspiracy of Germans and Jews, threatened France. The Anti-Semitic League eventually took an active part in a plot to overturn the French republic, resulting in the rifle-toting Guérin's receiving a ten-year sentence after holding off five thousand troops in a month-long, Waco-style siege on the organization's headquarters in the rue Chabrol. During Zola's trial, the duke of Orléans provided an additional stipend of fifty-six thousand francs to the Anti-Semitic League. And while a howling mob of anti-Semitic thugs lobbed tomatoes and spit at Zola outside the courthouse, Opal's Angel Father, Henri d'Orléans, representing the family, made a dramatic appearance outside the courthouse to shake hands with and praise the real traitor, Major Esterhazy.

The association of anti-Semitism with French monarchism has lasted to the present day. When I began my research, the French Embassy in Washington gave me the phone number of a man in Houston who was said to represent the current pretender's interests in the United States. I spoke with this affable Texan on the phone. He seemed to be involved in efforts to restore various European monarchs to their thrones and was most optimistic about Simeon of Bulgaria but said he had severed his connection with the "support group" for the d'Orléans claim because there was a competing claim, which had attracted the support of some of his "European buddies" in the Knights of Malta, and he noted also that he had discovered anti-Semitic elements were involved in the d'Orléans cause.

It's no wonder that the reactionary nun took to Opal and her d'Orléans name. Opal in turn took on the repellent ideology of the d'Orléans family, explaining in a letter as late as the 1930s, when Hitler was firmly entrenched as German chancellor, that the First World War had been the result of a German Jewish conspiracy.

Opal's politics were always tied in to her current image and changed as she reinvented herself. As a Junior Christian Endeavor worker she had lobbied against alcohol and didn't approve of dancing—positions she later shed. When she learned that the d'Orléans family championed reactionary French and anti-Semitic nationalism, she took that on board. But essentially her politics, if they could be called that, were really always about Opal.

Now in her thirties, Opal was described as "a shabby little woman" by an English friend, Elizabeth, countess of Iddesleigh. No longer was she referred to as a child. But despite her fading charms, she was still able to mingle with important people. She was mentioned in occasional society columns and was asked to preside at the opening of the La Sagesse Convent School in Golders Green.

Years later the countess of Iddesleigh said she met Opal after her return from "the East" at the home of Lord Grey, but only Lady Grey was present. Before the first meeting, Lady Iddesleigh quoted Lord Grey as saying, "We have a French Princess coming to tea—you will have a lot in common because she is a Roman Catholic."

A widower when he had met Opal in Boston and been enchanted, Lord Grey had now remarried. His new wife, who believed she had a connection to the d'Orléans family through an illegitimate birth in her own family tree and who was also interested in the occult, took to Opal immediately.

Lord Grey's interest in her, however, cooled. Her appeal to him had been as a delightful, pure child, and he had even offered to help support her. After she'd been a year in England, Opal wrote Sedgwick that she had seen Lord Grey "but once" since her return to England and that he had given her a reference to live in the Catholic hostel in London.

Lady Iddesleigh, who said that Lady Grey had told her Opal had been denounced to the Inquisition, perhaps in some fracas with the nuns in Vienna, commented, "I liked the poor thing. You could see she was poor." Opal's source of income at this point was a mystery. She seems to have continued to receive handouts from well-wishers in America.

Lady Iddesleigh once wrote of her belief in Opal's noble origins, "What is there not to believe?" but when the countess was asked by authorities in England if she didn't think Opal's claims had been "one great hoax," she was quoted as replying, "It is funny you should say that because although [she] stayed with very important people and seemed to have a large circle of friends in Catholic and Anglo-Catholic circles, nevertheless, when I took her to see my mother on one occasion, my mother said afterwards 'I think the woman is bogus.' " Lady Iddesleigh's mother was Marie Belloc Lowndes, the detective novelist, whose novel about Jack the Ripper *The Lodger* was perhaps her most famous work. The puzzled countess said, however, she was sure Opal was "a lady" and described her as "a pathetic little figure."

She also reported that Lord Grey had never quite made up his mind about Opal's bona fides, an opinion backed up by a letter about Opal from publisher Constant Huntington to the countess of Warwick that said Grey never considered her "a conscious impostor."

In July 1929 Opal was living in Kensington near the Natural History Museum at 42 Emperor's Gate, a charming triangular square with a tiny triangular gated garden in its center. She was back in touch with Ellery Sedgwick in Boston and attempted to sell him a series of articles about India, which she said was a description of her continuation of her father's geographic work. Since the death of her grandmère, she explained, she would have to earn her own living. The duchess of Chartres had indeed died while Opal was in India. Marie Mullen had read about it in the papers and sent her the news. The letter to Sedgwick pitching the book was signed Françoise de Bourbon-Orléans with "Opal" in quotation marks tucked into a corner. The d'Orléans were related to the Bourbons, but no family members used this double-barreled form, and there is no explanation of how Opal came to use it.

Sedgwick immediately wrote to Dr. Richard C. Cabot, saying he had heard from Opal and wanted to discuss the situation in person, noting, "I am not certain whether she is quite normal." Why did he want to talk to Cabot, who had suppressed the diary six years before and spirited away the manuscript? To get his professional opinion of her sanity? A memo from someone on *The Atlantic Monthly* staff, while saying the material had charm, began, "I am afraid of her. Is she or is she not sane? And she wants us to take enough to fill the magazine for a couple of years and to pay her large sums." In an interoffice memo, Sedgwick asked an assistant, "Do you think the child [Opal was then thirty-one] is entirely herself?" The reply: "I fear we had better keep entirely free from her."

But Sedgwick seemed unable to do so. He kept stalling and dangling the possibility of publishing some of her articles. Was he nervous that she would reveal she had been forced to sign a document that was clearly not in her best interest? Or was he genuinely enchanted by her and unable to resist, despite all the trouble he'd been through on the last go-round? Or both?

When Opal offered him the India stories, he told her that he saw the same charm that he had seen in her diary and that his children often asked after her. Sedgwick did turn down the same book that Putnam had refused, about the Indus River, describing it as "disorganized and wandering," but he said he would be interested in a piece titled "The Children's Kingdom." He insisted, however, on some proof of its authenticity on the grounds that while thousands of people had enjoyed her diary, "other thousands, even though they liked the book, think it was written in mature years." He brought the Cabots, "your old friends," into it, saying that he would consult them about this but that "they are out west." He asked to see her passport and to get some people in India to vouch for her, so he would know she'd actually been there.

Opal's imperious reply demanded a full explanation for his rejection of the book about the Indus River and two thousand dollars for a series of articles with an immediate down payment of five hundred dollars.

She told him it was in his best interest to pay her well, for "if you do not I will simply not allow you the opportunities of having anything else." She pointed out that "many people will be interested in my journey because they loved the diary and many *thousands* will be interested in this series because it is so *unique*. It will never be done again."

Warning him against taking advice from others, she wrote bossily, "You are old enough and capable enough to decide about things for yourself. When you act alone, I trust you. When you act upon the advice given you by different people, I mistrust you. . . . I warn you to be careful about taking and acting upon the advice of your various 'friends' or else you will lose my trust again." Perhaps she thought that Dr. Cabot would advise Sedgwick she was mentally ill. She said she would not send him her passport as it was "quite against the law" but would arrange for someone in England to examine it and report back to him.

Somehow Sedgwick learned that Opal made her journey from India to Europe with a French passport in the name of Mlle. Françoise Marguerite Henriette Marie Alice Léopodine d'Orléans. Whether he saw this passport or not is not clear. It was most likely viewed by a third party in London, who passed along the information. Sedgwick said the passport stated that "the lady is given permission to return to France from her archeological journey in India."

Why a French national would need permission to return home is rather mysterious, as is how she got this passport in the first place. If she did have a passport with this name on it, it's strange she refused to show it to Major Pritchard when he demanded it, for it would have supported her story.

One of Opal's last aristocratic friends, Mia Woodruff, later said Opal got rid of her American passport in India and replaced it with French papers. Mrs. Woodruff saw a document in Opal's possession, bearing a tricolor, "very grand and official-looking," from the French consul in Madras, India. Mrs. Woodruff told documentary maker Ian Taylor in a video interview taped before her death that the document said, "This lady tells me she has lost her passport and honoring what she tells me I issue her with this travel document." Mrs. Woodruff said Opal was very proud of the document.

Now that he was again in contact with Opal, Sedgwick tried to get some back story on her time with the New York theosophists and he asked her how involved she had been with the legal struggles he and Hargrove had gone through. Sedgwick always remained entranced by Opal. He seemed to want to know if her antipathy had really been her idea.

Opal wrote Sedgwick, "No, I have never known anything which took place in yours and the lawyers [*sic*] discussions. I was never allowed to know anything except that you said I had a French dictionary." She said she had been under "complete restraint" from the day she arrived at the Millers' until she escaped a year and a half later. Any contracts she signed in that period, she maintained, were illegal, and then, perhaps giving Sedgwick pause, she added that Dr. Cabot "is *not* my friend— since he signed a treacherous agreement. . . . The agreement he drew up in Putnam's office had no consideration whatever."

She had a point there. If a lawyer had drawn up the agreement, she might at least have received a dollar in consideration to make it legal. She also informed Sedgwick that she had a copy of the Cabot agreement safely in the bank. Opal wrote, "He Dr. Cabot was to have my diary. . . . I had previously told him 'no' . . . always when he talked of the diary. I said I would take it home to France." This was not true. Actually she had turned it over quite willingly during the happiest period of her life when France seemed far from her mind. Now she said that because she had poured her love of her Angel Parents as well as "my dear little friends of the woods" into the diary, it belonged with the d'Orléans family. "It was all I had to bring back except my character of a good girl."

Opal said the diary fragments belonged not to the public but to "her and me," presumably the duchess of Chartres, and, mysteriously, "now this dear one who loves me dearer than life always keeps them [diary fragments] near her bed. In these fragments she feels given back to her a part of my sad years in America." There is no clue to who this person might be. It sounds like the duchess of Chartres, but she had been dead for some time. Opal signed off with "I won't tolerate other people interfering. I simply won't stand for it."

Meanwhile, just as he had years before, Sedgwick asked her for names of people to vouch for her veracity, and letters began to arrive from old India hands. Captain Handcock, who had bought her the one-way ticket to Marseilles, wrote back a starchy letter that seemed to imply Sedgwick was a cad for doubting her, and referring to her as S.A.R, presumably short for *son altesse royale*.

Lady Pinhey, a niece of General Chinese Gordon, and Lieutenant Colonel Hunt, whose wife had given Opal a cocker spaniel, also wrote effusively. Bapji's private secretary sent a cool note saying that Opal had stayed in Udaipur from September 1924 to about June 1925 and had "moved extensively about in the State." Chevenix Trench, who had thrown her boyfriend the swami off his property and plotted to get Opal kicked out too, sent a cagily worded reply. He reported she had worked for up to sixteen hours a day on her book and got genuine details of the lives and customs of the people. "I know that she penetrated to corners to which no European had ever before found his or her way, and witnessed rites and ceremonies to which no European had hitherto been admitted."

He said she'd had her own carriage, had attended a dinner for the prince and princess Arthur of Connaught, enjoyed the "rare privilege" of going hunting with the maharana, "and had an adventure with a charging tiger, which mounted, I was informed, her elephant." He added that Opal's "fearlessness and unconventionality involved her in situations not altogether free from danger."

In his correspondence with Opal, Sedgwick assumed that someone important—namely, the duchess of Chartres, must have paved her way. Opal replied that her success was based on her own efforts. She pointed out that she made contacts all by herself and that her openness to Indian culture and religion and her respect for Indians had given her an advantage over the British in gaining access.

Sedgwick wrote Opal back to say that he now believed she had been in India, but he wouldn't print the article under her royal name without proof that she was entitled to it. Opal had told him the duchess of Chartres, now dead, had accepted her but that other family members hadn't. He wanted an explanation to give his readers of just how Opal had made the "transition" to Françoise Bourbon-d'Orléans.

Opal, disgusted, asked him to send back *The Children's Kingdom*. The idea that linking "my true name with the nom-de-plume and sad life of Opal Whiteley in America might cause a great sale of the Children's Kingdom" was detestable to her. Anyway, she said she already had a book partly written, explaining how Opal had become Françoise. "I do not want idle curiosity beforehand until 2 or 3 years when I will have written the complete story of my life." She also objected to his use of the word "transition" to describe the metamorphosis. "[I]t was the princess in America, only incognito and treated generally as a nurse-maid."

Referring to her father's "ideal of work," which she said she shared, she explained, "We do not live by a great name but try to make our work worthy of that tradition by doing it thoroughly and as perfectly as possible with our whole heart and bodily force and soul devoted to the task at hand." The work, she said, would "stand on its own merits and does not need any romance to bolster it up." She added, "I *never* was an American citizen. I was always an Alien & *never* had an American passport."

A month later she had second thoughts. She cabled him that she would offer him *The Children's Kingdom* under the name Mademoiselle Françoise. Opal offered a promotional copy approach, suggesting he use the line 'Opal Comes Back'—explaining "that I wish only to be called Mlle Françoise—that I have gone on further explores than the Diary time (with many of the same feelings that I had then). As my name Françoise is mentioned in the diary Françoise going [on] farther 'explores' makes unnecessary any reference to my family."

In five separate envelopes she sent him twenty thousand words of material about India and said she would provide a total of thirty-five or forty thousand words for the upcoming magazine series. The book would be sixty thousand words. "I would appreciate receiving $2000," she wrote, going on for three pages to explain how special the work was, as it would include "the little animals" too, and how much she was loved in India.

It was too late. Sedgwick had finally had it. He met with Dr. Cabot to discuss Opal. In setting up the meeting, Cabot wrote, "The story I have to tell is extraordinary, but rather sad." Perhaps he was breaking it to Sedgwick that Opal, whom he had once loved, had mental problems.

After the meeting Sedgwick wrote Opal a letter that crossed with hers, saying that he couldn't work with her if she distrusted him and pointing out that he had discussed this with Dr. Cabot. Opal had expressly asked him not to discuss her with Dr. Cabot as "he is not my friend." On the subject of Dr. Cabot, Sedgwick explained: "So far as I know, he has done you nothing but kindness." He pointed out that she had a habit of turning on people and used Mrs. Griscom as an example. He also told her that whatever position in life she found herself in, it wouldn't hurt to be courteous to others. He ended the letter, "I am anxious and ready to help you if you give me the opportunity," and he returned all her manuscripts.

Sedgwick was also in communication with Opal's old friend Maude MacDonald of Myrtle Point, Oregon, on the subject of Opal. Mrs. MacDonald pleaded with him to publish Opal's work on India. She was also worried about Opal and believed there was a huge conspiracy surrounding her. She was convinced that Opal's mail was often confiscated by mysterious agents. Mrs. MacDonald said she had it on good authority that the duchess of Chartres had arranged for Opal's true name to be restored to her by the French government, that she had received letters from Opal in India, "where she was initially a prisoner," that someone with influence in "the legislature there" had interfered with the publication of her book on India "because it revealed facts . . . which officials did not want published."

Sedgwick wrote back to Mrs. MacDonald, hinting at insanity. "I have wondered how well she is. She often writes under a great strain, like a person whose mind is exhausted."

In her reply Mrs. MacDonald offered more details of the conspiracies that Opal believed swirled around her. Mrs. MacDonald, an unsophisticated woman in an isolated area, fully believed that "the most powerful and intriguing and shrewd system of detective's system on earth held her" and that Opal had been held captive on several occasions for years at a time. "Please destroy this letter," wrote Mrs. MacDonald. "I hardly know how much I dare mention." Noting that two of Opal's bitterest enemies had died, the pious Mrs. MacDonald expressed the unchristian hope that Opal's other enemies would die soon, so that "her grave danger of molestation will be over." Mrs. MacDonald conceded that at times Opal's mind didn't quite seem normal, but she felt the strains of international conspiracies would unhinge anyone. In another vein, Mrs. MacDonald tried to pitch some of her own writing to *The Atlantic* and said she had lots of short pieces that she thought were worth five dollars each.

Sedgwick's caution toward Opal's new material was understandable. He'd been through a huge mess with Opal the first time around. Since then he had been approached by an ex-actress named Wilma Frances Minor with a collection of love letters said to have been written by Abraham Lincoln, which Sedgwick had published and which proved to be forgeries (Minor's defense was that the letters came from the spirit world through her mother, a trance medium.) Attracted as he was to Opal, he couldn't bring himself to risk the embarrassment of billing her under the d'Orléans name.

Although Sedgwick eventually bailed out, Opal had been simultaneously selling a book on India to Putnam's. Constant Huntington of the London office had already given her half of a hundred-pound advance for a British version. Within a month of Sedgwick's rejection, Opal had dinner with George Palmer Putnam in London when he was visiting Europe, at Huntington's house, and she made her pitch for an American edition of this book about India.

When she didn't hear from Putnam within forty-eight hours, she fired off a letter, clearly composed with the help of someone who knew something about law and business. She said she needed a decision from Putnam and a contract for the book immediately because she needed money. She wanted two hundred pounds up front, but she didn't want the name Opal Whiteley connected with the new work in any way. She pointed out that she had signed their previous contacts under coercion at the Millers' and that she wanted the royalties she had signed away in the agreement with Dr. Cabot. She also complained that one of the contracts she'd signed with Putnam gave him the right to her family papers and life story, and she repudiated that clause.

The letter was very firm and included a complete copy of the ridiculous agreement Dr. Cabot had drawn up and Putnam and she had signed, a copy of which, she told Putnam, as she had told Sedgwick, was safely in the bank. "In 1919, 1920, 1922 and early in 1923," she wrote, "Dr. Cabot tried again and again to get my papers from me, particularly certain things relative to the family for his psychology studies. . . . That paper of March 1923 was pure treachery on his part. He and others, when they were not able to do what they wanted, hinted at my not being quite all mentally there."

Unfortunately, this makes Dr. Cabot, who later endowed a chair of ethics at Harvard and was the author of books titled *Honesty* and *The Meaning of Right and Wrong*, look rather shabby. He knew she was unstable. Nevertheless, he got her to sign away an important asset without any advice from anyone. She said the papers were "coaxed" from her on the grounds that there were people after her "like hounds," and the diary was given to him to be kept safe, a recollection not supported by letters she wrote at the time.

This letter seems to have got Putnam's attention, even though he had other things on his mind. His wife, Dorothy, a Crayola crayon heiress, was getting a Reno divorce from him that month, the marriage apparently busted up by Amelia Earhart. In a firm letter, Putnam told Opal not to make wild accusations about her friends and advisers and said he wouldn't change her contract with him regarding *The Story of Opal*. Her royalties had been withheld, he explained, to cover Putnam's cost of buying the plates from *The Atlantic Monthly*.

But he seemed to have had a change of heart. He subsequently told Huntington to go ahead and pay Opal $191.30 for the unpaid royalties that she had waived in the Cabot agreement and added, "In accordance with her request we are canceling the agreement of March 17, 1923 of which Dr. Cabot is a part." He also said he would also cancel the contract masterminded by Hargrove with the clause signing over her life story to Putnam. Putnam, now back in New York, put the offending contracts in an envelope, mailed them to London, and instructed Huntington: "Please destroy in her presence."

This solution to an embarrassing problem does not have the air of having been run by the legal department. Presumably, canceling the agreement in writing would have been more official. Of course, Dr.

Cabot still had the diary, or at least he was the last person to have had it. But the gesture seemed to have mollified Opal. George Palmer Putnam, however, was not out of the woods yet. Opal now began to write him letters declaring her love. Putnam, while negotiating the publicity fallout from his divorce and planning marriage to his protégée Amelia Earhart, was writing Opal frequently, trying to calm her down.

He now addressed his letters to Princess Françoise de Bourbon-Orléans, and they began "Dear Françoise." In January 1930, a month after he'd arranged to have her contracts torn up, he strongly advised against her coming to America: "I think the thing for you to do is carry on cooperating with Mr. Huntington." Two days later he again advised her not to come and said he'd be out of town anyway. A week after that, he again told her he'd be away a good deal and promised her an English visit soon. He wrote her on January 30 in the fourth letter in the month, that even if she came to America, she couldn't see him every day, and it would be "much pleasanter to meet in London."

By February she had backed off, and he was busy trying to sell magazine rights to her India material. But a few weeks later he informed her that he had to be "brutally frank" and that he was engaged to marry an American girl, and that he was too old for her anyway. (Actually, Opal and his fiancée were born only a couple of months apart.) Opal had written him that he reminded her of her "dear Angel Father." Opal apparently replied that she understood, but a few weeks later Putnam told her she must not write any more letters "in this vein," that he was in love with someone else, and that she, Opal, was being carried away by her emotions of the moment. Opal later wrote cryptically in the margin of this letter, "10 years is not a *moment*."

In November, Putnam and Earhart got a marriage license, and although there was no public announcement of any forthcoming marriage, Opal knew enough about it to send Amelia Earhart a note via Putnam, which he promised to forward.

Putnam seemed terrified of offending Opal. He made a point of giving her his new home and office address, keeping in touch. Eventually he broke the news to her that he had married Amelia Earhart and later thanked her for the "sweet" letter Opal had written Amelia, which she said he was sure Amelia would be answering soon. Among Opal's papers was a Christmas card from Putnam and Earhart, showing them in a cartoon airplane with photographed heads.

Why did Putnam treat her so gingerly instead of simply cutting her off? He seemed to have gone out of her life at this point, but Constant Huntington continued to cater to her, allowing her to use his office in London as an accommodation address, storing trunks and books for her for years, and writing her many kind and patient letters over the years about her India book, which never materialized.

Huntington did, however, manage to get *Queen* magazine to publish a series of articles on India, under the byline Princess Françoise Marie de Bourbon-Orléans. The articles were unevenly written and contained such sentences as "To dwell in Udaipur for long is but to become the weaver of a small portion of the loom of beauty, because one has so many materials with which to work, and there is an urge to find words for what cannot be described, but is a mantle to one's thoughts and a boat in which to journey along the river of imagination."

Mia Woodruff later said the article had been ghosted, but they clearly show Opal's hand. At one point she compared blue butterflies in India to the ones she knew in Oregon and the articles were full of praise for the maharana and Crown Prince Bapji, who she said were so kind and helpful when "an annoying Swami had been most troubling." The pieces were full of Mewar history and praise for the heroic qualities of the clans of Rajputana, and there were also pretty descriptions of birds, plants, and animals. Opal was a talented photographer, and her accompanying pictures were well composed. *Queen* readers learned that Opal had stopped off in Udaipur on her way to Dar Lac in Indochina, "my father's last field of exploration," and that the author was "the last descendant of the two great houses of France and the daughter of the explorer Henri d'Orléans." She referred at one point to "my *noblesse oblige* courage."

The Whiteley girls in Oregon saw a copy of one of the articles. They were shocked to see the author's picture accompanying it. Thirty-two-year-old Opal looked thin, tired, pale, and drawn, with circles under her eyes, her hair now bobbed. She was wearing a gigantic cross on a wide black ribbon.

Some old India hands who remembered her cutting a wide swath around the palace five years earlier saw the articles and looked her up. They too were shocked when they went to visit her and found her in a grim little one-room flat lined with portrait miniatures of the d'Orléans family.

Twenty

*O*pal had ordered the miniatures on her wall from a company in Paris that made antique reproductions. The wholesale firm of Léon Lévy specialized in furniture, paintings, engravings, prints, pastels, gouaches, and miniatures, among other objects. In reply to her first order, it assured Madame Marie de Bourbon, a new alias, that it would make an exact copy of the postcard she had sent, very finely executed on ivory, for three hundred francs or about twelve 1930 dollars, worth about $120 today. Turnaround time was two weeks.

Opal promptly sent five more postcards and ordered more miniatures of royal personages throughout the centuries who were related to the d'Orléans family. At one point there were sixteen in the pipeline, guaranteed to be made by hand. Correspondence about dimensions, oval versus rectangular frames, and materials, such as parchment and leather, flew back and forth across the English Channel, the Lévys once explaining they had trouble finding elephant ivory of the proper dimensions. Soon Opal owed the Lévy family thousands of francs, but they continued to do business with her, and she kept the flow of miniatures coming with occasional payments on account.

Opal became quiet friendly with Mme. Lévy, a war widow who ran the business with her children. The friendship lapsed, however, after Opal's outstanding balance proved too difficult to collect. Polite but firm requests for payment were tactfully paired with hopes she was not in ill health as it had been some time since they had heard from her. When Opal did settle, she tried to return a few of the customized miniatures for credit, which the ever-patient Lévys agreed to accept. The postcards of royal portraits came from another Paris business that specialized in reproductions of paintings in museums all over Europe.

The episode of the miniatures was yet another example of Opal's life taking on the details of a Gene Stratton-Porter novel from her childhood. In Stratton-Porter's *Freckles*, the scruffy orphan lad working in the wilderness for a timber company is presented a miniature on ivory of his dead mother when he learns he is actually of aristocratic birth, related to Lord and Lady O'More of County Clare.

Opal wrote Nellie Hemenway and reported that she was continuing "my father's books on geographical subjects." She also said she had been elected to many of the scientific societies to which her father had belonged. This wasn't strictly true. She had written to the societies, asking to join, and at least some were open to anyone who wanted to pay a membership fee. Opal also asked Nellie for pictures of her son, Tom, and pictures of the three children of Nellie's sister Florence. She wrote: "I am always praying God to send me a dear husband and babies. I hope He will some day." Nellie, whom she had always patronized, was now an object of her envy. While Opal had been racketing around the world, Nellie had led a much quieter life. She wrote Opal all about her thimble collection.

Opal's religious interests continued. During this period she sent a telegram to the pope, telling him about an encyclical concerning the Holy Ghost that God wished him to write, and signed it Françoise Paraclete Orléans, Paraclete being a name for the Holy Ghost. Opal moved for a time in the early 1930s to Oxford, where she hoped to be taken into All Souls Priory and take vows there. She spent many hours praying and saying the rosary.

In 1933 she made another attempt to sell her material on India to Sedgwick. Opal reported to him that she was hard at work on her "theology studies" and that she spent a lot of time in the Bodleian Library and prayed a lot. Sedgwick's long fascination with Opal continued. He wrote Nellie Hemenway, and asked if he could see all the letters Opal had sent over the years. Nellie replied, politely and very correctly. She had gathered intelligence on Opal for him many years before only because she'd had Opal's written permission to do so. She didn't think it would be right to share Opal's letters with Sedgwick because nearly every one of them enjoined her to silence. "Although I am of many minds about her story," wrote Nellie, "and though I think I see many flaws in it, I yet have a feeling of personal loyalty to her."

She may well have felt sorry for her too. Opal's letters had become repetitious and rather pitiful. They were filled with information about the d'Orléans family. In her letters, Opal often repeated that she was praying for a dear baby and a dear husband. "Do you have a garden?" she wrote Nellie wistfully. While Opal lived in tiny basement flats, Nellie had a large garden with stately oak trees and was an innovator in landscaping with native species. She was a prominent member of the Portland Gardening Club, at one time writing and editing its newsletter. She had a handsome shingled house in the Arts and Crafts style with some colonial touches. (Her brother Roscoe who designed it went on to be a very successful Portland architect.) The house was beautifully furnished with oriental rugs, a horsehair sofa with down cushions, and a special needlepoint fire screen designed by her architect brother. Nellie's nephew told me she was always in demand socially because she was intelligent and a good conversationalist. Her letters to Opal, however, tactfully played down her good fortune.

While living in Oxford, Opal was back in the news in America, and in *The Oregonian*, and Elbert Bede was back on the story. "There comes now from far India a strange sequel," he reported. A "Human Side of the News" syndicated column by Edwin C. Hill, a nationally known newspaperman and radio broadcaster, had appeared in newspapers around the country. This story was the source of many untrue rumors about Opal that have been since passed from source to source and have been accepted as fact.

Hill claimed that in secret files in the State Department "lies buried a romantic secret," a document signed by Charles Evans Hughes, former secretary of state, and possibly also signed by Lord Grey, about Opal Whiteley and her true origins. It went on to say that an American woman traveling in Udaipur who knew Opal claimed to have seen her in a bright carriage sitting up very straight under a crimson silk parasol. The carriage was flanked by a half troop of Indian cavalry officers on coal-black horses. The woman made inquiries and learned Opal was living in the palace. When she tried to visit Opal, she was told the ladies of the palace did not receive callers. The woman later learned from a British official in another princely state, Dr. Rushford Williams, that Opal was a child of the comte d'Artois, "of the old royal house of France," and a Hindu princess, and "none other than the granddaughter of the old Maharana of Udaipur." The article claimed that Opal had left America in March 1923, "not with an ordinary passport but with a confidential document signed by the Secretary of State of the United States and by the Ambassador of the King of England and the Emperor of India."

Hill quoted Ellery Sedgwick at length from what he said was "a letter to this writer." Sedgwick said Opal had sent him the material on her trip to India from London, noting that she was said to be following the footsteps of Henri d'Orléans. Sedgwick added that he'd seen photographs of the trip and had written to several maharajas, "and from the secretaries of at least two of the courts I got formal assurances of the correctness of her story. Opal Whiteley never told me under whose auspices she went, but I think beyond question the old Orléans dowager, now dead, countenanced her. At any rate she was everywhere accepted as an authentic princess, and I received several letters from Englishmen of position saying that they had seen her at important levees, and that she had been shown signal favor in accompanying one maharajah at least, on a tiger hunt, with all the trappings appropriate to a visit of royalty."

Despite what the Hill article said, Opal had never lived in the palace but in a hotel and later a guesthouse. She was not escorted by troops of cavalry and was not accepted as a long-lost member of the royal family. The maharana had three daughters, but they lived in strict purdah. The idea that they would be free to date and presumably marry Henri d'Orléans on his way through town is ridiculous. The article also implied that Opal was living in India in 1933 and had been seen in Udaipur quite recently when actually she had been living in England for five or six years.

The idea that Opal had a special diplomatic passport arranged by Lord Grey and the American secretary of state Charles Evans Hughes seems to be another completely unfounded rumor originating with this story. Apart from everything else, Lord Grey had left Washington years before Opal arrived there. And if any high-powered people helped her, they certainly didn't provide her with enough money to live well or to get back. She arrived broke on a one-way ticket. Nor did these worthies back her up when the local authorities were trying to figure out who she was and how to get her to leave town.

Sedgwick may well have been the unwitting source for the whole story and not simply for his long statement, which he later claimed was misquoted. Sedgwick wrote Opal after the story broke, saying that a friend of his youth, Mrs. Sherwood, a distinguished painter, wrote to tell him that a friend of hers had spotted Opal driven through the streets in a gleaming carriage and that he had quoted her in letters to others.

Meanwhile, living among nuns at Oxford, Opal had outlived her welcome. The Mother Prioress banished her and her pet hare, Beatissima. It is easy to see how someone like Opal could be barred from a communal living arrangement such as a convent. Monastic life requires discipline and order. Opal was notoriously untidy her whole life, and her belongings were always in a state of disorder. Even at bohemian El Alisal, Lummis had been infuriated by her piles of papers. Nuns were expected to own things communally, something a packrat like Opal would have found difficult, and they were also expected to mend napkins, polish brasses, scrub floors, and do other household tasks, something Opal hated her whole life. Many nuns have said that of the three vows— poverty, chastity, and obedience—it is obedience that is the most difficult. Opal was simply too volatile to obey anyone for long, as even the controlling Fairy Godmother and Fairy Godfather had discovered.

After she left the priory, two friends there, Sister Mary and Sister Mary Baptist, wrote her affectionate letters, telling her how sorry they were she couldn't come back. They were completely charmed by Opal and mended her clothes for her even after she moved back to London. They asked after Beatissima and regularly sent her two shillings and sixpence, apologizing to Opal if it was late, just like the rich ladies from Los Angeles who continued to send Opal money. All her life people gave Opal money. Even nuns who'd taken a vow of poverty.

In Oxford she became quite a pest to her priest, Father Stuart, barraging him with notes, sending him roses and dates, and constantly asking for appointments. He apparently allocated her one half hour a week, his letters often beginning, "I could not possibly. . . ." At one point he sent her a papal dispensation she had asked for that would allow her to take mass five times a week after some liquid nourishment, and he commented that it was a pity she was getting unpleasant letters but good news that her book was progressing nicely.

On another occasion, after Opal had become infatuated with an aspiring priest, he wrote, "You must give up all idea of marriage with Mr. Sheppy Green. He has chosen his vocation and I know that in any case he has no thought of any such thing." On another, Stuart said firmly, "I am sorry but you cannot possibly accept an invitation to open or even to take any part in a Church of England fete such as you describe."

Later her affections transferred from Mr. Sheppy Green, who went on to become a priest, to Father Bede Jarrett, a middle-aged theologian and medieval scholar. Monica Baldwin, an English nun who left the convent after twenty-eight years and wrote about it in a 1949 memoir, *I Leap over the Wall*, described Jarrett as "the famous Dominican," and wrote that he was a man of "deep humor, profound learning and wide experience." She added that he had "unforgettable" eyes, "intent, yet curiously brooding."

Father Stuart asked Opal to "stop kneeling in a conspicuous place and keep your eyes fixed on Fr. Jarrett in such a way that everyone notices it . . . I cannot wonder that he is annoyed." Opal was concerned that a devious Miss Lane had become her rival for Father Jarrett's affection. She wrote him overwrought declarations of her love, and when he died in 1934, she apparently made a scene at the funeral, throwing herself sobbing on his coffin. Later she prayed to him in heaven and indulged in speculation that he might be canonized. Opal also took an interest in the Prince of Wales and asked others to pray for his conversion to Catholicism, "as I so desire this." Despite her religious excesses, she seems to have managed to have some kind of social life, often with Roman Catholic aristocrats. One of her friends was Oscar Wilde's litigious old boyfriend Lord Alfred Douglas, aka Bosie, now married and a Catholic convert.

Opal, despite her Catholic piety, had taken up astrology and was casting horoscopes, and Lord Alfred Douglas, equally heretical, was scrambling to get his exact date of birth from his mother so Opal could do his. He signed himself "Your Affectionate Friend A.D. (Fleur de Lys)." Bosie also seemed to think that another friend, the countess of Warwick, could help Opal get things straightened out with her d'Orléans relatives who weren't accepting her as one of the family.

Frances, Lady Warwick was also known as Daisy and was supposedly the inspiration for the song "A Bicycle Built for Two," which begins, "Daisy, Daisy, give me your answer true." She was the mistress of Edward VII when he was the Prince of Wales, who was said to have given her an ankle bracelet engraved with the words "Heaven's Above." When Opal met her, the countess, pushing seventy, was enchanted.

Opal had sent her the manuscript of her book on India, and angled for an invitation to the countess's place in the country. Lady Warwick, saying the garden wasn't at its best, proposed a meeting in London, where they could talk and said she knew all about Henri d'Orléans's "wonderful research."

In a letter a month later to "My dear Mademoiselle," she suggested that Opal come to tea at her London flat to plan a visit to her in the country. "I shall be so glad to meet you," wrote the countess, but in a postscript with a foreshadowing of things to come, she asked how she should address Opal—as mademoiselle or princess.

Apparently the answer was the latter. Soon the countess was writing to "Dear Princesse" and visiting her in town.

Opal was invited to come finish writing her book at Easton Lodge in the country, where the countess lived. She was also encouraging Opal to write a biography of "your wonderful (and sad) life!" Lady Warwick's enthusiasm lasted well into the summer, when she was addressing Opal as "My darling little Princesse Françoise" and vowing to make her life "less harassed and cramped." By July, when she invited Opal to lunch at the Connaught Hotel, "affectionately" had given way to "lovingly" above the signature.

But things began to cool down. There was the ticklish matter of Opal's title. Soon after the scheduled lunch at the Connaught, Lady Warwick wrote Constant Huntington at Putnam's, with "Very private and confidential please" scrawled across the top of the letter. The countess feared Opal was an impostor. She wrote Huntington that she had heard "distinctly different" stories from Opal of her birth and child-hood. She had also been talking to some members of the d'Orléans fam-ily, including her friends Queen Amélie of Portugal and the duke of Guise. They told her that Henri d'Orléans had never married and said they had never heard of Opal.

Having heard the story that Opal had spent time with the duchess of Chartres at Chantilly, Lady Warwick learned that Henri's sister had lived with the duchess the whole time at Chantilly and denied Françoise was ever there. (The d'Orléans family always maintained she wasn't one of them. As late as 1992, the head of the family, the count of Paris, Henri d'Orléans's nephew, wrote to filmmaker Ian Taylor that his father, Henri's brother, had often spoken of a Françoise who had taken the fam-ily name "abusively" and that he considered her an impostor and *une dérangée mentale*.) The countess mused that perhaps Opal had been the daughter of some old family retainer of the d'Orléans family since she seemed to know so much about them. She noted that Opal was highly strung and imaginative and that the superior at the convent where she had stayed was "not favourable to her story. . . . I am truly puzzled. I do not know what to make of this little woman."

Opal had been demoted from lady to woman, and in a PS, the count-ess wrote even more cuttingly, "She has none of the family traits of the Bourbons . . . Françoise is quite insignificant." Lady Warwick called the whole thing "most mysterious, as she no doubt has many miniatures of the family."

Innocent of Opal's hobby of commissioning heirlooms, the countess continued to fret about Opal's bona fides. The French Embassy re-ported there was no such person. Opal was scheduled to arrive at Lady Warwick's on August 12 for an extended stay. Her long-suffering priest, Father Stuart, encouraged her strongly to go there and finish her book. Shortly before her arrival the countess wrote Opal a long letter con-fronting her. Pleading with her to be "sensible," she said she could not introduce Opal to her friends under a name that "you cannot prove to any of us." She begged her to "be honest about all this, dear" and said her friends would appreciate her for herself.

When Opal refused to budge, Lady Warwick rescinded her invita-tion, and accused her of snobbery.

Opal was also friendly with Lady Baden-Powell, wife of the founder of the Boy Scouts, and boasted of her friendships with the countess of Iddesleigh, the niece of Hilaire Belloc, and with a Christian Iraqi general, Jafar Pasha, mentioned in Lawrence of Arabia's book. She also dropped the name of Sir Oliver Lodge, a psychic researcher, and a great friend of Lady Grey's.

Another friend during the 1930s was the Michigan-born actress Doris Keane, who had played Juliet in London with Ellen Terry as the nurse. She was a fin de siècle beauty, with huge, liquid dark eyes and the tiny cupid's-bow mouth so prized during her heyday. When she befriended Opal, Doris Keane was living in Hanover Square. As with the countess of Warwick, the friendship began enthusiastically. Miss Keane had her to tea, to "a comfy dinner," and invited her to a lecture on Egypt. She shared Opal's interest in Catholicism and sent her curtains, cash, money for a ticket to see the Max Reinhardt production of *A Midsummer Night's Dream*, and a hamper from Fortnum & Mason at Christmas as well as a check "for your Christmas dinner if you are not invited to a friend's home." Miss Keane also gave her castoff clothing, including a fur-lined velvet coat, which Opal later claimed had been a gift from the old duchess of Chartres. Doris Keane also made solicitous inquiries. "Have you heat in your room? I am glad you have the fur-lined coat for cold days." While she always had an excuse not to see Opal at Christmas, she made a point of having her around on Boxing Day or New Year's Day.

But a new obsession of Opal's threatened this friendship. Opal now began to tell people that she had been promised in marriage as a child to the heir to the British throne. She had taken to writing the Prince of Wales. The Home Office had bulging files of her love letters to him, beginning "Dear David," in which she lamented their separation. She also wrote to other members of the royal family.

After hearing Opal on the subject, Doris Keane told Opal that she could not see her any more unless she stopped pursuing the Prince of Wales.

Opal's obsession with the Prince of Wales prompted her to take a flat near Buckingham Palace after she moved from Oxford back to London, and she occasionally tried to see him. One indignant letter to Dear

David read, "I came out to Belvedere to see you the other evening, but the detective drove me away. It seems impossible in what is called a democratic age."

About this time, as Opal's behavior was becoming more and more eccentric, she was befriended by Mia Woodruff, a daughter of Lord Acton and a devout Catholic. Her father's title meant she was officially called the Honourable Mrs. Woodruff. Mia Woodruff was devoted to Opal but was never under any illusion that her friend was sane. She was so concerned that Opal, now verging into stalker territory, would make some kind of scene at the coronation of Edward VIII that she arranged for Opal to visit her in the country. Opal had changed since the days she taught little children about nature. She didn't like the country, and when she was asked to take some children out for a walk, Mrs. Woodruff reported that "they loathed each other" and quarreled on the walk. "She obviously didn't like children," said Mrs. Woodruff, who also tried to get her into some kind of shelter, which Opal was hurt to discover was "an almshouse."

In the late 1930s, Opal was writing to members of the d'Orléans family, asking them to drop by while they were in London and telling them she had applied to be naturalized as a British citizen. She duly applied but was never granted citizenship. In 1936, Opal made a third attempt to sell Sedgwick material about her time in India and also suggested he buy her autobiography. This time, she said, she'd reveal the parts of her life before she arrived in Cottage Grove, and just as she had in 1919, she pitched him a Steinbeckian view of life in a lumber camp, including the hooker with the heart of gold and loggers going through delirium tremens and little Opal bringing them food. Sedgwick hadn't bitten then, shifting her to the more innocent diary and suggesting "the seven-year-period," and he didn't bite now. This was her last recorded attempt at publication. Opal's mental state was such that she was no longer able to pretend to write.

By the 1940s Opal was living in a cheap basement flat in Hampstead. Her bibliomania had turned her into a looter, as she grubbed around through the rubble of the blitz, stealing books. According to Mrs. Woodruff, "she rather enjoyed picking through the ruins and finding a dead cat and that sort of thing." She pushed a baby carriage full of books around the neighborhood, shouted at neighborhood children, and wandered around the streets screaming for her lost love, the alleged swami whose attentions had caused her to be driven from Udaipur many years before. Her flat was full of rows of bookshelves made from hundreds of empty wooden gin boxes. She lived in a sort of island in the middle. During the war she took to filling up many notebooks with numbers, creating strange coded messages, and believed this was an important part of the war effort.

In 1948 neighbors complained that her apartment smelled foul and that she was shouting in the street. Now fifty, she was taken to a mental hospital and diagnosed as suffering from "paraphrenia with paranoid features." Paraphrenia has been defined as late-onset schizophrenia with delusions and hallucinations. She was detained as a person of unsound mind under the Lunacy Act of 1890 and was said to be hallucinating, "believing herself to be persecuted by international bodies and also that various people are trying to steal her property and work."

The Cassandra-like prediction of Opal's biggest critic, Maud Bales, who in 1920 declared to both Ellery Sedgwick and Elbert Bede that Opal would end up in an asylum, had come true. Opal was committed to Napsbury Hospital.

Twenty-one

Opal was not, however, immediately forgotten. British economist and policy expert Barbara Ward, later Baroness Jackson of Lodsworth, arranged for a public appeal for money for her. The Opal fund was publicized in a piece by Ward in *The Atlantic Monthly*, explaining to readers who might have remembered the diary that Opal had had to be removed from "the tiny room in which she lived surrounded by her beloved books and her relics of France and the French royal family."

Opal, readers learned, had not fulfilled her early promise because in India "she fell victim of a sunstroke from which she never fully recovered. She lost her powers of concentration and although she continued to delight people by the delicacy of her artistic ideas and of her imagination, she could not write." The aristocratic name of Lord Grey, now deceased, was mentioned. Miss Ward appealed for funds that would enable Opal to live in a private hospital where she could get better treatment and privacy and presumably live among a better class of lunatic.

Sedgwick, now retired in Arizona, sent in the first check. Other checks arrived. The fund was administered by Mia Woodruff, who used it to pay storage fees on Opal's huge collection of books, which was kept by London governmental authorities, and to take Opal to a Harley Street specialist. The doctor, who charged fifteen guineas, said she would never be happy and might benefit from a lobotomy, or more specifically a leukotomy. Whether she had it or not is a matter of speculation.

Despite her diagnosis of a late-onset disease, Opal had been mentally fragile since late adolescence. The madness had finally consumed her. After a series of breakdowns, beginning with her episode of mutism as an adolescent and followed by similar bouts in California, Boston, and New York, she had become increasingly irrational. As time went on, the episodes were less cyclic, and irrationality eventually became her normal condition.

After her commitment, Opal wrote many angry letters to old acquaintances in Oregon complaining about being in the hospital and insisting she was being ill-treated and didn't have enough to eat. When these old Oregonians sent her a few dollars, she wrote back thanking them and saying she needed the money for food. Besides these gifts, Mia Woodruff sent Opal twenty-five pence a week pocket money, which she steadfastly refused to spend, although if Mrs. Woodruff was late, Opal wrote her to ask for it. She also resisted the chance to earn pocket money by washing eggs, serving tea, or doing other domestic chores around Napsbury. Opal had hated housework her whole life, and she wasn't about to do any now.

The first to revisit the story of Opal after her hospitalization was Elbert Bede. In 1948, noting that he had covered her for thirty years, Bede, then living in Portland, where he edited *The Oregon Mason*, wrote to *The Oregonian* to advise its readers that Opal was now in "an institution for the feeble-minded in England." In retirement, he wrote a book about her for an Oregon publisher. *Fabulous Opal Whiteley: From Logging Camp to Princess of India* appeared in 1954. When I visited Bede's daughter, Beth Simkin, at her home in Port Angeles, Washington, she told me, "Papa wrote it right here in the basement of this house." Bede rose early, wrote until lunch surrounded by his research papers, then played golf with the local Episcopal minister, a fellow Mason, often discussing the Bible on the links. He had a highball with the minister back at Beth's house, ate dinner, and played with the grandchildren until bedtime.

Opal didn't think much of his book. She wrote a letter to the publishers from Napsbury, saying she had counted more than 340 lies in it. She was especially annoyed with Bede's final sentence: "Tragedy has stilled the mind of a genius, though the body lives on for a time."

"I am very sane," wrote Opal, "and as soon as I get out of this hell I intend to write my life story: I am not mental at all but was kidnapped. . . . I was put away because of my child marriage to the Prince of Wales by the Revolutionary Tribunal which is against the law."

A few years later a British educator, Elizabeth Bradburne, later Elizabeth Lawrence, took an interest in Opal. Her first professional involvement with Opal was in 1958, when she worked in educational programming for the BBC. She produced a radio documentary about two authors, Marjorie Fleming, a child diarist who died at the age of eleven, and Opal. At the time she was told Opal had been dead for ten years. After the program came out, she received a letter from a listener who said she believed Opal was the "the little person we knew in Hampstead as 'The Little Princess.' "

Mrs. Lawrence, determined to find out more about Opal's life, tracked her to Napsbury Hospital, where she assumed Opal had died. She wrote the hospital to see what she could learn, and the reply included the startling sentence "The lady in fact is not dead, but is still a patient here."

She went to meet her and described the occasion in her 1962 book *Opal Whiteley: The Unsolved Mystery.* "The impact of this first meeting with Opal was something I was not prepared for. She had about her a dignity which I had not expected to find, which made me think at once of Queen Victoria. . . . Though shabbily dressed in a badly fitting brown woollen jumper [sweater] and skirt, she had an undoubted graciousness and charm. She held out her small hand to me, a gesture which almost made me feel I should bow over it.

"I particularly noticed her hands. They were not the hands of a labourer's child."

Mrs. Lawrence repeated this thought to me many years later. "It wasn't the personality, the attitude of a lumberman's child. Her hands were so small and delicate. That struck me very much. It wasn't the hand of a laborer's child."

"Could you see the child at the same time as you were talking to the woman?" I asked.

"No. And that I was rather sad about because the child had been so real to me for so many years. . . . And here was this old lady, interesting in itself but [she] hadn't got the quality that attracted me to the diary." Soon Mrs. Lawrence was at work on the book that would include a reprinting of the diary, with additional historical material.

She got in touch with Elbert Bede and an ailing Ellery Sedgwick and corresponded with other people from Oregon, including the son of Mrs. MacDonald, the motherly preacher's wife with whom Opal had spent a happy summer in 1916. She also wrote to the Honourable Mrs. Woodruff.

Mrs. Woodruff wrote Mrs. Lawrence that she had read some of Bede's book and received "a horrid letter" from him to which she had not replied. From Mrs. Woodruff, whom Mrs. Lawrence described as "a fervent Catholic," she also learned that the London County Council, the local governmental authority, had arranged for the storage of Opal's belongings in an old school after her commitment to Napsbury Hospital. "She told me the papers were all in the store in the East End of London and she paid for the storing of them. She gave me permission to go down to the East End and take what I wanted. It was astonishing! She [Opal] used to buy gin boxes from the local pub." Later estimates put the number of gin boxes full of books and papers at five hundred. Mrs. Lawrence had a taxi waiting. "I picked up what was obviously interesting and took it all home and I've still got it now." The haul included some original pages of the pieced-together published diary.

Mrs. Lawrence's book stated that these original diary pages she had found among Opal's papers had been scientifically analyzed and that the crayons were of a type used before World War I, as was the paper.

This would mean Opal could have faked the diary only by hoarding paper and crayons from childhood, then producing the diary in 1918 or 1919, knowing that sometime in the future forensic science might be able to date the materials.

Mrs. Lawrence told me she had originally sent the pages off to a graphologist, or handwriting analyst, to see if the writing was that of a child, and she hadn't asked him to date the materials at all. "I sent them off to a graphologist. And asked him to please tell me how old the writer was. He did everything except that."

"So you were trying to find the age of the writer, not the age of the paper?"

"Yes. The age of the writer. In order to see if it was genuine or not . . . The thing is he kept the material for ever so long. Eventually he sent me a long report and a huge bill."

He kept the papers ever so long indeed—about a quarter century to be precise. Among Mrs. Lawrence's papers, which she kindly allowed me to examine, I found a communication from her accountant who referred to the expert as "a queer customer" and suggested in 1961 that they offer him ten pounds instead of the sixty he was holding out for.

(Apparently it didn't work, and the graphologist held on until 1984, when Robert Nassif, who had befriended Mrs. Lawrence during his own research for his musical *Opal*, tracked him down, paid the sixty pounds, and reclaimed the diary pages and other material.)

In happier days, however, Mrs. Lawrence and the graphologist were quite friendly. He was clearly excited by the story. He went with Mrs. Lawrence to meet Opal at Napsbury Hospital and later wrote, "I thoroughly enjoyed every moment of the whole outing." The two of them discussed a plan to get in touch with the duke of Guise, whom the graphologist referred to as "the Princess's uncle."

I have examined a copy of the graphologist's notes that remain. There is no summary or final report. If it ever existed, no one knows where it is. Instead the graphologist made copious and sometimes cryptic notes on old envelopes and junk mail, some of it notes from books he consulted about how to date paper, citing page numbers.

It seems odd for an expert to remind himself of the principles of his craft by writing such statements as, "The basis of all paper is cellulose fiber in one form or another, the grading of the paper depends largely on the length and regular quality of the fibre." And "Crayons Harnian p. 25—mixture of waxes & oil-soluble dyestuffs."

When Mrs. Lawrence first engaged him, in 1958 or 1959, his letterhead proclaimed that he did "handwriting analysis, consultant graphology and psychology," with expertise in "personnel selection and vocational guidance." During this era, job applicants were often asked to apply in their own handwriting, so it could be analyzed.

Later, after he had had the diary pages for a quarter of a century, and presumably after his sessions with the how-to books, he added "Examiner of Questioned Documents" to his letterhead.

Even if he were an expert, what conclusions there are seem inconclusive, to say the least. While Mrs. Lawrence quoted him on the age of the crayons, stating that they were of much higher quality than crayons available during World War I, there was also a note about one diary sample he examined that said it was "made for very cheap (wrapping) purposes just before or during 1914–18 war," or when Opal was between sixteen and twenty.

The questions surrounding the age of the paper and crayons are not likely to be resolved any time soon. All the remaining pages are now in the possession of either Mrs. Lawrence or Robert Nassif. I asked both of them if they would be willing to have the pages they hold examined by forensic specialists with a view to dating them properly, if possible, but they both refused.

Mrs. Lawrence visited Opal's early haunts in the 1980s. "I went with a friend who's from Oregon, and we didn't know where to begin to look. All of a sudden as we came round the corner, we saw this fingerpost that said 'Wendling.' We went down there, and we found the creek, and I paddled in that in the fields where probably her home was."

When she visited there, Mrs. Lawrence reported, the locals said of Opal, "When she was going past, our parents called us in because they said she was a witch." Of the denizens of Cottage Grove during Opal's time, she commented, "I think the people at that time were very backward . . . uneducated and superstitious."

In 2000, Mrs. Lawrence published a second book on Opal, *Opal Whiteley: The Continuing Mystery*. It contains much of the material from her 1962 introduction to the diary. Just as it went to press, she received some information from Oregon, in the form of forwarded e-mails describing information from the Internet.

"What I guess is . . . and this goes back to this Web site, which I discovered just before the book was published about the French royal family and this priest that escaped from France, that filled in that gap which I always felt I couldn't understand . . . where her knowledge of French and the Catholic religion came from. That accounts for it all, and my guess is . . . that somebody connected with the royal family was given the job of finding a home for this child and approached the Whiteleys, and quite possibly they didn't even know who she was."

The e-mails in question note, among other things, the existence of the grave of a royalist French priest exiled from France in 1903, who had wandered around Washington and Oregon for two years and been in Colton and Wendling; the fact that the d'Orléans family gave money to a Catholic diocese in Walla Walla, Washington, in the nineteenth century; and the existence in Oregon of a town named Orleans, now abandoned. Mrs. Lawrence concedes that the case is highly circumstantial. "It's only a guess," she said.

Mrs. Lawrence has put in fifty years pursuing the story of Opal. She spent almost twenty years before that as a fan. Her interest goes back to her days as a student in the 1930s. Like all Opalites, she was enchanted immediately and has reread the diary often. She told me it has shaped her ideas about nature and childhood. "I had grown up with her, really," she said.

When she began researching her book in the late 1950s, her activities aroused the attention of Martin Schmitt, then head of special collections at the University of Oregon Library in Eugene.

Schmitt realized that Opal, whom he characterized as "Oregon's greatest (probable) fraud in the world of letters," was about to get back in the news. He already had some boxes of notebooks she had left behind, one of which had emerged during the remodeling of a women's dormitory. His goal was to get all her papers and to see if any unpublished manuscripts remained to be added to his collection.

Schmitt asked English Professor Carlisle Moore, who was going to England on sabbatical, to represent the university in what he called "this rather strange, and possibly delicate business."

Dr. Moore, saying he would act with as much tact and discretion as possible, made his way to Winchester, where Mrs. Lawrence then lived. He was warned by Schmitt not to voice any doubt about Opal's royal birth to Mrs. Lawrence, who was a true believer. Moore left Mrs. Lawrence's house empty-handed, recording in his notes, "She has many letters and photos from warehouse." Moore also had tea with Mrs. Woodruff and met Opal herself at Napsbury. He described her as "short, faded, stoutish, weak-eyed and a twist at her mouth yet somehow dignified." She was up-to-date on her latest *Oregonian* publicity, reviewing Bede's book, and lambasted Bede, saying his book was full of lies. Moore also talked to her doctor about her well-being and the need to preserve her papers, perhaps by her writing a will. The doctor said she refused to write a will. (When Schmitt heard this, he expressed derision that an incompetent would be allowed to make one in any case.) Moore suggested to the doctor that one be written for her.

When Moore confronted Opal directly about leaving her books and papers to the University of Oregon in a will, she said she'd have to consult with her family, by which she meant her husband, the duke of Windsor, whom she said she had married in 1902 in a child marriage. Moore reported, "Opal of course hates Mrs. Windsor, a common woman and divorcée who stole him and ruined him. Opal could have been Queen of England!" Moore also went to where the boxes were stored, and climbed around among them, writing down some of the book titles and searching for any unpublished work. His search was thorough enough that he believed he could state there wasn't anything of the kind.

Despite all his efforts—Schmitt even had a cultural attaché at the U.S. Embassy on the job—he never got near the papers. Schmitt was astonished to learn that the British authorities took Opal's claims to the d'Orléans name seriously, weren't ready to take his word for it that the patient in Napsbury was Opal Whiteley, and were demanding to see her birth certificate and a family tree. In their report on Opal, attempting to find out who she was, the British authorities seemed confused by her social class, noting that she had been put in "a working-class" foster home in Oregon and elsewhere that the countess of Iddesleigh had said she was "a lady." Schmitt wanted the British authorities to write a will leaving all her effects to the University of Oregon, and over the years they wrote Schmitt a series of vague, chilly letters, which his internal memos indicate he found condescending and slightly loony.

In the 1960s, Opal heard once more from her old friend Nellie Hemenway Price, who had lost her husband to a heart attack during World War II, an event tragically followed by the death of her twenty-one-year-old son and only child, Tom, fighting in Europe. Nellie wrote Opal that she had the consolation of her home and wonderful friends. Opal offered her condolences and wrote Nellie, "You are more fortunate than I am as my wonderful friends died long ago; they were older than me." She explained to Nellie that she had been taken by the Revolutionary Tribunal "and considered mental because I would not tell them the sealed date of my child marriage with the Prince of Wales. . . . I lived very quietly in Hampstead working on several good books and the code books. I am quite sane." She also asked Nellie to tell her about the Whiteley children, carefully listing all their names and birthdays. She wanted to know whom they had married and where they lived, but said, "I don't want to get in contact with them."

Later, Elwin Whiteley's widow, Helen, got in touch with Opal in Napsbury, and they corresponded. Helen Whiteley wouldn't give Opal the addresses of the Whiteley sisters, as she had requested, fearing that family bitterness remained, but she did express an interest in getting possession of Opal's books and papers on the ground that her son might want to write about Opal. This seems to have been the first contact Opal had with the Whiteleys since she left Oregon in 1918.

As the years went by, Opal's papers, and her finances, received more and more official attention from British authorities. William McBryde is a retired lawyer and a former assistant official solicitor for the Supreme Court. His office, the Court of Protection, became involved with Opal when someone from the hospital asked it to take care of Opal's financial affairs. "The only assets she had were a collection of books which had been removed from the room in which she was living . . . which had been stored by the then county council," he told me.

Bill McBryde's office was also asked to step in when a reorganization in London government had resulted in a local council's asking someone please to deal with Opal's stuff. It was no longer responsible for her effects, as another local council now had jurisdiction. The material, mostly books, was stored in five hundred boxes, two trunks, and several tea chests. These were stacked eight feet high, and the whole collection was estimated to weigh seven tons.

As Professor Moore had done some years before, McBryde checked it out. He thought it would be irresponsible not to go through it in case any of the books were valuable, but he realized it would be impossible to go through it all where it was being stored, jammed into the ward of an old hospital. At the time he was treasurer of his local church, and he rented himself the church hall and rounded up a lot of friends to act as volunteers to go through the boxes.

"A team of us volunteers worked in absolutely filthy conditions . . . The dust! You have no idea. We had to wear masks. We also wore protective clothing. It took two runs of water in the bath to get yourself clean."

The collection was long on genealogy, royalty, and Roman Catholic theology, with many Catholic postcards and devotional items. There were the notebooks full of numbers—the "important code work" she said she was doing for the navy during the war. There were, said McBryde, few books about nature. Opal's interest in the natural world had long ago been replaced by her obsession with the d'Orléans family and traditional religion, which had replaced the spiritual awe she had experienced in forest glades of her childhood.

A few valuable books emerged: an unsigned copy of Lord Grey's *The Charm of Birds*, a book by Grey's stepson, Stephen Tennant, inscribed to Opal, and other books with authors' inscriptions, as well as valuable illustrated books. These McBryde arranged to have auctioned off by Sotheby's. The rest of the collection was sold in a lot to legendary bookseller Richard Booth, and it ended up in the bookish village of Hay-on-Wye on the Welsh border.

The volunteers also went through Opal's papers. One of the volunteers was a professor at Cambridge, an Orientalist who became interested in Opal. The professor, a Buddhist, believed, according to Mrs. Woodruff, that Opal's conviction that she was the daughter of Henri d'Orléans could be explained by reincarnation. McBryde turned the papers over to her, on the grounds she was a responsible academic and would be a good guardian of them.

Eventually, after Opal's death, the Cambridge professor delivered these papers to the University of London Library, in accordance with a will that Bill McBryde wrote for Opal. The library now has this collection, recently cataloged and preserved in acid-free envelopes, but some material, including the original diary pages, is not there.

Writer Benjamin Hoff, for one, who has researched and written about Opal, thinks that all of Opal's papers should be professionally archived and available to scholars and has said so in his book. I asked McBryde if there had been any thought that the papers that Mrs. Lawrence had should be united with the rest of the collection at the University of London Library.

"It was discussed, but in fact, I took the view that they got in her possession at a time when Françoise was capable of making a judgment and she'd given them to Mrs. Lawrence," said McBryde. "The library consulted me on it, and my advice was 'Don't rock the boat.' " He added, "Since I also personally like Mrs. Lawrence I didn't want to disturb her." Stickers on the boxes of Opal's papers Mrs. Lawrence has indicate that she wants them to go to playwright Robert Nassif after her death. He already has original diary pages he collected from the graphologist when he paid the decades-old bill.

McBryde shares with Mrs. Lawrence the opinion that Opal was not a Whiteley and was probably a member of the d'Orléans family. "My own view," he said, "is that very possibly she was an illegitimate child. The dates seem to be about right. She seems to have been moved to Oregon after [Henri d'Orléans] died, and that coincided with things like the Dreyfus affair in France . . . the monarchists had hopes that they might be on the way back."

His theory is that an illegitimate child by a relative of the monarch wouldn't have been a political liability unless it was the result of a liaison between Henri d'Orléans and a social equal. McBryde thinks, for reasons not entirely clear to me, that it might have been a cousin. "Purely speculation, but it seems to fit in with the facts," he said confidently.

Twenty-two

*I*n the early 1970s, Jane Boulton, a Californian, borrowed a copy of the diary from a friend. "I was so charmed by the whole diary that I thought it should not be lost, and so I made notes of some of my favorite parts because I knew it was a book long out of print," she told me. "I took notes of a few of the segments and just filed them away. So when we were living several years later on a sheep ranch in Alberta, Canada, I was going through my files on a snowy, snowy day and found them, and I said, 'Oh, these are still charming,' and I took some of my excerpts and mailed them to *Ms.* magazine, which was still quite new in those days. This was in '72 or '73, And they did a very nice spread, I guess it was four pages."

When I arranged to meet Jane Boulton, she described herself to me as "the aging blonde in the white Taurus." She is a petite, charming, animated grandmother and she likes to laugh. When I met her, she wore bright pink lipstick and nail polish to match her polo shirt. She said she was old enough "so that my kids are already divorced and on their second marriages."

Boulton thought of the diary as having adult appeal, but *Ms.* magazine chose to use her excerpts in a regular feature titled "Stories for Free Children." "I received a lot of fan mail, saying, 'What happened next?'" She'd also attracted the attention of an editor at Macmillan, who asked her if she wanted to put together a book based on the diary, as she indeed did, under the title *Opal: The Journal of an Understanding Heart.* She followed up some years later with a picture book version for young children, *Only Opal*.

In the first book she did, Boulton arranged the lines so they looked like poetry rather than prose, in chunks like verses.

> *I did see the pensée girl*
> *With the faraway look in her eyes*
> *And the man of the long step*
> *That whistles most all of the time*
> *Come walking through the woods.*

She made other changes. "I changed the order of the diary because in the first place Opal made long lists of trees she passed and how many butterflies she saw and all this . . . which became quite boring, and then also she would get onto one subject and go on it for a long time so I broke it up and I started it at a different point, so I made those kind of arrangements but the words were all hers." Boulton also changed the names of the pets. "I shortened them because she would have five names, so I shortened a few of the names." The crow Lars Porsena of Clusium, for example, because simply Lars Porsena. The words, she said were all Opal's, but it's clear that the syntax and grammar were edited to make the prose more grammatically correct and some content was also changed, rendering the story more credible.

After the book came out, Boulton went to visit Opal. She described Napsbury Hospital as a "very big estate run by their [the British] government." She went there in 1975. "My friend and I went together, and we had tea with her in this big room, and I asked her questions . . . I could tell she had perfect recall of . . . her childhood. She could remember the people, she could remember the things that happened. . . . I mean, it was just amazing, But then there were times of her mental disturbance, and all of a sudden that would creep in."

Boulton and her friend returned for a second visit with fresh fruit. "Apparently they didn't give them many fresh fruits in their diet there . . . She was very thrilled to have company, no doubt of it. And you could tell that her life was kind of a lonesome, bored life . . . She was a little dumpy, little tiny squat, little plump woman. Sort of flashing brown eyes. She was a talker. She really loved talking, and she loved the attention, and it was an experience."

Opal received other visitors in the 1970s, and she continued to communicate with many people from Oregon. Some of Lizzie Whiteley's cousins came to see her, and several people interested in her story, including Whiteley relatives, wrote her. Word went out around Cottage Grove that including five dollars guaranteed a reply. A religious woman from Cottage Grove whose husband's family had known Opal as a girl visited to try to convince Opal to repent and admit she had lied when she said she wasn't a Whiteley. Opal stuck by her story. A Lane County Historical Society volunteer went over and taped her describing her life in a pleasant, genteel little voice with an American accent and English cadences. The story of her origins had now become much more lurid. At one point she claimed she had been promised in marriage to the duke of Windsor when a child. Now she was a child queen, who had actually married the duke of Windsor in a child marriage in 1902 and been kidnapped by the IRA in 1904. The Whiteleys had then kidnapped her to hold her for ransom for the crown jewels of England.

Opal had by now come to fear space aliens, who worked in collusion with the duchess of Windsor and the IRA. She referred to the nurses as "prostitutes from Shanghai," perhaps because of an unkind rumor about the duchess of Windsor, who gossips claimed picked up some tricks while working as prostitute in Shanghai that allowed her to keep a hold on the duke. The space aliens, the IRA, and the duchess of Windsor all were part of a "Jewish-Protestant" conspiracy against Catholics to take over the world, though why the IRA would be part of a Protestant conspiracy was not clear. Interwoven with this material were flickers of her real past, sometimes astonishingly accurate, including such things as the correct street address of El Alisal and the precise date on which a long-ago event had occurred.

The writer Benjamin Hoff wasn't aware of Mrs. Lawrence's book, or Jane Boulton's, when, one morning in 1983, as he was reaching for a book on a shelf in the Multnomah County Public Library in downtown Portland, his eye fatefully strayed to the volume next to it. It happened to be *The Story of Opal: The Journal of an Understanding Heart*. He took it home, spent the next sixteen hours reading the diary and Opal's and Ellery Sedgwick's introductions, and fell completely under its spell. Opal was to become a part of his life for years to come.

Hoff, an Oregonian, had a degree in Asian art from Evergreen State College in Washington State. After college he worked for two years as a tree pruner in Portland's Japanese Garden, his surroundings informed by Shintoism, Buddhism, and Taoism. The garden is considered one of the most authentic of its kind outside Japan. During this time he wrote his first book at night and on weekends. *The Tao of Pooh* uses Winnie the Pooh as an introduction to Taoist thought for Westerners. Now in its fortieth printing, it is a steady seller and commands a devoted following.

The *Tao of Pooh* (later followed by *The Te of Piglet*) came out the same year Hoff discovered Opal's diary on the library shelf and provided him with the opportunity to pursue his research into her life.

"I just had to know who Opal Whiteley was," he told me. ". . . It's not like I found out definitely who she was. Opal Whiteley is a very elusive personality."

Hoff's investigations in the 1980s included interviews in Cottage Grove with many people, now dead, who had known Opal and the Whiteleys. He also traveled to England and visited Mrs. Lawrence and the Cambridge academic, who each had a portion of Opal's papers. (He said the two women, who had had a look at the other's materials, were quarreling about who owned what, and he was asked to serve as a go-between.) Eventually, in 1986, he brought out the diary with his own editorial material added, under the title *The Singing Creek Where the Willows Grow*.

Hoff's introduction gives the historical background and paints a vivid picture of the young Opal during her Oregon years. Hoff had come to the conclusion that Bede and others had defamed Opal, that the diary was genuine, and he was determined to prove it and vindicate Opal before she died. An afterword, "Napsbury and Beyond," chronicles his attempts to get the diary republished after twenty rejections and his thwarted attempts to visit Opal in England.

In his book he reported that the two-year effort left him "considerably in debt," with his literary career possibly "wrecked," and that eventually the overwork and frustration of the task resulted in his nervous collapse and his being rushed to a hospital in an ambulance after an episode of vertigo, racing pulse, and numbness. Most compelling are the passages where he went to Napsbury Hospital on borrowed money to try to meet Opal. The administration never answered his letters requesting a meeting, so he arrived anyway and was refused access. He contemplated sneaking onto the grounds but thought better of it.

On a second visit he reached the cottage where Opal lived. He talked to a nurse through a window, trying to get her at least to deliver a letter to Opal. He quoted the nurse as saying, "Post it," before drawing the curtains. Eventually he was ejected from the employees' cafeteria by a sarcastic security guard. A visit to the office of Opal's psychiatrist was equally fruitless. He was told he was not on a list of approved visitors.

It's pretty dramatic stuff. Hoff described his anger and frustration as he tried to get past the gauntlet of officials, got the run-around and icy treatment, read the diary for solace, and imagined the young Opal while the old woman she had become, lay tantalizingly close behind locked doors.

The book included a second afterword, in which Hoff outlined a theory of impending ecological doom, revealed by changing migration patterns of animals, climate change, volcanic activity, and changes in ocean currents, as well as by predictions of "seers, around the world." He was concerned that without a cleanup of toxic waste, natural life on earth, including human life, would die out and said it was possible that "we have little time left." He went on to say that what time was left would well be spent "applying the values expressed in the writings of Opal Whiteley." The version of *The Singing Creek Where the Willows Grow* currently in print eliminates this ecological warning, and some of the other personal material seems less emotionally fraught. Hoff seems to have taken some distance from his subject over the last fifteen years.

Hoff believes that the diary was an authentic product of childhood, but that Opal was schizophrenic and that this was what accounted for her belief that she was a d'Orléans. Expanding on the fact that the farther one gets from Oregon, the more likely one is to believe she isn't from there, he commented, "I mean, my mother was an Oregon pioneer family descendant. The general attitude that people have who believe in Opal's French parentage is that people in Oregon were just a bunch of hicks, who couldn't even read probably, let alone have access to books. Well, that just isn't true at all."

Hoff seems to think Opal had psychic ability. "She could, as far as I can tell, know what animals and plants were saying, thinking, whatever. Also, according to some people she could do things like levitating—things that are beyond the abilities or at least the knowledge of most people."

A professor at the University of Oregon who runs an Opal Whiteley Web site, had told me that Benjamin Hoff was in love with Opal, an impression I had also received from reading his book. I asked him if he had fallen in love with her.

"I would say so," he replied matter-of-factly. "Maybe not in the usual way. Spiritually maybe. I think people do. I think that's a big reason for her appeal. She's a very charismatic figure."

The second edition of Hoff's book included a friendly letter from a new administrator at Napsbury Hospital who had read his book and made it clear Hoff was now free to visit Opal. But he never did. I asked him if he regretted never having met her or if he felt that it was somehow not meant to be.

"Both," he said with a little smile. He said that after his foiled attempts to see her, "I figured I wasn't really geared up for another one. . . . I don't know if I could have endured a visit with Opal, emotionally."

"Did you feel if you did meet with her, it would take too much out of you?" I asked.

"No, I just thought it would have been totally depressing because a young woman from Australia started a correspondence with me, and she went to Napsbury, sneaked her camera in, which is illegal, photographed Opal, interviewed her, and was out of there before they even knew what was going on, and so she sent me some pictures of her, and she was a real mess."

I had seen this picture. It was indeed alarming. Opal seemed to have had a stroke, her tongue was lolling in her mouth, and she, who had loved to be photographed, seemed completely unaware of the camera.

After seeing the picture, Hoff appeared to be over his desire to meet Opal. But she was still to play an important part in his life. Some years ago he gave a reading of Opal's journal at an event he called "a spiritual retreat during some sort of earth awareness weekend." A woman named Deborah introduced herself to him after the reading. "She was sort of acquainted with me because my cousins who lived in West Linn, Oregon, loaned her *The Tao of Pooh*, so she knew who I was, so she knew about this book on Opal Whiteley, so she sort of met me through Opal." Deborah, an artist, is now his wife. She is small, slender, and pretty, with long dark hair and looks rather like the young Opal.

While Hoff was trying desperately to meet Opal at Napsbury Hospital, Robert Nassif was visiting her regularly. Robert Nassif writes musicals. His one-acter *The Flight of the Lawnchair Man* was directed by Harold Prince and got great reviews when it premiered in Philadelphia in 2000. Under Harold Prince's auspices he also wrote the music and lyrics for *Eliot Ness in Cleveland*. His *Honky-Tonk Highway*, for which he wrote the music, lyrics, and additional dialogue, had an Off Broadway production, and he worked for three years with Arthur Miller on a planned opera of *Death of a Salesman*.

For his musical *Opal*, he wrote the book as well as the music and lyrics and won the Richard Rodgers Award, which provided the funds to finance a full production. It was produced Off Broadway to warm reviews.

Opal Whiteley had an big impact on Nassif's career and on his family. "Opal has transformed all our lives so drastically," he told me. "She's really charted our courses. And she'd love to know that."

Rob Nassif has crisp dark hair, brown eyes, a mustache, and an old-fashioned courtesy that seems to come from an earlier age. He has a pleasant, calm, low, measured voice, even when speaking of things he feels strongly about. And he feels very strongly about Opal. He first learned of her from a friend of the family's who called in 1980 while Nassif was home from college for the weekend. She read some of it over the phone to Nassif's mother.

"My mother said, 'You've got to reread this,' and put me on the phone. So I believe she read the passage about 'cheese squeaks.' . . . I was smitten, I was enchanted."

The cheese squeaks came from a wood rat named Thomas Chatterton Jupiter Zeus.

When I was most come here he did squeak more of his cheese squeaks. It was most hard—having hearing of him and not having cheese for him. I could hardly keep from crying. He is a most lovely wood rat, and all his ways are ways of gentleness . . . I just couldn't keep from crying. His cheese longings are like my longings for Angel Mother and Angel Father.

After that phone call, Nassif said, "I knew I wanted to do something with it musically. So the first thing I knew was that while there was time, I wanted to meet her. I know everyone feels this way about the diary. Opalites who hear it for the first time, they know it was written just for them. And we all have that tremendous sense of attachment and personalization. I wrote the hospital, and they said yes, come see her, and it was not a big deal.

"They called her the princess. Most of the time I visited her she had a small private room . . . it was lovely. It looked like an estate." In fact, at the end of her life Opal seemed to think that Napsbury Hospital, a large Victorian structure, was a royal palace.

In all he visited her seven or eight times. "I would stay and see her on three consecutive days. I always stayed at St. Albans, this charming village, a very upper-class village, gorgeous, with a marvelous market." He put up at various bed-and-breakfasts. "My favorite was St. Michael's Manor House with a duck pond and clotted cream and waiters in tuxes and hyacinths in the vestibule. It was just enchantment. You cannot imagine the discovery and sense of enchantment and magic in going to visit Françoise." He said that given a chance to meet anyone in history, "even now, of [all] the people in history, she would be the person I would choose. There's Jesus," he added with a smile. "Right under that would be Françoise."

There is no doubt in his mind that she was a princess. Or at least of royal blood, for illegitimate children do not inherit actual titles. "She was a princess. People who never met her are not qualified to comment on that. She was exactly what you would think a princess would be. Petite, enchanting, quite eccentric, fine-boned."

I laughed and said, "Princesses don't have big hands and feet?"

He laughed too. "Oh, please! She was little, petite."

I pressed him in a jocular way about the possibility of big-boned royalty.

He replied, "All that inbreeding . . . I think beautiful people select beautiful people, and so it goes."

He said her manner was also indicative of noble birth. "I felt most definitely I was being given an audience. You were presented to her. You were being granted [an audience]. And it wasn't fake. I'm pretty good at spotting fakes and pretension, and it wasn't that. I mean this was a woman in a little robe and housecoat and slippers, and she still had an aristocratic demeanor just because it's, I think, genetic."

"It was absolute magic. We'd sit there hour after hour. I'd often be there three or four hours." Nassif said she told him she no longer spoke French but pronounced "pardon" in the French manner and said *oui* for "yes."

Nassif always wore a coat and tie to the meetings and brought her presents: housecoats, several teddy bears, which she liked to hold, chocolates, and flowers. At her request, he also brought her Mentholatum, which she mentioned using to treat her pets in the diary. His mother, Barbara Nassif, made her an Opal doll that was later displayed in her room.

Nassif told me he was glad she was so well cared for at Napsbury. "Was it ideal? No. But she complained wherever she was. She was an artist; what can I say? There are worse alternatives. She would have been on the street."

Of her mental condition, he said, "I think there was child abuse. I think there was a sunstroke in India, and perhaps some genetic predisposition. In a very flimsy way it's sort of a proof—all that inbreeding that goes on in aristocratic families. It's not hardy stock."

On his visits he would ask her to describe Angel Mother and Angel Father and talk about her early life. "Year after year, and I visited her for twelve years, the answer never changed. "She said the Whiteleys were very attractive people. But she said they were atheists. Never went to church. She called them atheists and [said] that they were very mean to her, which is clear from the diary. I mean that's child abuse. They would arrest those people. It goes beyond even the harsh discipline of the time. . . . She was clearly an abused and neglected child . . . she was not only hypersensitized in the way abused children are, it undoubtedly contributed to her mental fragility. . . . With abuse a great sense of disassociation from the self occurs, and that in itself may be a definition of schizophrenia."

Nassif believes that the fact that Opal did not publicly declare herself to be other than a child of the Whiteleys until she moved away from Oregon is a characteristic reaction of abused children, who are trained not to tell the truth to the outside world.

On one visit in 1987 Nassif was with his mother and his sister Patricia, a law professor. He made an appointment to see the last of Opal's aristocratic English friends, Mia Woodruff, sister to Lord Acton, who befriended Opal in the 1930s before her commitment.

"I made an appointment to see the Honourable Mrs. Douglas Woodruff. I knew that Aunt Mia, as I came to call her, had known Françoise since the 1930s and went to visit her, and her nephew Richard was there. He and my sister struck up a conversation, and nine months later they were married."

Mia Woodruff's nephew Richard inherited his father's title and is the present (and fourth) Lord Acton, complete with a seat in the House of Lords. "So I don't see Françoise's story as so fantastical," said Nassif. "I mean . . . my father was the son of Lebanese immigrants who grew up in dire poverty. His daughter sits in the peeress's box in the House of Lords . . . curtsies to the queen, and on state occasions wears a historic tiara. So is Opal's story so fantastic? No."

Richard, Lord Acton described the purchase of his wife's gold and pearl tiara at an antique fair in Cedar Rapids in his own book, *A Brit Among the Hawkeyes*. The book is a collection of essays describing, among other things, what it is like to divide one's time between London and Cedar Rapids. *A Brit Among the Hawkeyes* also contains an essay about Opal, "To Live Again in Music: The Riddle of Opal Whiteley."

Opal told Rob Nassif that her mother was Her Imperial Highness Archduchess Margaret Mary of Salzburg, but Nassif is not so sure about that. "She looked like there was a mixture of French and East Indian.

She had this flat nose, these almost Oriental eyes." Nassif believes she was almost certainly illegitimate. "The details of her mother change according to what she is able to accept and able to finesse so she isn't illegitimate. Given her era, that would have had a stigma attached to it.

"I've had twenty years to think about it. [Henri] would have visited, as she recalls 'the happy days when Father would come,' but they were few. Because he and the mother were not married." After Henri d'Orléans died in Saigon in 1901, Nassif theorized, "the funds would have dried up, especially if the child were a secret."

He wonders if she were somehow put on an orphan train in New York, ending up in Oregon. In his play, Opal and her parents are shipwrecked off the coast of Oregon and she is washed ashore, but this, he said, was more of a dramatic device. He believes the diary was written when she was a child, and that anyone else who does *has* to believe in her d'Orléans parentage, because of the clues in the text. But he adds, "I have no investment in whether or not the diary is true. [It] has no bearing whatsoever on the value of my play. I do not deal with [the issue] in the play; in fact, *The New York Times* gave me some credit for wisely avoiding that issue. I deal with the diary . . . on a personal level.

"That being said, I absolutely think it is the only full and logical explanation. Only a child could have written it. It was written by her. All the writing bears the trademark of her hand. There's no question. But she absolutely lost the gift as she aged."

Curious about Opal's astounding ability to charm and captivate others, I asked Nassif about the qualities she had that charmed him.

He said, "She seemed amused by the world. She had laughing eyes. Very dark eyes. I don't remember her moving a lot. She had a sense of composure. I mean, it's regal. A sense of composure that is almost, I think, in the blood. Here's an example. When Prince Charles was shot at, what was his reaction? He was quite composed. He was bred to stand up. And you almost cannot learn that; you have to be that. That quality of noblesse oblige—is that the word?— . . . And always when I'd go she'd say, 'Good-bye. Next,' it was never 'Oh, Robert, don't go.' "

"Would you say you loved her?" I asked.

"Absolutely. Like a grandmother."

He described her feelings for him as "the way the queen feels about

Prince Charles . . . she knew I loved her, and I was definitely special to her, but there was a barrier, like with a queen."

"She wouldn't say, 'Robert, how are you?' or 'I'm worried about you?' " I asked.

Nassif said, "No! It would be more 'What can I tell you about *myself*?' " He laughed. " 'That's why you're here!' And [she would be] *loving* it."

Bill McBryde, who handled Opal's financial affairs for decades, said that although the case fascinated him, he felt no emotional attachment to Opal herself. He met her only once in almost thirty years. "When I did go and see her, I went with Rob Nassif . . . and she was quite an invalid, unable to communicate at all. I don't think she knew that I was there. . . . Rob had seen her several times before. He thought she [recognized him], but I was sitting quietly on the other side, and I had my doubts.

"She could hardly speak. She was pleasant and smiled. She was quite a pretty old lady really. . . . It was a distinguished face, very good bone structure, and compared with the women she was sitting with who were very much of the same vintage and condition, she did stand out."

Twenty-three

By the end of her life, Opal was getting boxes of fan mail from American schoolchildren. One of the most astonishing aspects of Opal's story is her nearly complete rehabilitation and the use of her diary in schools.

In 1920, after the scandal broke, Frances Lee of Miss Lee's School in Boston canceled an upcoming arrangement by which Opal was to take her pupils on nature outings. "Although in literature there may be some excuse for calling fiction fact I feel in dealing with children such an attitude is quite foreign to the policy of my school," wrote Miss Lee. Today, however doubts about the authenticity of the diary have been dismissed as irrelevant, reflecting, perhaps, modern scholarship's open-mindedness about the reliability of texts. The version of the diary most often used in schools today is that of Jane Boulton, which in its current printing is billed as "based on the childhood diary of Opal Whiteley, adapted by Jane Boulton." It has been in print for most of the time since 1976, and its current publisher provides an online teachers' guide, which describes it as "the magical diary of a six-year old orphan girl written at the turn of the century" and "a compelling, true-life story." It is praised for its "allure as an American primitive and the evidence it provides that Opal was probably descended from French nobility."

The text has, however, not been subjected to linguistic analysis for over seventy years. When the diary was first published in 1920, at least one scholar took a hard look at the text. Dr. Robert Max Garrett, an associate professor in the English department of the University of Washington, wrote, "All teachers of language and composition will agree with me that participial forms and gerunds are not innate in the child—that they must be taught carefully and laboriously. It will take a great deal of persuasion to believe that it is humanly possible for a six year old child to make use of the following expressions: There I found the Mamma's thimble, *but she said the pet crows having taken it was as though I had taken it*, because he was my property. . . . [his italics]."

Garrett was a medievalist with a Ph.D. from the University of Munich, whose main interest was Chaucer and the medieval revival. He was also a westerner, who had received his B.A. in Idaho and his master's degree in Seattle. And he was interested in linguistics. As a member of the American Dialect Society he had done research in northwest logging camps, compiling slang and occupational vocabulary. He was suspicious of the use by a child from this environment of "one's" in the phrase "Thinking of these things makes it a joy to share one's bread and jam . . ." and of her claiming to have gathered "cornflowers" in local meadows, although whether this was on botanical or linguistic grounds is not clear.

"Also," he wrote, "an observing child who has lived in a Western lumber camp does not pass the age of six without knowing the difference between praying and a quite different use of holy names," quoting, "That Rob Ryder was out there by the chute shouting at God in a very quick way. He was begging God to dam that chute right away. Why if God answered his prayer, we'd be in an awful fix. The house we live in would be under water if God dammed that chute."

Garrett was also intrigued by the information Opal is said to have gleaned from the two copybooks "which contain such marvelous information. *The Atlantic Monthly* would do humanity a real service if it were to search the world for those priceless texts which taught a child before the age of six, all that is usually learned by a college graduate of Greek mythology and philosophy, Latin literature with due notice of Lucian and Pliny, French, Italian and English history with criticism enough to call Edward the First 'good,' musical and art history with the thoroughness to know even birthdays . . . only a Woodsworth enthusiast would know enough about him to name that tree for him 'around where the little flowers talk most.' " Garrett had a point. The most bizarre aspect of the story is the idea that the diary was full of erudition taken on board by the child Opal from the two notebooks left her by Angel Mother and Angel Father and hidden from the Whiteleys in the secret compartment of a box.

When the diary first appeared in England, a reviewer suggested it had been plagiarized from Opal's favorite childhood author, Gene Stratton-Porter. But the reviewer missed another potboiler of Opal's teenage years, when she was reading a lot of bestselling literature, which does not appear on her official reading list.

Edgar Rice Burroughs's 1914 novel *Tarzan of the Apes*, which was published when Opal was sixteen, tells the story of the young Lord Greystoke, separated from his parents, Lord and Lady Greystoke, and left to fend for himself in the jungles of Africa. This foundling, despite foster parental guidance from lower primates even less cultivated than the Whiteleys as described by Opal in the diary, manages to teach himself English from two books left behind by his aristocratic parents, an illustrated primer and a dictionary. Burroughs wrote, "Squatting upon his haunches on the table top in the cabin his father had built—his smooth, brown, naked little body bent over the book which rested in his strong slender hands, and his great shock of long, black hair falling about his well-shaped head and bright, intelligent eyes [an accurate physical description of Opal]—Tarzan of the apes, little primitive man, presented a picture filled, at once, with pathos and with promise—an allegorical figure of the primordial groping through the black night of ignorance toward the light of learning."

Tarzan aside, what was most damning in Garrett's view, on the grounds of either subconscious confession or intended irony, was the use of the name Thomas Chatterton Zeus for Opal's pet wood rat. Garrett pointed out that Thomas Chatterton was an eighteenth-century adolescent plagiarist who, starting at the age of twelve, created fictitious fifteenth-century poems attributed to a monk named Thomas Rowley, that initially fooled a lot of people, including Horace Walpole. Walpole later broke off communication with him when Chatterton's plagiarism was exposed. At age seventeen Chatterton committed suicide by taking arsenic and his body was found in an attic surrounded by his manuscripts torn into shreds in the manner of the diary. Like Opal, mentally unstable, talented, lower-middle-class Chatterton rebelled against his life of drudgery as an apprentice, striving in vain to become a poet. Garrett believed they also had fraud in common. As far as I can tell, no other scholar had analyzed the text on a linguistic basis ever since.

I went back to the University of Washington, where, since Dr. Garrett's time, a department of linguistics has been established. The chairman of the department, Julia Herschensohn, seemed admirably suited to the task of casting a trained eye over both Opal's text and Dr. Garrett's opinions, since her specialties are Romance linguistics, French syntax, and second-language acquisition, and she kindly agreed to do so.

After examining the diary and Dr. Garrett's comments, she replied, "I think that Dr. Garrett's comments are very well taken. The prose is clearly pretty sophisticated, containing many complex sentences and vocabulary well beyond the writing ability of a child. It seems much more likely that she constructed it when presented with the possibility of publication. The proof should rest, I believe, with the publishers, since the reconstruction story seems pretty implausible." Dr. Herschensohn added that the sampled text she read "does not at all look like it contains mistakes 'typical' of native French speakers. The strange syntax is rather quite English. What strikes me particularly is the use of 'periphrastic do' as in 'this road did have a longing to go . . . they did build it a bridge. . . .'"

"Periphrastic do," she explained, "came to be used in negatives like 'John did not leave' and interrogatives like 'Did John leave?' and began to occur with significant frequency at the beginning of the fifteenth century and steadily increased in frequency until it stabilized into its modern usage by the mid-seventeenth century. "It is . . . used for emphasis in modern English, but in earlier centuries was used in regular declaratives too. So Opal's use of it is weird-archaic. There is nothing like do-support in French."

(Do-support is used in the King James Bible, with which Opal was very familiar and which influenced *The Fairyland Around Us*, with its odd phrase "the mole eateth of worms." The headline IT IS WRITTEN on the front of her *Fairyland* brochure is another biblical touch.)

"Another syntactic device that she seems to use a lot," said Professor Herschensohn, "is compounding, putting two words together to make a new one, as the examples in the preface, 'star-songs, star-gleams, earth-voices.' "

Compounding, she said, happens a lot in English and doesn't in French. Her conclusion is that "the French words in the text seem to be gleaned as do all the names."

The truth about the diary remains elusive. What does seem to be proved is that Opal did keep a diary, at least from the age of twelve or thirteen, and that her sister Faye tore up some of it. There are several witnesses to this. But nobody ever saw a diary on butcher paper written in crayon. They saw cursive writing on lined paper in composition books. All that said, there's much that simply cannot be explained. Producing a fake childhood diary is one thing. Tearing it up into neat little pieces requiring that it be laboriously put back together, then leaving it behind in a hatbox, a small package, and five other cartons, if that is what happened, is simply bizarre. For one thing, unless Opal had a confederate who would guard the boxes and mail them when needed, it was very risky. The results of all that labor could easily be thrown out. In fact many of the papers Opal left behind in California were burned by Ruth Gentle at Mrs. Bales's house.

In the end, those who love the diary and revere Opal the most tend to say that the authenticity of the diary ultimately doesn't matter.

Mrs. Lawrence, while explaining why she wouldn't permit another forensic test of the diary fragments she has, said, "I think it's irrelevant, I think it's putting everybody's attention on what doesn't matter." What's important, she said, was to "get inside the mind of a child. I think everybody should read the diary because it gives you an insight into how a child feels."

Robert Nassif told me, "If the diary were to turn out to be a hoax, I would only admire the author all the more. What an astonishing accomplishment! . . . It doesn't matter to me. It's a phenomenal work of literature. I love Françoise, and so of course I care that she cares, but I am sophisticated enough to be objective, and it doesn't matter to me if her story is true or false. It was true for her, that's all that matters."

In 2001, Opal's image, based on the photo of her with butterflies on her hands and her hair, was painted on the entire side of a two-story brick building on Main Street, in Cottage Grove, part of a series of murals with which the Chamber of Commerce is brightening up the town and celebrating its history. Millions of people have seen this particular Main Street. The payback scene from the 1978 movie *Animal House*, in which the Deltas disrupt the Faber College homecoming parade with smoke bombs and the Deathmobile, was shot here. The Chamber of Commerce was also considering a John Belushi mural somewhere in town, commemorating this event. The editor of the *Cottage Grove Sentinel* told me that everybody in town has a John Belushi autograph. Opal Whiteley, born in 1897, outlived John Belushi by a decade.

Carol Reeves owns The Flower Basket across the street from the Opal mural and is the head of the Chamber of Commerce mural committee. She told me there was some controversy about putting the giant image of Opal's face on Main Street. Some of the "old-timers" objected, she said, quoting them as saying, "Oh, she's a farce."

Reeves said her response was "But hey, it's part of history." By including images of a white painted covered bridge near Opal's childhood home and the Walden School, which Opal attended in 1904 and 1905, the mural became more of a historical artifact than an endorsement. "It softened the blow, and made it more positive," Reeves said.

There was some similar quiet grumbling a few years back when a bronze statue of the child Opal was unveiled at the Cottage Grove Library, and the pro-Opal forces were triumphant. Before that, local anti-Opal feeling had prevailed when some citizens of Cottage Grove mulled over the idea of naming a new middle school after the town's most famous daughter. The idea never got very far. Instead it was named Lincoln Middle School.

About fifty miles up Interstate 5, however, in Portland, there is a public charter school named after Opal Whiteley. Its director is quoted on its Web site as saying that Opal School offers "approaches that challenge both children and adults to think outside the box and then to redesign the box we call 'school.'" A section titled "Background Information on Opal School," says, "Opal, who saw herself in relation to all things, understood the *pedagogy of listening* as a way to live in the world. She has been described as a child Saint Francis 'with gifts we are told children have until they are educated out of them.' . . . *Opal School strives to honor her dream.*"

Steve Williamson, the Opal researcher in the Cottage Grove area believes she did write *The Story of Opal* when she said she did, and he has spent years following up clues he finds in it in order to authenticate it.

"You can find everything in the diary if you just know where the road goes three ways," he told me at entrance to the Row River trail. ("Row" is pronounced to rhyme with "cow," having been named after a fight between two pioneers.) "Where the road goes three ways" is, he said, how Opal described the spot where we were now standing.

Williamson's business card reads "Research Assistant, Opal Whiteley Project," making him, as far as I can tell, the only professional Opalite in the world. He has been hired by the University of Oregon's Department of Education to find material for its Opal Whiteley Web site. The site is funded with money from a four-hundred-thousand-dollar federal grant, "Special Education—Technology and Media Services for Individuals with Disabilities/Steppingstones of Technology Innovation."

He is not only the world's first professional Opalite but the founder of the Opal Whiteley Memorial, and he helped build Opal Park on top of nearby Cerro Gordo Mountain, the nearly abandoned site of a self-styled "intentional community and ecovillage," which the Cottage Grove old-timers call Rattlesnake Hill. Unfortunately, a storm blew many ancient firs down all over the park, which has since been allowed to "return to nature." Because of his personal Opal Whiteley Web site, he also serves as a sort of clearinghouse for people interested in Opal.

A large, friendly, bald man with glasses, a big smile, and more than a trace of a folksy accent from his native Louisiana, Williamson dresses like one of the loggers pictured in vintage photographs of Cottage Grove at the turn of the last century in plaid shirts with wide suspenders.

In the parking lot of the Row River trailhead, he pointed at surrounding landmarks. We were at a spot where one road meets another. "A child's imagination being what it is," said Williamson, "she sees Mosby Creek Road going two ways. See those oak trees over there? Those oak trees follow a little creek. Her house was on the other side of those oak trees, kind of back up where that little green meadows is."

I asked him if there was any trace of Opal's house.

"No. I walked back there and found the old garbage pile. What I found in that garbage pile was an old Castoria bottle. I've got it at the office."

Opal mentioned Castoria in her diary several times. *"My big problem was what to carry water in when I go to make prepares to give my pets foot-baths and neck-and-ear washes. I have tried thimbles to use for wash-pans when I do wash the hands of my pets, but thimbles hold not enough of water . . . but mostly now I do carry Castoria bottles full of water when I start on my way to wash the neck and ears of my animal friends."*

"It's exactly the same kind of Castoria bottle," he said, "which was a common medicine. A lot of times they threw things in the creek. In fact, that's where the Castoria bottle was."

Across the road from us was "the ranch-house where the grandpa does live," which appeared in the published diary's opening paragraph: *"To-day the folks are gone away from the house we do live in. They are gone a little way away, to the ranch-house where the grandpa does live. I sit on our steps and I do print. I like it—this house we do live in being at the edge of the near woods. So many little people do live in the near woods. I do have conversations with them. I found the near woods first day I did go explores. . . ."*

Williamson has been over the house looking for signs of Opal. He has a patch of some floral wallpaper, which he thought was in the house when Opal lived there.

"Where we're standing here is really close to Mosby Creek. That white covered bridge, that's the Mosby Creek bridge. In the diary it's set upriver a bit, maybe a hundred yards. When she is talking about going over a bridge over the *rivière*, that's the bridge she's talking about."

Williamson got help in his Opal research from his now-deceased mentor, John Wilson, a local historian whose family had lived around here since 1852. "He remembered Opal. He gave me introductions to people in the historical society and helped me make it kind of a legitimate interest around here instead of a crackpot joke or embarrassing local history." Wilson told Williamson that as a child he and a friend mischievously let loose a huge collection of hundreds of butterflies Opal had in a cage near her house and that an irate Opal ran out of the house in her bloomers, yelling and throwing a book she had been reading at the two boys.

Williamson had brought along a ringed binder full of Opal-related documents in plastic sleeves. He showed me a picture of a reunion of the McKibben family taken in 1905, right exactly where we were. "It's the only known picture of the McKibbens and the-man-who-wears-gray-neckties-and-is-kind-to-mice."

The binder contained every possible connection to Opal, including a large diagram of an ice pick entering an eyeball, illustrating the kind of lobotomy he thought Opal might have had at Napsbury in the 1950s.

Williamson felt his survey of the terrain bolstered the idea that the diary was written by Opal as a child. At one point he told me, "This marks the westernmost point of Opal's exploration." Williamson showed me a spot near Star, a small community farther away from Cottage Grove where Opal lived for a time. "Somewhere right around here is where the diary was torn up, and I do believe that." He got the story from an old school friend of Opal's named Ida Wicks, one of four teenage girls present at the time.

I asked him if the diary that Opal pieced together in Boston was the one he said was torn up here. He believed the destruction of the diary took place on more than one occasion, "but this is the time that's dramatic and the time that I think the diary fragment I found comes from." Williamson's diary fragment appears on his Web site, and he has donated it to the University of Oregon.

"It's enchanting the way I got it. I was at the one hundredth Dorena birthday party put on by the post office, and this woman comes in there. I have a little booth set up of Opal Whiteley stuff . . . so this older woman comes in there and she has this big thick book and it's a history of central Oregon, and she comes straight up to me and she says, 'This book's been in my family for a long time. I want to give it to some group 'cause I'm afraid if something happens to me, my family is just going to throw it out and they won't care.' So I start flipping through it, and inside, there is this folded piece of paper, and inside that piece of paper is . . ." He opens his binder to the photocopied fragment.

The writing does look like Opal's with its characteristic backslant, and he said he was hoping to get the writing carefully analyzed. It appeared to be a diary written in a composition book, as it began "Dear composition . . ." The fragment described gathering flowers and encountering a snake and a deer. It is displayed on his Opal Web site, which notes: "This piece of paper has NEVER been in Los Angeles or Boston—it could not have been 'made up' later. And it is clear that it was deliberately torn into quarters." He dated it from when Opal was twelve, later than the period in the published diary.

He said, "I got a list of the schoolchildren [at Star] and Opal and Pearl and Faye [Whiteley] are in that school, and also Fairy and Lizzie who are named in that fragment. I think it's real possible . . . it's known that she gave some parts of her diary to various local people—bits and pieces."

Twenty-four

*J*ulie Clark and her sister-in-law Tanya Van Alstine are also fascinated with the story of Opal. The two blond, energetic young mothers in Hood River, Oregon, do not believe the diary is a work of genius and doubt it was written in childhood. Nor do they believe Opal was a d'Orléans. They got hooked on the story because Julie's grandmother Bertha C. Arrington, now ninety-six, started out life in Cottage Grove as Cloe Whiteley, the second-to-last child of Lizzie and Ed Whiteley. The last official word on the Whiteley children had come from Elbert Bede. In his 1954 book, he reported that the family, hounded by the press and humiliated in their hometown, changed their names, and vanished. What had happened to them?

Widower Ed Whiteley remarried soon after the scandal broke. His second wife, Florence, was much younger than he. Florence's sister, who still lives in Cottage Grove, told me he was a wonderful, kind man and a good husband to Florence. Laughing, she quoted Florence as saying happily, "I'd rather be an old man's lover than a young man's slave." But Whiteley's reticence, commented upon by Bede, was a lifelong trait. The second family he had with Florence knew so little about his early years that his death certificate lists neither his parents' names nor his place of birth. A son of Ed and Florence Whiteley told me that he had heard that Opal Whiteley was a half sister, but the matter was never discussed. One of Ed and Florence's daughters asked me if I could enlighten her on the family's ethnic heritage. Noting that many Whiteleys were dark, she asked, "Is there Indian in me?"

Ed and Florence moved to southern Oregon, where Ed continued working in the woods. The Whiteley sisters, Pearl, Faye, and Cloe, and little Elwin went their own ways. Ed Whiteley died in Jacksonville, Oregon, in 1948, a few months after Opal had been taken to Napsbury Hospital.

While Opal was in India explaining to Major Pritchard that she was traveling incognito, having hacked off the last syllable of the name d'Orléans, coming up with D'Orlé, the Whiteley children in Oregon were living incognito and had hacked off the first syllable of Whiteley. Their new last name was Ley.

Julie told me, "They also used what appeared to be their middle names as first names. Pearl became Geraldine. Cloe became Bertha. And Faye used various names during her life, including Jean, Gay, Gale, and Garnet." Julie said this was because she was "a scammer and needed lots of names." Little Elwin remained Elwin. Julie characterized the Whiteley siblings as "extremely intelligent but unstable—all of them."

Julie is the mother of three boys and lives in a big modern and immaculate house on top of a tall hill overlooking the Columbia River Gorge. Her husband, Tanya's brother, is a computer administrator for the county government. Interestingly, it is a much nicer place to live than the description I have read of the tiny, shabby flat in France where the current pretender to the French throne, Henri d'Orléans, great-nephew of Opal's Angel Father of the same name, lives with his chain-smoking wife. Press reports indicate that his father, Angel Father's nephew, died in 1999, having run through the family fortune, selling off heirlooms, including Marie Antoinette's jewels. About thirty-eight million dollars were declared missing at his death. He also quarreled with his children, predicting gleefully that they would inherit "crumbs" and "only tears."

Julie reported that her grandmother's generation never talked about Opal. Once in a while Elwin, an alcoholic, would start in on it when he was drunk, referring to the big secret and the Whiteley name. "What happened was no one knew the story until my mom and dad were on vacation and stopped in Eugene and in a store they found these books by Elbert Bede and Jane Boulton in a display. Somehow, my dad said, 'I think that's what my mom's last name was' . . . and they took these home and they read them, and they started piecing things together. "They did not dare talk to Geri [Pearl]. They talked to Geri's kids and Elwin's son, Roger. Those were the next generation. I don't think Geri ever acknowledged it. They got Grandma once, that entire time, probably in the mid-eighties to acknowledge that Opal was her sister. It was just never brought up."

Julie investigated some more, found some long-lost cousins, and also got hold of some pictures of the Whiteley children when they were very young that someone had found in an old trunk and was displaying on the Internet. She took some of them to show her grandmother.

"I showed her the pictures. She loved looking at them. She said, 'Where did you get these?' " One of the pictures, however, was a shot of Opal, about four or five, sitting in a little rocking chair on the porch with Pearl and Faye nearby. Cloe was upset to see Opal's image and said, "That must be the girl who used to go house to house to tutor children. That's the only reason she got in our picture." Julie thought that was sad, but she didn't believe her grandmother when she said Opal wasn't a Whiteley. Julie said her goal that day was to find out if what people had said about Lizzie, that she was abusive and cruel, was true. "I said, 'Grandma, what kind of mother was your mom?'"

"She said she was very doting, very caring, and that education to her was more important than anything and that the biggest thing that really concerned her when she was on her deathbed—she was only forty— was would her children be able to continue their education. Grandma says that was the number one thing she was concerned about.

"She said she was never, never abusive. She said that there were always books and things; they always had music lessons." Julie added, "There are times Grandma talks about being so poor they were without shoes."

I asked Julie what had happened to the Whiteley children. Pearl married an electrician and raised two children as well as her baby brother. It had been Pearl's idea to leave town with her siblings and change their names. She told the others not to reveal their real names, just as Opal later claimed she was not allowed to tell the people of Cottage Grove she was really Françoise.

Cloe, however, got left behind. ". . . I do know that about a year later when they did move to Portland she got very sick. . . . Basically her grandma took care of her. When she was living with her grandmother, there was a box of Opal's, clothes, some Indian dolls, and Grandma wanted to play with them. Grandma's still twelve, thirteen years old, and they were so afraid the neighbors would see these items that were Opal's that . . . they took these things from her, and they burned them."

Eventually Cloe joined the others and worked for a time with Pearl at the Portland department store Meier & Frank. When Cloe was eighteen, she went to live with Ed Whiteley and his new family. "She took care of the house." Ed's daughter by Florence remembered Cloe but had no idea she was a half sister. Cloe met her husband, Lloyd Arrington, there. He worked in the mill alongside Ed Whiteley.

Faye, like Opal before her, went to Hollywood to seek her fortune. "My dad said that she was totally into the Hollywood scene. Totally. He said she would live it up like no other, yet she was only like a secretary for a producer . . . my dad always said she was a plump little short thing, dark hair . . . not very tall.

"Really the last time [Mom and Dad] saw her she had come for a visit for a couple of days . . . and when she had left, they started getting phone calls from someone demanding his money back. . . . They kept getting phone calls from this guy for a week. He would not leave them alone. He would call and say, 'I want my money. I was told you'd give me back my money,' and my mom was hanging up on him. Finally Mom asked him who told you that? . . . [He said,] 'Jean [one of Faye's many names] said you were going to pay back the money I gave her. . . . ' That's the last time they saw her."

Julie said that Faye always wanted attention. "I think it was almost like a starvation for attention. My grandma tends to be very self-centered. If you're talking about something and it's not related to her, forget it. And I think Elwin was the same way. Pearl was the same way." Elwin, said Julie, was very intelligent and went to college at sixteen. He started an electronics business in his garage, which eventually became Ley Electronics in Portland. "He was a millionaire by the time he was thirty."

Julie shares one trait with the woman she believes was her great-aunt. Like Opal, she can tell you the date of an event many years ago.

She told me it drives her husband crazy. She can tell you that the first day she lived in a new house when she was three years old was August 3, 1971, and if she ever hears anyone's birthday just once, she can never forget it. She remembers the birthdays of children she knew when she was seven or eight, who moved away years ago.

Julie and Tanya believe Opal was a fraud. Tanya once ended up at a party of teachers who were fans. "They were so passionate," she said. "Lots of the teachers use her book . . . but it's the edited version [Jane Boulton] and the children's version. That's not even the real story." Julie and Tanya also found it funny that the teachers' guide, which they read online, backs Opal's claims. They found Bede amusing too. "Bede cracked me up," said Julie. "Some of the stuff he came up with! He was so funny about it."

But she found poignancy in his book too. "It's really sad because Bede talks about how close [Opal and Lizzie] were as mother and daughter."

Of Cloe, she said, "It's sad because a lot of people would like to talk to my grandma or at least have me talk to her . . . it's not something I have been able to crack. . . . When I brought those pictures, you know the first thing she said was 'Are you writing a book?' And I'm like, 'Whoa, no!' The thing is there's still that sense of distrust."

I asked, "What would happen if I went in there and asked, 'Did Faye tear up the diary?' What would she say?"

"She'd say, 'What diary?' She would chase you out of there."

Julie believed all the Whiteleys of Opal's generation had emotional problems. She didn't know if it was part of their makeup or the result of something that had happened. Julie also said, "My dad is very sensible. Extremely sensible. The good thing is it hasn't been passed down." She added that when she and her sister Justine first learned about Opal as young teenagers, "we thought, 'It only happens to the girls.' " They told each other, "We've got to take care of each other and make sure we don't go screwy!"

She laughed, then added seriously, "We were worried, though. Luckily we had stable parents."

Tanya laughed. "Maybe it was the water," she said. "I think they were drinking out of lead pipes!"

Julie and Tanya joked about it, but Julie knew that the pain that the Whiteleys were said to have endured back in 1921 was real to them, and that it still hadn't gone away. Julie said that when she decided to ask her grandmother about Opal and about Lizzie, Cloe described her mother's death "as if it happened yesterday. She stopped me. I said, 'What about Opal?' She said"—and here Julie lowered her voice to an intense whisper to quote her grandmother—" 'I can't talk about this. It hurts *so bad.*' "

"I told her, I said, 'I am sorry, Grandmother, I promise I will never [ask about this] again.' "

There were no Whiteleys present at Opal's funeral. It took place in St. Ethelreda's in London, one of the only English Catholic churches that, because it was a private chapel, survived the Reformation intact. Four excellent male voices sang the traditional Latin mass from a balcony up above. The Latin required a special dispensation. The priest had a magnificent voice exactly like Alec Guinness's, and he used part of the homily to explain how in some ways the Latin mass captured certain theological principles more aptly. The mourners included several nurses from the hospital, as well as Lord and Lady Acton, née Nassif; the Honorable Mrs. Woodruff, wearing a Russian-looking fur hat and sitting to one side in her wheelchair; and Mrs. Lawrence, who read from the diary.

When I visited Mrs. Lawrence, we watched a tape of Opal's funeral. It had been made by documentary maker Ian Taylor, who at that time was in preproduction on a British television documentary that, like so many film projects, wasn't produced. "The taximan was so interested in the story he didn't charge me," said Mrs. Lawrence, referring to her arrival at the funeral.

Taylor also filmed the graveside service at Highgate Cemetery, a quirky note being provided by the priest's saying some words of the service twice so it could be filmed from two separate camera angles. The final frames of the tape showed clods of earth landing on the crucifix-topped coffin in its grave surrounded by ivy and twigs. Finally, the London clay obscured the nameplate Françoise de Bourbon-Orléans.

I read the name aloud.

Mrs. Lawrence turned to me and said, "None of them questioned that."

"Who?" I asked.

"The family." She meant that the d'Orléans family had apparently raised no objection to Opal's being buried under their name.

"Did they even know?" I asked.

"It was in the *Times*," she said with a slightly contemptuous, case-closed air.

Mrs. Lawrence told me she was grateful to Bill McBryde for managing Opal's estate properly, allowing for this dignified funeral and her plot in Highgate. "Otherwise she would have had a pauper's grave," she said.

When he heard she had died, Bill McBryde arranged for "the full Latin requiem she would have preferred . . . I was quite pleased," he said. "We went up to Highgate Cemetery, and she had a private grave there. . . . It came out of the estate, as did the headstone. There are not very many spaces left. There are some single spaces, and we managed to get one. They're very expensive. I think we paid twelve hundred or two thousand pounds."

McBryde also arranged for her tombstone which reads

Françoise Marie de Bourbon-Orléans
(Opal Whiteley)
Died 17th February 1992
Aged 95 Years
"I Spake as a Child"

The truth of the first and last lines of this inscription has never been resolved to everyone's satisfaction.

To those who believed, the funeral was a moving tribute, a dignified burial for a troubled soul. To those who didn't believe, the posh cemetery, the noble name on the tombstone, the Catholic mass for someone who may never have been baptized in the Catholic Church, and the scriptural implication that the diary had been written in childhood were Opal Whiteley's last con.

The idea of the child as one who understands God in a pure, unfettered way through nature has been around for a long time. For Lord Grey, Elizabeth Lawrence, Rob Nassif, Benjamin Hoff, and many readers, Opal's gift to others was to see lucidly as a child and be articulate enough to share that vision. To them, the fact that the diary is written more cohesively and is a better book than *The Fairyland Around Us* is proof that it was written first, not second, and by a child. Their view is that we don't get better with practice. We lose our innocence, and it ruins our art. Inez Fortt, a librarian at the University of Oregon, wrote an article in 1961 with a unique theory. Postulating that the diary was faked, she said that it was also written when Opal was mad and had *reverted* to childhood and as such was psychologically, at least, an authentic document of childhood.

There are many visions of Opal besides the wise child or the con-artist. There is the New Age Opal, offering spiritual solace through communion with nature; there is the abused Opal, a child victim; there is the spunky, brave Opal, who triumphed anyway with goodness and humor; there is Opal the genius, whose gifts were robbed from her by madness. There is diva Opal, ecofeminist Opal, royal Opal. And of course, there is Mrs. Bales's take. The Hollywood landlady called her a "new kind of adventuress," a publicity fiend Opal.

Opal was indeed a child of her times in that she came of age along with the mass media. She subscribed to movie magazines, sent out press releases, posed for publicity shots. Those trees Ed Whiteley was felling were made into telephone poles. The information age was at hand.

She can be placed firmly in a historical and cultural context as a child not of the frontier but of its aftermath. She was, in her own small way, a cuspate figure who came of the age just as the West was reinventing itself. When Opal wrote of weeping at the death of a tree, Michael Angelo Sanzo Raphael, whether she wrote it as a child or as a young woman, she was heralding the fact that the West had been won. Now the forest could be exploited in popular culture, as in the works of Gene Stratton-Porter.

In 1909, when Opal was eleven, the organization that was to become the American Camping Association was formed to establish standards for organized camping for children. It was designed in part to bring children into contact with nature for the purposes of spiritual uplift, an idea that has endured in American culture. While Ed Whiteley and the other men in her community were chopping down trees, the teenage Opal was traipsing through the landscape with younger children in tow, examining flora and fauna. Opal's pupils later waxed rhapsodic about her tutelage. Her greatest success may have been her work with children, many of whom who genuine learned a love of nature from her.

I cannot say I fully understand her obsessions or her ability to charm. In the end, all that seems indisputable about Opal is that she was a bright little girl who loved God and the outdoors, that she had a magnetic presence and an amazing capacity to enchant, and that she struggled against madness and lost.

In 1977 she wrote to University of Oregon Professor Carlisle Moore from Napsbury Hospital complaining, "These Jewish slave drivers from outer space Mars, Jupiter, Venus, Pluto, Planet of the Apes" were impersonating dozens of people she had known in Oregon sixty-five years before and were planning to invade Oregon. She wanted the address of *The Oregonian*, so she could warn everyone. Ever mindful of her publicity and with her uncanny ability to remember dates, she noted correctly that *The Oregonian* had published articles about her from March 1915 to 1970.

In the midst of this horrible, sad letter came a glimpse of the Opal that was once, or perhaps the Opal that could have been, flickering out from behind the mask of insanity.

Apropos of nothing, she wrote: "I used to sit out on a stump after dark by the lumber shanty Taylors lumber camp 1908–1909 & watch the shooting stars. There were myriads of shooting stars. I called it the valley of the shooting stars."

That little Opal, sitting on that stump in the damp of a Northwest valley, is perhaps the real Opal, momentarily freed from madness. She is the Opal who has captivated others for almost a century.

FOR THE BEST IN PAPERBACKS, LOOK FOR THE

In every corner of the world, on every subject under the sun, Penguin represents quality and variety—the very best in publishing today.

For complete information about books available from Penguin—including Penguin Classics, Penguin Compass, and Puffins—and how to order them, write to us at the appropriate address below. Please note that for copyright reasons the selection of books varies from country to country.

In the United States: Please write to *Penguin Group (USA), P.O. Box 12289 Dept. B, Newark, New Jersey 07101-5289* or call *1-800-788-6262.*

In the United Kingdom: Please write to *Dept. EP, Penguin Books Ltd, Bath Road, Harmondsworth, West Drayton, Middlesex UB7 0DA.*

In Canada: Please write to *Penguin Books Canada Ltd, 10 Alcorn Avenue, Suite 300, Toronto, Ontario M4V 3B2.*

In Australia: Please write to *Penguin Books Australia Ltd, P.O. Box 257, Ringwood, Victoria 3134.*

In New Zealand: Please write to *Penguin Books (NZ) Ltd, Private Bag 102902, North Shore Mail Centre, Auckland 10.*

In India: Please write to *Penguin Books India Pvt Ltd, 11 Panchsheel Shopping Centre, Panchsheel Park, New Delhi 110 017.*

In the Netherlands: Please write to *Penguin Books Netherlands bv, Postbus 3507, NL-1001 AH Amsterdam.*

In Germany: Please write to *Penguin Books Deutschland GmbH, Metzlerstrasse 26, 60594 Frankfurt am Main.*

In Spain: Please write to *Penguin Books S. A., Bravo Murillo 19, 1° B, 28015 Madrid.*

In Italy: Please write to *Penguin Italia s.r.l., Via Benedetto Croce 2, 20094 Corsico, Milano.*

In France: Please write to *Penguin France, Le Carré Wilson, 62 rue Benjamin Baillaud, 31500 Toulouse.*

In Japan: Please write to *Penguin Books Japan Ltd, Kaneko Building, 2-3-25 Koraku, Bunkyo-Ku, Tokyo 112.*

In South Africa: Please write to *Penguin Books South Africa (Pty) Ltd, Private Bag X14, Parkview, 2122 Johannesburg.*